THE MAKING OF THE NORTHERN ONTARIO
SCHOOL OF MEDICINE

The Making of the Northern Ontario School of Medicine

A Case Study in the History of Medical Education

EDITED BY Geoffrey Tesson, Geoffrey Hudson, Roger Strasser, and Dan Hunt

McGill-Queen's University Press

Montreal & Kingston • London • Ithaca

© McGill-Queen's University Press 2009
ISBN 978-0-7735-3649-4

Legal deposit fourth quarter 2009
Bibliothèque nationale du Québec

Printed in Canada on acid-free paper that is 100% ancient forest free
(100% post-consumer recycled), processed chlorine free

This book has been published with the help of a grant from Laurentian University.

McGill-Queen's University Press acknowledges the support of the Canada Council
for the Arts for our publishing program. We also acknowledge the financial support
of the Governmentof Canada through the Book Publishing Industry Development
Program (BPIDP) for our publishing activities.

Library and Archives Canada Cataloguing in Publication

The making of the Northern Ontario School of Medicine: a case study in
the history of medical education / edited by Geoffrey Tesson ... [et al.].

Includes bibliographical references and index.
ISBN 978-0-7735-3649-4

1. Northern Ontario School of Medicine – History. 2. Medical education –
Ontario, Northern – Case studies. I. Tesson, Geoffrey

R749.N67M34 2009   610.71'17131   C2009-901904-3

This book was typeset by Interscript in 10.5/13 Sabon.

Contents

Preface

This book tells the story of the creation of the Northern Ontario School of Medicine (NOSM), an important event in the history of medical education in Canada. The Ontario government announced the decision to create the school, with campuses at Laurentian University in Sudbury (the Northeast) and Lakehead University in Thunder Bay (the Northwest), in May 2001. The first students arrived on campus in September 2005. At the time of writing, the school has just received its full accreditation and is preparing to graduate its first class of students.

Like all developments that mark a significant break with the past, this event had a highly visible public face, evident in the political debate that preceded it and the intense regional media interest that ensued. The public discourse was about the need for a bold gesture to redress the chronic shortage of doctors willing to practise in Northern Ontario. It touched a nerve in the resource-based communities of Northern Ontario, which had long felt alienated from the Southern Ontario monopoly over professional training programs – a monopoly that seemed more designed to meet metropolitan than rural needs. There were issues of regional pride and regional rivalries.

But at a deeper level, the creation of a new school signalled changes in thinking about medical education that had been taking place for some time in various schools across Canada, the United States, and other parts of the world experiencing problems related to preparing physicians for practice in regions with dispersed populations. The fact that the new school started from a blank slate meant that its designers were able to incorporate many innovations (which had been proven in other contexts) into a new kind of program. The ambitious goal was not just to respond to the doctor shortage in Northern Ontario but also to create a new medical education program that would produce graduates with a wide range of superior skills applicable to both rural and urban environments. Even more significant was the goal of rethinking the configuration of generalists, specialists, and other health professionals – a rethinking that would not simply replicate what was found in urban metropolitan centres but, rather, would be appropriate for northern, rural, and remote settings. This is not something that a medical school can achieve on its own, but it can have a significant impact, both in the form of the skill sets it offers students and, especially, in the culture of practice and the ability to work with others that it instills in them during their clinical learning.

An important first task for this book is to provide a historical account of the public debate and the mechanics of the decision-making process that led to the new school's being created. But a second, equally significant task is to describe the complex process of translating the dream of a custom-designed medical school for Northern Ontario into a coherent workable program rooted in the experience of other pioneers in this field. This being the case, *The Making of the Northern Ontario School of Medicine* is addressed to a wide audience. The communities of the North, who have shown such a strong interest in their school as well as a growing appreciation of the complexities involved in meeting all their medical education needs, will find their story told here. The creation of the school is testimony to their intense interest and involvement, which played such a key role in convincing the government of the day to take this step. But the book is also aimed at medical education and health and human resource experts and policy makers in Canada, the United States, and other parts of the world, especially those who have tried to solve the problems of delivering health care to dispersed populations. It will be of particular interest to those who have sought to redirect medical education in order to more closely meet community needs. They will see how the design of the school is grounded in an appreciation of earlier experiments and how every effort has been made to apply the lessons of this new experiment to future endeavours. It is written with the conviction that this project offers valuable lessons for those attempting to do similar things in similar geographic regions.

The Making of the Northern Ontario School of Medicine is a multi-authored work and is divided into three parts. Part 1 relates how the decision to create the new school was taken and describes the social and geographic context of that decision. It also lays out the thinking behind a new approach to medical education. Part 2 is devoted to the content of the new school. It describes the development of an admissions process, the building of a new curriculum, and the establishment of a novel governance and organizational structure. Complementing these administrative details is an account of the experience of the first students to enrol in the program. Part 3 reflects on some of the lessons that may be drawn from the building process. I now turn to an overview of the chapters of this book.

In chapter 1, Geoffrey Tesson and John Whitfield, each of whom held the position of vice-president academic at their respective universities (Laurentian and Lakehead) and each of whom co-chaired the northern working group (which produced the first substantive proposal for a new school), provide a chronological narrative detailing how Northern Ontario's desire for its own medical school first became a concrete proposal and then a reality. They provide an overview of the lead up to the decision to create the school and offer a prelude to the following chapters. They describe the growing capacity for medical education in the North and the mixture of politics and popular support that combined with new government-sponsored policy analyses to coalesce into a rationale for creating a new school.

In chapter 2, Raymond Pong, director of the Centre for Rural and Northern Health at Laurentian and a long-time advocate of paying greater attention to rural health human resource needs, provides a review of the history and geography of Northern Ontario: its resource-based economy and the problem of providing health care to rural and remote populations there and in other parts of Canada. He portrays the creation of a northern medical school as a response to the failure of piecemeal measures to provide a sustainable solution to chronic doctor shortages in Northern Ontario.

In chapter 3, Roger Strasser, the founding dean of NOSM, highlights the innovative nature of the school's design. He shows how its development built on worldwide historical trends in medical education in the latter part of the twentieth century. These trends included case-based learning in the classroom, rural and community-based medical education for clinical learning, and electronic distance education. NOSM provides students with high-quality clinical and educational experience in a diverse range of social, cultural, and health service settings.

In chapter 4, John Mulloy, a family physician who became a leading advocate for a new northern school, provides insight into the motivation for practising doctors to become involved in medical education. A largely personal account, it describes how a network of northern physicians became convinced of the need to assume more responsibility as medical educators in order to ensure that there would be a new generation of practitioners to continue their work. It underscores the importance of distributed family medicine residency programs in developing a broad base of physician-educators, and it describes the challenges and rewards of northern and rural practice.

Part 2 of the book focuses on the process of actually building the school. In chapter 5, Jill Konkin, the associate dean responsible for developing the NOSM admissions process, describes how admissions criteria were designed by looking at research that had been conducted on the kinds of students most likely to opt for practice in northern, rural, and remote environments. She also describes the input of different communities, especially the Aboriginal and francophone communities, in the admissions process and shows how the social composition of the charter class of students closely reflects the social make-up of Northern Ontario.

In chapter 6, Joel Lanphear, the associate dean of undergraduate medical education, provides an account of the historical evolution of medical school curricula as a background to explaining how the NOSM curriculum was designed specifically to meet its northern and rural mandate. The challenge in developing the curriculum was threefold: first, it had to meet the demanding standards of the accreditation process; second, it had to recognize the population health issues of people in Northern Ontario as well as the special features of rural and remote health care; and, third, it had to be capable of being delivered in distributed sites throughout Northern Ontario and, hence, required the extensive use of information technology.

In chapter 7, Geoffrey Tesson, Hoi Cheu, and Raymond Pong provide an account of the experience of the first cohort of students. Hoi Cheu, a specialist in film from the Department of English at Laurentian carried out extensive video interviews with NOSM students. This chapter offers a sample of those interviews, together with material drawn from questionnaires administered to each incoming class. It explores the students' motivations for choosing this program, describes their experience during its early years, and explores their career aspirations in relation to NOSM's rural and remote mandate.

In chapter 8, Arnie Aberman, the former dean of the University of Toronto's Faculty of Medicine and a consulting dean to NOSM, and Dorothy Wright, NOSM's chief administrative officer, describe the unique governance structure devised to meet the various demands placed upon the school. NOSM was established as a distinct legal entity whose governing board was structured to reflect both its commitment to serve the different cultural communities of Northern Ontario and its relationship to the two northern universities. The school has developed as an organization whose staff and faculty members are distributed across two campuses and many communities, all of which are supported by advanced information technology and administrative systems.

Part 3 discusses some of the lessons learned from the experience of creating NOSM. In chapter 9, Geoffrey Hudson, a medical historian on the NOSM faculty, and Dan Hunt, the school's vice-dean, academic activities, address the challenges of making a medical school that is responsive to the communities it is designed to serve. NOSM's mandate is not only to respond to the needs of the different cultural groups that make up Northern Ontario but also to involve those communities in the design, management, and delivery of its programs. This chapter explores the history of socially accountable medical education and analyzes the development of the school's engagement with the Aboriginal, francophone, and rural and remote communities of Northern Ontario.

In chapter 10, Geoffrey Tesson and Roger Strasser explore NOSM's historical uniqueness as a school specifically designed to meet the health care needs of northern, rural, and remote populations, their purpose being to draw lessons for other jurisdictions with similar health care delivery issues. They analyze: (1) the decision to create a new school, (2) the development of an admissions process and a curriculum that would best meet regional needs, (3) strategies for involving communities, and (4) the governance structure. Finally, they offer some general conclusions regarding the future importance of community-based medical education.

A word about the authors: there are twelve in all, and each has had a significant role to play in creating and building NOSM. In planning the book, it was decided that the value of the collective experience of these central actors would outweigh any difficulties that might arise in trying to meld their different contributions into a single coherent work. Because of their involvement (whether past or current), it might be argued that the authors lack the necessary objectivity to provide a critical perspective on the developments they are describing. Certainly they all share an evident pride in and enthusiasm for the school and a strong commitment to ensuring its long-term success. And this is apparent in their writing. But all are also keenly aware that NOSM's stature among Canadian medical schools will depend far more on the quality of the educational experience of its graduates and the range of skills that they bring to their practice than on any amount of cheerleading from its principals.

A final note to the reader: NOSM has gone through some name changes during its progress from original conception to current status. Since these names and their ubiquitous acronyms appear in the early documentation and, consequently, throughout the text, a brief statement of the history of the changes might prove helpful.

NORMS – NORTHERN AND RURAL MEDICAL SCHOOL

When, in his report to the Government of Ontario, Robert McKendry first floated the idea of a new school located in Northern Ontario, he acknowledged that the problem of physician shortages was as acute in southwest rural communities as it was in Northern Ontario. Consequently, he recommended that the school be designed to address the needs both of northern and rural communities. The pan-northern working group that developed the first full proposal took up this idea, named itself the NORMS Liaison Council, and submitted its proposal under the name NORMS.

NOMS – NORTHERN ONTARIO MEDICAL SCHOOL

When the Ontario government announced in May 2001 that it intended to fund a new medical school in Northern Ontario, it specified that the school would focus primarily on northern needs. It had other plans (detailed in the report of the Expert Panel) for decentralizing clinical education in rural parts of southern and southwestern Ontario. So the word "rural" was dropped from the name, and the embryonic school flew under the NOMS flag.

NOSM – NORTHERN ONTARIO
SCHOOL OF MEDICINE

When the school was officially established as an independent entity and had achieved its first provisional accreditation status, its new Board of Directors chose a new name that would distinguish it from its mixed ancestry and announce to the world that it had come of age. The official name of the school is now the Northern Ontario School of Medicine – and it is expected to remain so for the foreseeable future.

Acknowledgments

Coordinating the contributions of twelve authors, who were not only from quite different backgrounds but also spread over different parts of the country, represented a more serious challenge than we imagined. At the outset, a Hannah Development Grant from Associated Medical Services enabled our authors to meet face-to-face to map out the manuscript and, in the final stages, Joanne Richardson's rigorous editing lent a new cohesion to our manuscript. Kathryn Needham organized our various meetings and teleconferences and, together with Nicole Lauzon and Natalie Raymond-Marois, ensured the smooth flow of communication between us all. Cara Blasutti and Amy Roy helped to make sure our tasks were completed on time. We are indebted to all of them.

Chronology of the Development of NOSM

Pre-1990
Since their inception in the mid-1960s, both Lakehead and Laurentian universities had frequently lobbied the provincial government to develop medical schools on their campuses. These efforts met with little success.

1972
McMaster University develops a program for some of its students to undergo periods of clinical experience in northwest Ontario (Northwest Ontario Medical Program [NOMP]) under the leadership of Dr John Augustine.

1991
Creation of family medicine residency programs in Thunder Bay (as an extension of McMaster's program) and in Sudbury (as an extension of the University of Ottawa's program).

1997
The Ontario government funds the Northern Academic Health Sciences Network (NAHSN) with a range of undergraduate and postgraduate medical education initiatives targeted for communities across Northern Ontario.

July 1999
In the face of growing concerns about physician shortages, Dr Robert McKendry was commissioned by the Ontario Ministry of Health and Long-term Care to report on issues of physician supply and demand in the province.

September 1999
A brief was submitted to Dr McKendry from Lakehead University
and Laurentian University, indicating the readiness of the two institutions to work with their respective clinical education organizations and their regional hospitals in the development of a northern
rural medical school.

December 1999
The McKendry Report was published and included among its recommendations the creation of a new medical school located at
Laurentian and Lakehead universities and designed specifically to
meet northern and rural medical training needs. The report included the Laurentian/Lakehead brief as an appendix.

January 2000
(1) Minister of Health Elizabeth Witmer announced the formation
of an expert panel, under the chairship of Dr Peter George, to
advise the government on the implementation of the McKendry
recommendations.
(2) A working group named the Northern Ontario Rural Medical
School (NORMS) Liaison Council was formed to develop a full proposal for a new school. The council, co-chaired by the two northern
university vice-presidents, included representation from the two
northern family medicine residency program organizations (NOMP
and NOMEC), the two regional hospitals, and a leading community
member from Thunder Bay and Sudbury, respectively.

May 2000
Meeting in Toronto of five mayors with Minister of Health Elizabeth
Witmer to press the issue of the Northern Ontario rural medical
school. The minister shows interest in the proposal and indicates
her willingness to have the George Panel receive a proposal.

June 2000
A proposal for the development of a northern rural medical school
(NORMS) with sites at Laurentian and Lakehead universities was
submitted by the NORMS Liaison Council to the Expert Panel on
Health Professional Human Resources. The proposal outlined a
model for a new stand-alone medical school specifically designed to
meet the needs of northern and rural populations in Ontario and

drawing on the existing network of physicians across the North involved in family medicine residency programs. The school's conception drew on the experience of successful rural medical education initiatives in Australia, the United States, and Europe.

August 2000
Presentation of the NORMS proposal by representatives of NORMS Liaison Council to the Expert Panel.

December 2000
Leaks from the Expert Panel suggest that the committee was only prepared to recommend a gradual approach to the northern school, beginning with the expansion of clinical education in the North. The mayors' coalition and the NORMS Liaison Council collaborate to publicly denounce this satellite model, saying that it falls far short of northern expectations.

January 2001
Toronto Star leaks key elements of Expert Panel report – *Shaping Ontario's Physician Workforce*. The report includes a wide-ranging set of recommendations aimed at expanding the number of undergraduate and postgraduate training slots in Ontario. Sudbury and Thunder Bay (together with Windsor) are designated as clinical education centres at which the clinical education of rural stream students will be established, with the development of a fully independent new northern school envisaged only as a probable subsequent outcome.

February 2001
Mayors' coalition meets with Minister of Northern Development and Mines Dan Newman, who commits $40,000 to the funding of an international symposium on rural medical education.

April 2001
International Symposium on Rural Medical Education is held in Sudbury. Presentations from leading medical educators from Australia, Norway, Finland, Canada, and the United States describe successes in rural medical education initiatives in their countries to a wide-ranging audience of physicians and health care professionals, academics, community leaders, and government officials.

May 2001
Minister of Health and Long-term Care Tony Clement and Minister of Northern Development and Mines Dan Newman jointly announce the intention to create a northern medical school, to open in 2004 and with fifty-five places to be based at Laurentian and Lakehead universities. Unlike the NORMS proposal, which envisaged dual campuses, this announcement designated Sudbury, in Northeast Ontario, as the main campus and Thunder Bay, in Northwest Ontario, as a clinical education campus. There was considerable disappointment in Northwest Ontario at the lesser role accorded to Thunder Bay.

October 2001
Premier Mike Harris announces the formation of the Northern Ontario Medical School Implementation Management Committee (IMC) together with $3 million to set the process in motion. The mandate of the IMC, to be chaired by Sudbury mayor Jim Gordon, is to produce a business plan with implementation guidelines that would see the new school open its doors to the first students in September 2004.

January 2002
Dr Arnie Aberman, the former dean of medicine of the University of Toronto, is appointed as "consulting dean" to the northern medical school project.

April 2002
Dr Roger Strasser, the former head of the School of Rural Health at Monash University, Melbourne, Australia, is appointed as founding dean of the Northern Ontario School of Medicine (NOSM). Dr Strasser is widely recognized as a leading international authority on rural medical education.

May 2002
Premier Ernie Eves (assuming the premiership of Ontario after Mike Harris's retirement from politics) includes in the Throne Speech a commitment to a dual campus model that would give an equal role to Lakehead University and to Laurentian University.

August 2002
The IMC submits its business plan, together with implementation guidelines, to the minister of training colleges and universities. The

business plan closely reflects the community-based distributed learning model outlined in the original NORMS proposal. It endorses the dual campus model, according an equal role to Lakehead and Laurentian, and it recommends the establishment of NOSM as a distinct legal entity (a not-for-profit corporation) that would be recognized, through their respective senates, as the Faculty of Medicine of both universities. However, NOSM would be answerable to its own Board of Directors, which would represent the two universities and the communities of Northern Ontario.

May 2003
Premier Eves announces a $95.3 million investment in NOSM over three years (capital and operating grants). This announcement closely reflects the start-up and operating expenditures envisaged in the IMC Business Plan and also makes capital expenditure provision for the development of separate buildings to house the new school at both the Laurentian and Lakehead sites.

December 2003
Inaugural meeting of the NOSM Board of Directors. The board chair is to alternate between the presidents of Lakehead and Laurentian universities. The thirty-five-member board represents diverse professional, regional, and linguistic communities throughout Northern Ontario.

June 2004
NOSM announces provisional accreditation of its year 1 program by LCME/CACMS.

September 2005
Official opening – charter class of fifty-six students arrives on campus.

Acronyms

AAMC	Association of American Medical Colleges
AFMC	Association of Faculties of Medicine of Canada
AMA	American Medical Association
CACMS	Committee on Accreditation of Canadian Medical Schools
CAUT	Canadian Association of University Teachers
CBL	case-based learning
CBM	case-based module
CBME	community-based medical education
CCC	comprehensive community clerkship
CLS	community learning session
CMA	Canadian Medical Association
CMPA	Canadian Medical Protective Association
CRaNHR	Centre for Rural and Northern Health Research
DCEL	distributed community-engaged learning
DFS	discipline-focused session
DTS	distributed tutorial session
FMN	Family Medicine North
GPA	grade point average
HIRC	Health Information Resource Centre
ICE	integrated community experience
IMC	Implementation Management Committee
LCME	Liaison Committee on Medical Education (US)
LHIN	Local Health Integration Network
MCAT	Medical College Admission Test
MCS	module coordination session
MMI	multiple mini-interview
NAN	Nishnawbe Aski Nation

NAHSN	Northern Academic Health Sciences Network
NOMS	Northern Ontario Medical School
NOMEC	Northeastern Ontario Medical Education Corporation
NOMF	Northeastern Ontario Family Medicine
NOMP	Northwestern Ontario Medical Program
NORMS	Northern and Rural Medical School
NOSM	Northern Ontario School of Medicine
NOSMFA	Northern Ontario School of Medicine Faculty Association
OSCE	objective structured clinical examinations
OHIP	Ontario Health Insurance Plan
OMSAS	Ontario Medical School Applications Service
OTSS	Ontario Trust for Student Support
PBL	problem-based learning
PCS	primary care session
PRCC	Parallel Rural Community Curriculum
SCS	structured clinical skills
SES	specialty enhancement session
SLG	Senior Leadership Group
TOS	topic-oriented session
UAP	Underserviced Area Program
VARs	virtual academic rounds
VC	videoconference
WGS	whole group session
WHO	World Health Organization

NOSM Charter Class, Fall 2005

PART ONE

The Context

1

For the North, by the North, in the North: From Dream to Reality

GEOFFREY TESSON AND JOHN WHITFIELD

The vigorous public debate that both preceded and accompanied the creation of the Northern Ontario School of Medicine was largely focused on the school's being a solution to the physician shortage in Northern Ontario. Viewed from a broad perspective, creating more doctors is only one part of what is required to deliver good-quality health care to the dispersed population of Northern Ontario. Problems relating to attracting enough doctors to the North have been compounded by the difficulty of keeping them there once they came. The long-term solution was to be found in a whole range of initiatives, such as seeking to attract students with an affinity for working in the North, devising curricula that would provide them with the skills that would help them to meet the challenges they would face, and developing different configurations of health professionals that would be more suited to northern conditions. But the idea of creating a new school to produce more doctors for the North focused energies in a way that no mere listing of measures for improvement ever could. Once the rough and tumble of the political dynamic was over and the school was announced, then the task of shaping it and its curriculum – the purpose of which was not only to create more doctors but also to transform the nature of northern and rural practice – began.

This chapter relates the events that led up to the announcement that the school would be created: the early aspirations, the increasing involvement of northern physicians in medical education initiatives, the reports that preceded the decision, the importance of political factors, and the role of the different institutions and individuals involved. Its aim is to set down what happened and to recognize the role of the central actors involved. Subsequent chapters address the more complex issues arising from the development of the school's curriculum, its admission policies, and its governance and administrative structure.

THE DREAM

Lakehead University and Laurentian University were created in the 1960s as part of the expansion of postsecondary education in the Province of Ontario. As regional universities serving primarily local populations, they offered a full range of science, arts, and professional programs at the undergraduate level, including a number of health-related programs. Later, they developed a select range of programs at the MA and PhD levels. Both universities aspired, at the outset, to develop medical schools, although they had not envisaged this as a cooperative venture between the two of them. But it was not to be. The prevailing wisdom at that time was that medical schools should be associated with larger, more well-established universities with close links to a teaching hospital. When Ontario created a new medical school in the early 1970s it was at McMaster University in Hamilton rather than in the North. McMaster's School of Medicine turned out to be an important innovator in medical education, introducing problem-based learning and committing itself to community-oriented medical education, including in the North. The dream of developing an independent medical school in the North would have to wait until the right conditions were present.

GROWING CAPACITY IN THE NORTH: THE DEVELOPMENT OF NORTHERN CLINICAL PROGRAMS

The path to becoming a practising physician is a long one. In a typical case, students take a four-year undergraduate degree, four years in a Doctor of Medicine (MD) program, and then two years of residency in family medicine (or longer for other specialties). Only then can they be certified to practise medicine. An important part of the whole learning process involves the development of clinical skills, which takes place under the guidance of practising physicians in various health care settings, from teaching hospitals and community clinics to doctors' offices. Because the clinical learning experience plays an important role in shaping the student's perception of the practice of medicine in general, its form and location often exert a strong influence on where the student chooses to practise upon graduation. It has been recognized for some time that students who experience most of their clinical learning in urban settings are more likely to opt for urban than for rural practice, whereas the opposite applies to those who experience most of their clinical learning in rural areas (Kaufman 1990; Rosenblatt et al. 1992; Rourke 1996). The faculties of medicine at McMaster University and the University of Ottawa have been leaders in Canada in decentralizing parts of their clinical programs to Northern Ontario, with the goal of encouraging more of their graduates to practise there. And it is their efforts that must be credited with establishing foundations in Thunder Bay and Sudbury for later development.

In the Northwest, Dr John Augustine led the development of the Northwestern Ontario Medical Programme (NOMP), which, in 1972, started accepting students from McMaster for part of their clinical experience. In 1978, students from other medical schools started coming to NOMP for northern clinical experience, and, in 1991, northern residency programs for postgraduate residents in family medicine were instigated in both Thunder Bay (which took residents from McMaster) and in Sudbury (which took students from the University of Ottawa family medicine program). John Mulloy, the first director of the Sudbury program, describes these developments in more detail in chapter 4.

These northern family medicine programs were widely viewed as successful. Not only did they appeal to medical graduates from the region but they also drew top-quality students from across the country. More important, research tracking the subsequent career choices of these northern graduates showed that they displayed a much stronger preference for northern and rural practice than did graduates from urban-based programs (Heng et al. 2007). This provides strong support for the theory that doctors trained in the North would practise in the North.

The success of the family medicine and other programs at the two northern sites encouraged more ambitious projects, and, in 1997, a battery of new initiatives known as the Northern Academic Health Sciences Network received funding. The projects included new training opportunities for undergraduate students, a support program for allied health professionals (such as physiotherapists and occupational therapists), a program for heightening the awareness of health career possibilities among school-age northerners, and the development of residency training positions in such general specialties as psychiatry and general surgery. None of these projects was, in itself, a big head-line maker, but they were all important in a number of ways. First, they were an acknowledgment that providing better health care in Ontario's north required not merely sending more doctors but also creating the right mix of health professionals working in teams. Second, they signalled the North's growing capacity to manage medical education programs without going through existing medical schools. More important, they showed that there was a network of physician educators and other professionals in the North – people who were willing to take on new responsibilities and who were developing a taste for managing their own affairs.

MCKENDRY COMES TO THE NORTH

In July 1999, amid growing concerns about physician shortages, Dr Robert McKendry was commissioned by the Ontario Ministry of Health and Long-term Care to report on issues of physician supply and demand in the province. As part of his fact-finding mission, Dr McKendry visited Sudbury and Thunder Bay to meet with key stakeholders; and, during encounters with mixed groups of physicians and municipal and university officials, he floated the possibility of developing a new northern and rural medical school. It was an important moment. For the first time, the growing aspirations of the physician community and municipal and academic leaders were mirrored by a government-appointed expert who was about to make recommendations on how to address the physician shortage. The idea of a northern medical school was no longer simply a pipe dream.

In December, McKendry's report was published (McKendry 1999) and included among its recommendations the creation of a new medical school located at Laurentian University and Lakehead University and designed specifically to meet northern and rural medical training needs. The report, with its scholarly discussion of issues of physician supply and demand, gave new weight to the view that Ontario was suffering from a shortage of doctors and that the established medical schools had paid insufficient attention to preparing students for rural and northern practice. The report's cautiously framed conclusion that the physician needs of underserved areas such as Northern Ontario could best be met by building a new medical school in the region met with some scepticism from the existing medical schools (Walker 2001; Sullivan and O'Reilly 2002), but it generated a growing wave of popular support in Northern Ontario.

As is usual when substantial new policies are being contemplated, the minister of health, Elizabeth Witmer, announced the formation of an expert panel on health professional human resources, under the chairship of McMaster University president Dr Peter George, to advise the government on the implementation of McKendry's recommendations.

THE NORTHERN PROPOSAL

Northern advocates for the school recognized that they needed to be proactive in ensuring that McKendry's proposal did not die on the vine for want of a clearer idea of what could be achieved. The approach was two-pronged: academic and political. First, there were the logistic issues of putting together an academically credible proposal. A working group known as the Northern Ontario Rural Medical School (NORMS) Liaison Council was formed to flesh out a detailed proposal for a new school and to underscore the willingness of the key stakeholders in Thunder Bay and Sudbury to work together on the project. The Liaison Council, co-chaired by the two northern university vice-presidents (the two authors of this chapter), included the administrative heads of the two northern Family Medicine Residency Program organizations (Jim Kraemer at NOMP and Miriam McDonald at NOMEC); the two regional hospital chiefs of staff (Dr David Boyle at Sudbury and Dr Blair Schoales at Thunder Bay); two physician educators (Dr Bill McMullen, the chair of the NOMEC board, and Dr Rick Almond from the NOMP program); and, finally, a prominent community member from Thunder Bay (Dr John Augustine) and one from Sudbury (Maureen Lacroix). A lot of the work of the group was carried out by the Office of Health Initiatives at Laurentian University and relied heavily on the organizational and planning talents of two key staff members, Ann Pegoraro and Ann Moro. The work was funded by a grant from FedNor, a federal agency with a mandate to promote economic and social development in Northern Ontario. The proposal was intended for submission to the government's Expert Panel.

Second, it was clear that this technical approach had to be paired with a political initiative that would put pressure on the provincial government to take this proposal seriously. In the face of the apparent reluctance of the panel to receive submissions, the mayors of five major northern municipalities (North Bay – pop. 63,681, Sault Ste Marie – pop. 78,908, Sudbury – pop. 155,601, Thunder Bay – pop. 121,986, and Timmins – pop.43,686)[1] met in North Bay to plan a strategy to ensure that the government gave the project the support they felt it needed. Subsequently known as the Mayors' Coalition, the group agreed unanimously to support the development of a northern medical school and sought a meeting with Minister of Health Elizabeth Witmer to press their case. The minister showed interest and indicated her willingness to have the Expert Panel receive a proposal.

In June 2000, the proposal for the development of a northern rural medical school with sites at Laurentian and Lakehead universities was submitted by the NORMS Liaison Council to the Expert Panel on Health Professional Human Resources (NORMS Liaison Council 2000). This was the first time that a document actually spelled out what a Northern Ontario medical school might look like, and it included estimates of what it might cost and how long it might take to establish. The proposal outlined a model for a new stand-alone medical school, which, following the suggestion in the McKendry Report (1999), would be specifically designed to meet the needs of northern and rural populations in Ontario, hence the name: Northern Ontario Rural Medical School (NORMS). The NORMS model, as it became known, drew on the existing network of physicians involved in family medicine residency programs across the North. The school's conception relied heavily on the experience of successful rural medical education initiatives in other parts of Canada as well as in Australia, the United States, and Europe.

A medical education design team involving innovative medical educators from across the country contributed significantly to the development of the model. This team was led by Dr Jim Rourke, one of Canada's leading advocates for making medical education more responsive to the needs of rural communities. At the time,

---

1 Population figures are for the Census Metropolitan Areas or Census Agglomerations cited in the 2001 Census.

Dr Rourke was a faculty member at the University of Western Ontario's School of Medicine and was responsible for a program ensuring that, as part of their MD program, all of Western's students were exposed to rural practice. The design team also included Dr John Mulloy, the director of the Northeastern Family Medicine Program; Dr Rick Almond from the Northwest program; Dr Tom Scott from Newfoundland; and Dr David Topps from Calgary. Both Scott and Topps subsequently became involved in the development of NOSM. The Society for Rural Physicians of Canada, whose president at that time was Dr Peter Hutten-Czapski, a physician from a rural Northern Ontario community, provided further support to the project. Jim Rourke's leadership helped crystallize the team's strong emphasis on a distributed model that was especially suited to the Northern Ontario context.

The NORMS vision was:

> To establish an innovative, community based medical school in Northern Ontario to train physicians for practice in rural and remote environments with the goal to provide improved rural and northern health care. NORMS is born from the conviction that Northern Ontario cannot meet the health needs of its population through dependency on expertise concentrated outside of the region. The North has reached a point in its development where it has the capacity, the organization and the will to build its own health education and research institutions and to shape their products to meet the health needs of northern and rural populations. (NORMS Liaison Council 2000, 12)

NORMS's focus was "on rural, underserviced, Aboriginal and northern health care. It will provide state-of-the-art, high-quality medical education that produces graduates who have the knowledge, skills and interest to practice in rural, northern and underserviced communities" (8). During their education, students were to be exposed to a variety of clinical settings in different cultural communities, with special attention being paid to Aboriginal and francophone communities.

The proposal demonstrated a number of strengths. To begin with, it showed that there was a capacity and a taste for expanding medical education in the North. It laid out a model for an entirely new school – one that would not be dependent for its curriculum and its administration on an existing school. It demonstrated that people from different sectors – the physician community, the hospitals, the municipalities, and the universities – could lay aside their territorial rivalries and effectively work together towards a common goal. In particular, it showed an effective working relationship between the Northwest and the Northeast. The project was able to attract high-profile support from outside of the region: its advisory group included Dr John Evans, the former president of the University of Toronto, who had also served as McMaster's School of Medicine's first dean; and Dr Robert McMurtry, the former dean of medicine at the University of Western Ontario. Both these men were influential figures in the world of Canadian health sciences. A presentation of the NORMS proposal was made to the government's Expert Panel on 23 August 2000.

RE-ENTER POLITICS

By October 2000, the expected report from the Expert Panel had not yet appeared, and, in the North, doubts were emerging regarding the committee's readiness to recommend the creation of a new school. In Thunder Bay, Lakehead University president Dr Fred Gilbert voiced the suspicion that, on the panel, there was opposition to the idea ("Northern Medical School Decision a Month Away," *Thunder Bay Chronicle-Journal*, 24 October 2000). And Sudbury mayor Jim Gordon suggested that it might be time for politics to weigh in on the issue: "it's time for us, the Councils in the North, to move politically on this" ("Gordon Says North Must Keep Pressure on for Medical School," *Sudbury Star*, 26 October 2000). As the New Year opened, it became increasingly clear that the now overdue report would fall far short of northern expectations for a stand-alone school. In February, the *Toronto Star* published details of a leaked version of the Expert Panel's findings, confirming northerners' anxieties ("Create New Med Schools, Report Says," 16 February 2001). The recommendation would be that Thunder Bay and Sudbury, together with Windsor, become clinical education campuses, offering extensions of the MD programs of existing medical schools. While there was clear acknowledgment of both the overall shortage of doctors in the province and the more acute problem of rural and northern areas, the leaked recommendations nevertheless reflected the view of the medical education establishment that these needs could be best met by developing new streams within existing medical schools.

It is ironic that, had this proposal for extending undergraduate medical education in the North been made a year earlier, the North would no doubt have welcomed it with open arms and heralded it as a great victory. However, when it became apparent that the government's Expert Panel was going to recommend the more modest approach of building satellite campuses rather than a stand-alone school, throughout the North a whole torrent of discontent was unleashed. There is a respected political theory that maintains that revolutions occur not as a result of absolute deprivation but, rather, in response to rising expectations. The North's reaction can hardly be called a revolution, but there was a general public outcry because people's hopes had been raised and then been dashed. Mayors met and pronounced their dissatisfaction, newspaper articles and editorials appeared not only in Thunder Bay and Sudbury but also in North Bay, Timmins, Sault Ste Marie, and Kenora, all condemning the short-changing of the North and urging the government to keep faith with the original McKendry proposal. "Satellite Campus Not Enough" shouted an editorial in the *Sudbury Star* (24 February 2001), echoing the general sense of frustrated ambition. Adding its voice to the rising chorus of injured northern pride, the business community weighed in, with the Sudbury Chamber of Commerce offering a strong statement of support ("North Has Proven Med School Needed," *Sudbury Star*, 15 January 2001). Aboriginal communities proclaimed they were being cheated out of a promise of better health care. It was a remarkable exercise not only in political lobbying but also in public education. Ordinary citizens talked in an informed way about what sort of medical school would be best for the North, and, perhaps most important of all, they identified it as *their* medical school, which was being denied them. There is no doubt that this widespread community response gained the government's attention and made a difference.

With the Expert Panel's recommendations not only prematurely leaked but also roundly condemned as inadequate by those whose needs they were intended to meet, the actual appearance of the report (Government of Ontario 2001a) was a non-event. Its less controversial recommendations regarding, for example, increasing medical school enrolment and adding more northern and rural postgraduate residency positions, appeared subsequently as items in the government's Action Plan, which was announced in its April Speech from the Throne (Government of Ontario 2001b). Other than that, there was no official launching of the report. Meanwhile, the northern mayors had been busy. Spurred on by the support of the Federation of Northern Ontario Municipalities, they sought a meeting with the government ("Mayors Unite on Medical School," *Sudbury Star*, 24 May 2001). The minister whose attention they caught was Dan Newman, the newly appointed minister of northern development and mines. The minister was sufficiently sympathetic to the northern lobby to promise funding for an international symposium on rural medical education ("Experts Coming to Sudbury to Discuss Medical School," *Sudbury Star*, 1 March 2001).

THE INTERNATIONAL SYMPOSIUM

The offer to fund the symposium was an important signal that the provincial government was attentive to the disappointment over the Expert Panel recommendations and was providing a forum for the North to publicly make its case for a new school. Drawing on Jim Rourke's international rural health contacts, an impressive array of expertise in rural medical education was hastily assembled, including Dr Richard Hays, the founding dean of Australia's newest medical school, James Cook University, in Queensland's subtropical north; Dr Arthur Kaufman of the University of New Mexico, a long-time advocate of community-oriented medical education; and Dr Vinjar Fonnebo, the medical education dean at the University of Tromso, Europe's northernmost university, which lies well within the Arctic Circle. The symposium, held on Sudbury's Laurentian campus, achieved two important goals. First, it provided concrete examples of successful rural medical education initiatives in regions with similar issues of medical underservicing to those of Northern Ontario. Hearing others confidently describing their successes helped counter the view that the northern medical school project was a highly risky venture that was unlikely to succeed. Second, it created social and political momentum, engaging a broad span of community, government, and health leaders in a groundswell of public opinion in favour of the new school. Thus was the groundwork laid for a government announcement.

THE ANNOUNCEMENT

In fact, the government used the occasion of the build-up to the symposium to declare its intention to create a new medical school in the North. On 24 April 2001, a backgrounder to the Throne Speech included a commitment to a "made-in-the-North" medical school; and on 25 April, just two days before the planned symposium, Northern Affairs Minister Dan Newman made the much awaited announcement at a hastily convened press conference in Sudbury. While the magic words "made-in-the-North medical school" were reassuring to northerners, the announcement was still frustratingly vague on details – understandably, perhaps, since few either inside or outside government knew what was actually involved in starting a new medical school.

The real announcement came a month later – "real" because it came with details of how the school would be organized and a promise of funding that would set in motion the actual process of establishing it. On 17 May 2001, Tony Clement, Ontario's newly appointed minister of health, came to a packed auditorium in Sudbury to announce the government's intention to create a new medical school in Northern Ontario. This time it was clear that there would be a stand-alone school that would not be dependent on existing schools – a school that would create its own curriculum, which would be tailored to preparing students for northern, rural, and remote practice. The plan was to accept the first cohort of fifty-five students in 2004, and there was a promise of a budget of $3 million to start the process (Government of Ontario 2001c).

However, in the months to come, one detail in the announcement was to place a severe strain on the coalition of northern advocates of the school. All the previous planning had been based on a dual role for the Lakehead and Laurentian campuses, but this announcement assigned Sudbury's Laurentian University as the main campus and Thunder Bay's Lakehead University as a clinical education campus – in other words, a satellite campus. The reaction in Thunder Bay to this unforeseen asymmetry was one of outrage and disappointment. The two regions had worked together in a partnership of equals, and now one region was being assigned a junior role. Proponents in the Northwest felt betrayed, with Thunder Bay mayor Ken Boshcoff commenting: "We as a community have had our hearts ripped out" ("Med School Plan Sparks Outrage," *Thunder Bay Chronicle*

Journal, 18 May 2001). In the Northeast, the excitement at the announcement and the undeniable sense of pride that the region had been chosen as the favoured location was quickly tempered by an appreciation of the huge disappointment in the Northwest and of the fact that re-establishing the earlier, more balanced, partnership would require a lot of work.

A delegation of Sudbury community, medical, and academic leaders, led by Mayor Jim Gordon, flew to Thunder Bay to meet with their Northwest counterparts. The goal was to seek a compromise that would allay Northwest concerns about its role without jeopardizing the promised project. The meeting produced a commitment to work together to develop a business plan for the new school that would address the allocation of functions between the two centres as a matter of detail. Both mayors diplomatically pronounced themselves satisfied with the outcome ("Mayors Unite on Medical School," *Sudbury Star*, 24 May 2001). The issue was far from being resolved, but a common language had been found, and this was key to working towards a solution.

There was a second consequence of the decision to put a greater focus on the Northeast than on the Northwest, and that was the perception within a number of Aboriginal communities that their needs were being ignored ("NAN Leads Fresh Call for Full Med School," *Thunder Bay Chronicle-Journal*, 15 January 2002). As shown in Chapter 2, the Aboriginal population of Northern Ontario is proportionally more represented in the Northwest of the province than in the Northeast. The government's tilt to the Northeast was thus seen as a slight to the medical education ambitions of Aboriginal communities. The proposed program had made much of the intention to have the new school be more responsive to the dire health conditions of Aboriginal communities, and the communities themselves had shown a strong interest in becoming involved in the development of the school with regard to such issues as governance, curriculum, and admissions.

In an interview at the time of the NOSM inauguration, Goyce Kakegamic, the deputy grand chief of the Nishnawbe-Aski Nation, representing a large proportion of Northern Ontario's Aboriginal population (especially in the Northwest), stressed how important it was to have a full campus in the Northwest: "Many live in First Nations in our territory and ... in the Northwestern Ontario communities they will depend on the availability of qualified doctors and specialists. That is one of the reasons why we got involved in it as the Nishnawbe-Aski Nation, in the dream of a medical school in Northwestern Ontario. We took a proactive role to ensure that a Northern medical school becomes a reality, a real Northwestern Ontario school in Thunder Bay" (NOSM 2005, 8). In the event, the strong interest of Aboriginal communities in the project and their desire to be involved in the development process were no doubt persuasive factors in re-establishing a dual campus model in which both the Northwest and the Northeast played an equal role.

For francophone communities, the large majority of which lie in the Northeast of the province, the issue was posed somewhat differently. For franco-Ontarians, the primary issue was the extent to which the proposed school's program would be available in the French language. Laurentian University is, by charter, a bilingual institution and offers its programs in both English and French. The hope was that the proposed school of medicine would have the same bilingual structure. As the project moved into the implementation phase, it became clear that the provincial government was not willing to fund parallel English and French programs. The high cost of medical education in general meant that contemplating dual French/English programming would have placed the cost estimate of building a new school beyond the bounds of political acceptability. Francophone school board officials, while recognizing this reality, were concerned that bright franco-Ontarian high school students contemplating careers in medicine would switch their studies to English if they thought that there would be no opportunity to use their French in the new school. Assurances that high-quality premedical studies at the undergraduate level would still be available through Laurentian University and that every effort would be made to ensure that students would be given as much exposure as possible to francophone clinical settings went some way to allaying these concerns.

IMPLEMENTATION

It was not until the end of the summer that the provincial government announced the next steps in the process of establishing the new school. Most of the early efforts of the school's proponents had focused on the political process of convincing the government to make the necessary funding available. Now that that commitment had been made, attention moved to the task of assuring the school's academic credibility. All North American medical schools are subject to a rigorous accreditation process whose standards must be met before their graduates can be certified to practise medicine. A cautionary tale was circulating about an American school that had recently been denied provisional accreditation after it had already accepted students, and nobody wanted to repeat that experience. The planned 2004 opening date began to look daunting in view of the tasks that had to be accomplished on the academic front: the hiring of a dean and the recruitment of an academic team that could build a curriculum in time to meet the accreditation deadlines.

In October, Premier Mike Harris came to Sudbury to name a committee to devise a business and implementation plan for the school. The Northern Medical School Implementation Management Committee was also charged with consulting with northern communities and establishing a vision for the school. It was clear that, from the outset, the intention was to make this school responsive to the communities that it was created to serve. The committee was chaired by Sudbury mayor Jim Gordon and included two municipal councilors, Linda Cunningham from Kirkland Lake and Rene Larson from Thunder Bay. Geoffrey Tesson from Laurentian was named a member, and provision was made for the dean to be included as soon as s/he was appointed.

The committee realized at the outset that it needed to draw on outside expertise in the field of medical education and that the appointment of a dean, which was to be decided upon by the two universities, was an urgent matter. The committee named PricewaterhouseCoopers as a consultant with extensive health-sector experience to assist with the business plan, and the two universities jointly instituted an international search for a dean. As an interim measure, the universities appointed Dr Arnie Aberman, the former dean of the Faculty of Medicine at the University of Toronto, as a consulting dean. Dr Aberman brought much needed expertise in the structure and operation of medical schools to the implementation committee, and he enabled work to progress on the development of a business and implementation plan before a full-time dean could be appointed.

The naming of the committee, with a membership that included three from the Northeast and only one from the Northwest, reawakened concerns that Thunder Bay's role would be overlooked. Two things happened that would eventually allay those concerns. First, the implementation committee began working on an innovative governance model for the school that would place the two universities on an equal footing. Second, Premier Harris announced his impending retirement and, in so doing, opened the door to the possibility that his successor might be more open to a return to the original dual-campus model. Ernie Eves, the eventual winner of the Conservative leadership campaign, announced early in the race that he would support the dual campus model ("Let Universities Share Med School: Eves," *Thunder Bay Chronicle Journal*, 27 November 2001), a promise upon which he quickly delivered when he became premier.

In the meantime, work focused on translating the dream of a custom-designed medical school for the North into a clear plan regarding what was going to happen where as well as tying that plan to a rigorous accounting of costs. The committee followed the strong emphasis of the original NORMS proposal on a case-based approach, according to which students would work in small groups, learning both the basic science of medicine and developing their clinical skills in addressing the health issues typically presented by northern residents. The plan was for a distributed model of medical education, with students spending the vast majority of their learning experience in clinical sites across the North. Because this model was likely to cost more than a traditional classroom-based model, strong rationales were needed to justify it. However, one major advantage of the distributed model was that many communities in the North would come face to face with medical students, and this would increase their ability to identify with the school's mandate.

In April 2002, the dean search resulted in the appointment of Dr Roger Strasser as founding dean. Dr Strasser was, at that time, head of the School of Rural Health at Monash University in Australia, and he had an international profile as an advocate for rural medical education. He had played an important part in establishing Australia's leading role in directing medical education to serving rural population needs, and he was now ready to apply that experience to Northern Ontario. Even though he was not able to move from Australia until August, his appointment meant that he could participate in and influence the decisions of the implementation committee while it was completing work on the business plan.

THE GOVERNANCE MODEL

In North America, universities are the only bodies with the authority to grant degrees in medicine; therefore, faculties of medicine have to be part of a university. In the case of the Northern Ontario school, two important issues had to be resolved. First, how could one school of medicine be academically responsible to two different universities that were separated by a thousand kilometres? While there were several examples of faculties of medicine being related to more than one university, there appeared to be no example where more than one university was the degree-granting institution. Second, how could the school's governing structure be organized so as to make it more responsive to the communities it was designed to serve? It was Arnie Aberman who devised a solution, unique in medical school governance, whereby the school would be established as a distinct legal entity, answering to the two universities on academic matters and answering to an independent board on fiscal and administrative matters. This arrangement and its rationale are explained in detail chapter 8.

With Roger Strasser's appointment as dean, the whole process entered a new phase, with priority turning to securing government approval for the business and implementation plan. By August 2002, the Implementation Management Committee (IMC) was ready to submit its business plan, together with implementation guidelines, to the minister of training colleges and universities. The IMC business plan closely reflected the community-based distributed learning model outlined in the original NORMS proposal (NORMS Liaison Council 2000). It endorsed the dual campus model, according an equal role to Lakehead University and Laurentian University, and it recommended that the school be established as a distinct legal entity (a not-for-profit corporation) that would be recognized by both universities (through their respective senates) as the Faculty of Medicine but that would be answerable to its own Board of Directors, which would represent the two universities and the communities of Northern Ontario.

In May 2003, almost three years after the submission of the original proposal to the Expert Panel, Premier Eves announced $95.3 million in capital and operating costs for the Northern Ontario School of Medicine over three years. He also followed through on his campaign commitment to return to the dual campus model and, thus, finally put to rest the tensions created by the asymmetric model that had been proposed two years earlier. This announcement closely reflected the start-up and operating expenditures envisaged in the IMC Business Plan, and it included a capital expenditure provision for the development of separate buildings to house the new school at both the Laurentian and the Lakehead sites. That this major financial commitment, announced in the run-up to the coming provincial election, did so little to reverse the tide of fortune running against the incumbent Conservative government must be considered as something of a political irony. That the incoming Liberal government of Premier Dalton McGuinty not only honoured this commitment but also subsequently bolstered it with other commitments to the postsecondary sector is also an important milestone.

But politics and financial commitments just open the door to possibilities. The real work of building the Northern Ontario School of Medicine had only just begun. Dean Strasser now had the arduous task of assembling an academic team that, within a very short timeframe, could build a program and a curriculum that would meet stringent accreditation standards. The remaining chapters on this book tell the story of the real creation of the school.

2

A New Medical School in the Big Picture: Setting the Scene

RAYMOND W. PONG

INTRODUCTION

The Northern Ontario School of Medicine (NOSM), which officially opened in the fall of 2005, is the first medical school to have been built in Canada in over three decades. It is also the first Canadian medical school with a special mandate to train physicians to practise in Northern Ontario and/or in rural communities in other parts of Canada. What makes NOSM significant, other than the fact that establishing a medical school is a rare occurrence in this country? In this chapter I seek (1) to indicate the big picture within which NOSM is situated and (2) to understand how NOSM came about. These two objectives are interrelated as big policy decisions are rarely made in a sociopolitical vacuum. I argue that the founding of NOSM needs to be understood against a broad geographic, social, political, and health policy backdrop. In doing this, I hope to help set the scene for the chapters to follow.

In the next section, I describe the geography, population, and socioeconomic conditions of Ontario's northern region. I then offer a discussion of the health conditions in Northern Ontario; that is, the health status of the population, physician scarcity, and northern residents' concerns about access to medical care. After that I discuss attempts by the provincial government to deal with the physician-shortage problem and the emergence of a workforce strategy that places an increasing emphasis on rural/northern medical education. I conclude by situating the new medical school within the geographic, sociopolitical, and health workforce policy context.

ONTARIO'S PROVINCIAL NORTH

Northern Ontario covers an area of slightly over 800,000 square kilometres (more than twice the size of Germany), representing just under 90 percent of the land mass of Ontario. It is made up of ten territorial districts and has 152 municipalities, 104 First Nations, and over 150 unincorporated communities. It has several mid-sized or small cities, such as North Bay, Sault Ste Marie, Sudbury, Thunder Bay, and Timmins. Although these cities cannot be called rural, some are quite isolated. For instance, Thunder Bay is about 700 kilometres from Winnipeg and about 1,400 kilometres from Toronto. Some remote communities in Northern Ontario do not even have road access.

The population of Northern Ontario has been declining in recent decades, while the rest of the province has seen healthy population growth. With just over 800,000 people in 2005 (representing only 6 percent of the provincial population), Northern Ontario has a population density of about one person per square kilometre, compared to 111 persons per square kilometre in the south. About half of the Northern Ontario population resides in the five aforementioned cities, with the rest found in many far-flung towns, villages, and Aboriginal communities.

About 27 percent of the province's francophone population (about 147,000 in 2005) resides in Northern Ontario (mostly in northeastern Ontario). Also, of the 134 First Nations in Ontario, 104 are located in the North, accounting for close to half of the province's Aboriginal population and representing about 10 percent of the Northern Ontario population (recent immigrants and visible minorities account for smaller proportions of the population). The population in the North is also older than is the general provincial population.

Generally speaking, Northern Ontario lags behind the rest of the province in terms of socioeconomic development. Table 2.1 shows that the North had lower educational attainment, higher unemployment rates, and was more reliant on government transfer payments than was the rest of Ontario. The economy of many northern communities depends heavily on natural resource extraction, such as forestry and mining. About one-third of the incorporated municipalities are single-resource dependent, suggesting that the regional economy can easily be buffeted by widely fluctuating international

Table 2.1
Demographic and socioeconomic characteristics of northeastern Ontario, northwestern Ontario, and Ontario, 2001

	Northeastern Ontario	Northwestern Ontario	Ontario
Total population (2004)	567,900	242,500	12,392,700
Population aged 65 or above (%)	14.8	13.3	12.9
Population of Aboriginal identity (%)	8.0	15.9	1.7
Population who are recent (5–year) immigrants (%)	0.3	0.4	4.8
Unemployment rate (%)	9.8	9.6	6.1
Youth (aged 15–24) unemployment rate (%)	20.4	18.0	12.9
Percentage of female lone parent families	20.7	20.4	19.3
Percentage of population without completed high-school education	33.4	32.6	25.7
Percentage of income from government transfer payments	15.6	13.2	9.8
Percentage of economic families below low income cut-off	12.5	8.9	11.7

Sources: Socio-economic Indicators Atlas: North East LHIN (Toronto: Health System Intelligence Project, Ministry of Health and Long-Term Care, 2006); and Socio-economic Indicators Atlas: North West LHIN (Toronto: Health System Intelligence Project, Ministry of Health and Long-Term Care, 2006).

market prices for raw materials and that boom-and-bust economic cycles are frequent and devastating. The fact that, in the wake of uranium mine closures, Elliot Lake almost became a ghost town in the early 1990s (Heard 1999) illustrates the tenuous economic situation of many northern communities.

Canada's provincial norths, including Northern Ontario, have largely remained the cultural, economic, and social periphery of the nation – a vast hinterland whose utility appears to be solely for primary resource extraction – and they have been dubbed "the Forgotten North" by Coates and Morrison (1992). The fragile nature of the economy of Northern Ontario and the less than favourable social conditions experienced by many who live there have generated resentment towards and/or alienation from the rest of the province. As Weller (1990, 275) notes:

> The political patterns that are observable in northern Ontario are described here as the politics of disaffection ... The politics of disaffection are largely a reflection of a deep sense of grievance and alienation among many of the residents of northern Ontario. This sense of grievance is partly a reflection of a perceived ignorance of the north on the part of those in Queen's Park or the south in general. It is also partly because there are marked differences between the north and the south in terms of economic well-being, health status and services, education and educational services, and most other indicators. It is partly the result of an awareness that the region is unable to do much about its own situation given its relatively small percentage of the total provincial population and consequent lack of political influence.

Dunk (1991, 118) made similar observations when he described how working-class men in northwestern Ontario saw themselves: "They clearly perceive themselves as part of the hinterland. The feeling of alienation from the South is a fundamental feature of the identity of the whites who inhabit northwestern Ontario." The sense of disaffection and feelings of neglect occasionally boiled over and resulted in calls for Northern Ontario to become a separate province or for parts of the North to join Manitoba. The first of such calls for "independence" was made in the late 1870s by Simon James Dawson, the member of the provincial legislature for the District of Algoma, which, at the time, constituted a substantial part of what is now Northern Ontario (Weller 1985). In the early part of the last century, some Sudbury residents advocated the creation of a new province to be called "Huronia" (Coates and Morrison 1992). Such separatist sentiments have not completely dissipated, as is reflected in a recent study that examines the "costs and benefits" of Northern Ontario secession (Di Matteo, Emery, and English 2006).

HEALTH AND HEALTH CARE CONCERNS

Studies (e.g., Badgley 1991; Fair 1992; Wilkin 1992) have consistently shown that, compared to their urban counterparts, rural Canadians have poorer health status. Additionally, people living in the most remote areas are likely to have the worst health status (Mitura and Bollman 2003; Pampalon 1991; Romanow 2002). A national study by DesMeules and colleagues (2006) has shown that rural Canadians, particularly those living in small or remote communities, have shorter life expectancies and higher mortality rates.

The health status of Northern Ontario residents follows a similar pattern, as some earlier studies (e.g., Weller and Manga 1988) have found. Reporting more recent data, tables 2.2 and 2.3 similarly show that, compared to the provincial population, residents of northeastern and northwestern Ontario exhibit less favourable health status. They have shorter life expectancy at birth and are more likely to have activity limitations and higher mortality rates from various causes. In addition, logging and mining – activities commonly found in Northern Ontario – are some of the most risky forms of employment in terms of occupation-related injuries and fatalities. A study of the health of franco-Ontarians (Allaire and Picard 2005) notes that it is in northeastern Ontario – which has the greatest proportion of francophones among all regions in the province – that francophones were least likely to rate their health as "very good" or "excellent." Studies of Aboriginal health in Canada typically show that Aboriginal people experience poorer health status than does the rest of the population (Health Canada 2003; Diverty and Pérez 1998; Probert and Poirier 2003). Although information about Aboriginal health conditions in Northern Ontario is scarce, studies such as the one by Young (1988) suggest that Aboriginal people in this region tend to have poorer health status.

Poor population health status is rarely the result of a single factor, but mass media coverage of health issues in Northern Ontario suggests that the general public typically blames various health woes on difficulties in gaining access to health care. In particular, Northern Ontario residents have been complaining for decades about physician shortages. Because doctors and other practitioners are hard to find, small-town newspapers are full of stories about poor access. Even bigger communities, like Sault Ste Marie and Sudbury, often claim to have too few physicians to meet their medical care needs.

Table 2.2
Selected health status indicators for northeastern Ontario, northwestern Ontario, and Ontario

	North East LHIN	North West LHIN	Ontario
Female life expectancy at birth (years), 2001	80.5* (±0.5)	79.5* (±0.8)	82.1 (±0.1)
Male life expectancy at birth (years), 2001	75.0* (±0.5)	74.7* (±0.8)	77.5 (±0.1)
Low birth weight babies (1999–2001)	5.4%	3.7%	5.6%
Infant mortality rate per 1000 live births (1999–2001)	5.2 (±1.3)	5.1 (±1.9)	5.4 (±0.2)
Population who say their health is Excellent or Very Good, 2003 (age 12+)	53.7%* (±2.0)	51.0%* (±3.4)	57.4% (±0.7)
Population with an activity limitation, 2003 (age 12+)	28.3%* (±1.7)	29.4%* (±2.9)	24.6% (±0.6)

* Significantly different from provincial average based on assessment of 95% confidence intervals.
Sources: *Population Health Profile: North East LHIN* (Toronto: Health System Intelligence Project, Ontario Ministry of Health and Long-term Care, 2007); and *Population Health Profile: North West LHIN* (Toronto: Health System Intelligence Project, Ontario Ministry of Health and Long-term Care, 2007).

General political disaffection and specific concerns about health care feed on each other to sometimes become public outcries or provincial election issues. Physician shortages, crowded emergency departments, long waits for some medical services, insufficient hospital beds, and perceived inadequacy in health-related travel subsidies are often seen by the public or portrayed by the mass media as evidence of the government's lack of concern for the North. The importance placed on the Canada Health Act principles of accessibility and universality has also given northern residents powerful arguments with which to demand better access to medical care.

GOVERNMENT'S RESPONSE

Geographic maldistribution of physicians is not just a Northern Ontario phenomenon: it is a national as well as an international

Table 2.3
Selected age-standardized mortality rates per 100,000 population (avg. 2000–01)

	North East LHIN	North West LHIN	Ontario
ALL CAUSES	715.3	734.9	602.6
Infectious diseases	8.3	8.8	9.3
Neoplasms	203.9	206.2	181.4
Endocrine/nutritional disorders	29.3	37.7	26.1
Mental and behavioural disorders	17.8	22.5	15.0
Nervous system diseases	30.2	35.5	24.8
Circulatory system diseases	245.3	243.2	209.1
Respiratory system diseases	58.0	51.1	45.4
Digestive system diseases	27.0	29.9	22.6
Genitourinary diseases	12.8	10.4	11.1
External causes of mortality	51.2	64.5	32.6

Sources: *Population Health Profile: North East LHIN* (Toronto: Health System Intelligence Project, Ontario Ministry of Health and Long-Term Care, 2007); and *Population Health Profile: North West LHIN* (Toronto: Health System Intelligence Project, Ontario Ministry of Health and Long-Term Care, 2007).

problem. Physicians tend to be disproportionately located in larger urban centres. A study has found that just under 16 percent of family physicians and only 2.4 percent of specialists practise in rural Canada, where over 21 percent of all Canadians live. The situation in Ontario is no different. In 2004, 9.8 percent of family physicians and only 1.4 percent of specialists were located in rural Ontario, where about 13 percent of Ontarians lived (Pong and Pitblado 2005). As of April 2007, the Underserviced Area Program (UAP) of the Ministry of Health and Long-term Care designated thirty-seven Northern Ontario communities (including some larger ones like North Bay and Thunder Bay) as "underserviced" in family physicians, with a total shortage of 132 doctors. In addition, fourteen Northern Ontario communities were designated as "underserviced" in specialists, with a total shortage of 129 doctors.[1]

---

1 List of Areas Designated as Underserviced for General/Family Practitioners: April/May/June 2007 (Sudbury: Underserviced Area Program, Ministry of Health and Long-term Care, 2007); List of Areas Designated as Underserviced for Specialists: April/May/June 2007 (Sudbury: Underserviced Area Program, Ministry of Health and Long-term Care, 2007).

In response, the provincial Ministry of Health has, over the years, introduced many programs, including the UAP, with a view to recruiting and retaining physicians to work in Northern Ontario. It might not be a mere coincidence that the UAP was established in 1969, the very same year in which the Ontario Health Insurance Plan (OHIP) – the provincial Medicare program – was introduced. OHIP was intended to ensure universal access to needed medical and hospital care for all Ontarians regardless of their ability to pay. But removal of financial barriers is meaningless if providers and services are not available or are not readily accessible. Thus, as far back as 1969, the provincial government saw shortages of health care providers, especially physicians, in the North as an issue that needed to be addressed.[2]

Pong (2008) examines how the Ontario government has dealt with the problem of physician shortages in the North over the last several decades. He does so by tracing the use of various strategies and the introduction of various programs – such as those involving financial incentives, physician recruitment drives, medical practice support (e.g., access to continuing medical education), and service outreach (e.g., visiting specialist clinics) – as ways of improving access to medical care. However, after examining the numbers of physicians in Northern Ontario from the 1950s to the 1980s, Anderson and Rosenberg (1990) conclude that the UAP has not improved the supply or distribution of physicians in that region. Likewise, Weller and Manga (1988, 146) describe such programs as "band-aids" that "will simply continue to be applied to symptoms rather than an attack made on the sources of the problems." Instead, they, as well as others, recommend training health care practitioners in the North. The emergence of rural medical education in Northern Ontario could be seen as part of a more comprehensive strategy to address the physician-shortage problem.

Though small in scale, the Northwestern Ontario Medical Program, which started in the early 1970s in Thunder Bay, was the first medical education initiative in the North. The first substantial investment in northern medical training occurred in 1991, when two family medicine residency programs (the Northeastern Ontario

---

2 Lucas (1971) examined the availability of physicians in single-industry communities with a population of 30,000 or less in Northern Ontario in 1968, just before the launch of the UAP. Of the 240 communities studied, 176 (or 73 percent) were without a doctor, and another twenty-three had only one physician.

Family Medicine Program and Family Medicine North) were established in Sudbury and Thunder Bay, respectively. Since then, other northern medical education initiatives have been introduced, including the Re-entry Program in 1996, the Northeastern Ontario Postgraduate Specialty Program in 2000, and the Rural and Northern Clerkship Program in 2002. The biggest and most significant medical education initiative in Northern Ontario to date is the Northern Ontario School of Medicine. In formally announcing the establishment of a northern medical school in 2001, the then minister of health and long-term care, Tony Clement, said in a news release:

> Our government is committed to doing all it can to ensure there is the right supply of doctors in Ontario and that their services are available where they are needed ... We believe this "made-in-Northern-Ontario" medical school – the first new medical school in 30 years – will both train doctors and encourage them to practise in the North.[3]

Jointly located at Laurentian University in Sudbury and Lakehead University in Thunder Bay, NOSM accepted its first cohort of fifty-six students in the fall of 2005.

NEW DEVELOPMENTS IN RURAL MEDICAL WORKFORCE AND EDUCATION

The growing salience of the rural/northern medical training strategy, including the founding of NOSM, is by no means a matter of happenstance. As noted earlier, the traditional rural physician workforce strategies of financial incentives, practice support, and so on, while helpful and still widely used, have not solved the problem. It has become obvious that other strategies are needed not so much to replace conventional recruitment and retention programs as to complement them.

The last two decades have witnessed a growing body of knowledge on the relationship between rural medical education and rural medical practice (e.g., Brooks et al. 2002; Pathman et al. 1999;

---

3 "Government of Ontario News Release: Harris Government Announced New Northern Medical School and Increased Medical School Enrolment," Toronto, Ontario, 17 May 2001.

Rosenblatt et al. 1992; Rourke and Strasser 1996; Rourke et al. 2005; Tesson et al. 2006). Studies conducted in Canada and elsewhere generally support the notion that doctors with an extensive rural exposure during medical education and training are more likely to practise in rural areas. Research evidence specific to Northern Ontario has become available in recent years. These include studies conducted by the Centre for Rural and Northern Health Research (e.g., Heng et al. 2007; Pong et al. 2007), which found that the graduates of the two Northern Ontario family medicine residency programs were much more likely to practise in northern or rural areas than were graduates of other programs and that they had a high regard for the quality of their training. The accumulation of scientific evidence on the efficacy of rural medical education may have provided added impetus for provincial policy makers to seriously consider expanding rural medical education and training (including building a new medical school) in the North.

There is also a growing awareness of differences between rural and urban medical practice. For instance, rural physicians typically have a much wider scope of practice and are more likely to work in multiple clinical settings (Chan 2002; Hutten-Czapski, Pitblado, and Slade 2004; Olatunde, Leduc, and Berkowitz 2007; Pong and Pitblado 2005; Tepper 2004), mostly due to critical shortages of specialists in smaller communities and the need for rural physicians to fill some of the service gaps. Also, as noted earlier, rural or northern residents tend to have poorer health status and a heavier disease burden, and they may have greater or more complex medical care needs. Physicians trained in urban medical schools may not have sufficient confidence or skills to practise in small or remote communities, where they often work with little or no support. Not only does Northern Ontario require more physicians, it also requires physicians who are equipped with the requisite knowledge and skills to deal with special health problems in the region. Again, research has shown that physicians with a rural medical education background are better able to work in challenging rural environments than are physicians lacking such a background (Denz-Penhey et al. 2005; Worley et al. 2000).

There is also a growing realization that effective medical practice requires physicians to have a good understanding of the social, occupational, cultural, environmental, and behavioural contexts of their patient populations. Research has shown that the health of a population is shaped by a host of factors, the availability of medical care being just one of them (Lalonde 1974; Raphael 2004; Wilkinson and Marmot 2003). Northern Ontario has its own unique characteristics, as historical and sociological studies have shown (Dunk 1991; Lucas 1971; Stymeist 1975; Young 1988). Physicians from the area or trained indigenously may have a head-start advantage in this regard; transplanted physicians may take longer to become familiar with the historical roots, community structure, local lifestyles, and disease patterns of the population; and itinerant, or "revolving-door," physicians may never gain, or never care to gain, such insights. Thus, it makes sense for Northern Ontario to have some locally trained doctors who have a broad and deep understanding of the conditions that affect the health of northern residents rather than to rely entirely on imports from other parts of the country or the world.

Most important, there was a radical shift in perspective regarding physician supply. The official view in the 1980s and early 1990s was that Canada had a surfeit of doctors and that physician supply needed to be controlled (Barer and Stoddart 1991). This resulted in medical school enrolment cutbacks across the country and measures to restrict the number of international medical graduates allowed to practise. But concerns began to surface by the mid-1990s regarding potential physician shortages as a result of lower medical school intake and an anticipated massive retirement of doctors who graduated in the 1960s and early 1970s (Dauphinee 1996). The opinion pendulum has swung from Canada's having a physician surplus to Canada's facing a physician shortfall. This is reflected in a number of commission reports recommending an increase in physician supply in Ontario (Expert Panel on Health Professional Human Resources 2001; McKendry 1999), recent expansion of medical school enrolment, and measures aimed at enabling more foreign-trained doctors to practise (Dauphinee and Buske 2006). This change in attitudes may have been behind the building of a new medical school in Northern Ontario. Such a decision would have been unthinkable in the early 1990s, when medical schools were told to curtail enrolment.

CONCLUSION

The above is an attempt to show that NOSM was the result of a confluence of factors and that its founding was not fortuitous. The characteristics of the new medical school are also unique, reflecting specific needs and distinct circumstances. Situating NOSM within this broader historical, sociopolitical, and health policy context enables us to better understand how the newest medical school in Canada came into being and to better appreciate its mission and nature. The founding of NOSM could also be seen as the proverbial stone whose purpose is to kill two birds – to address some pressing medical workforce issues and to symbolically redress some sociopolitical grievances in Ontario's northern hinterland.

There are some practical medical workforce issues that NOSM can help to address, such as increasing the overall supply of physicians in the province and training physicians who are more likely to work in the North and who are more suitably prepared for medical practice in small or isolated communities. To this end, NOSM has adopted a set of social accountability principles and has developed a unique curriculum that pays special attention to rural medicine and rural population health issues. It is, therefore, not surprising that NOSM is the first medical school in the world to have adopted an integrated community clerkship model and to require its students to spend their third year living and working in small or remote communities in the North.[4] To address the problem of underrepresentation of rural students in Canadian medical schools (Hensel, Shandling, and Redelmeier 2007), NOSM has instituted special student selection criteria that give greater salience to rural or northern background and/or intention to work in rural or northern areas. Additionally, rural and northern health themes have been integrated into the medical curriculum, with a view to preparing physicians who have a better understanding of population health issues, particularly those with a rural or northern focus.

The creation of a school of medicine in Northern Ontario is also seen as a response to the inability of piecemeal measures to effectively overcome the doctor-shortage problem in northern areas. Although a single medical school will never be able to train enough physicians to meet the personnel needs of the North, it is an important physician workforce strategy and it will complement other programs. The emergence of rural medical education in Northern

---

4 "News: Northern Ontario Medical School First to Require Community Clerkships," *Canadian Medical Association Journal* 176 (5 June 2007): 1695.

Ontario reflects changes in rural health workforce strategic thinking, and NOSM is the latest and most ambitious project in a series of rural medical education initiatives in the North (Pong 2008). It is also a strategy that is backed up by a growing body of research evidence from Canada and abroad, which shows that rural background, training, and exposure do have an impact on where and how physicians practise.

Geographic maldistribution of doctors and lack of access to medical care due to physician shortages have resulted in calls by Northern Ontario residents for political action. Viewed from this angle, NOSM may also be seen as a symbolic political gesture, which shows that Queen's Park cares, has recognized the concerns of northerners, has done something about it, and has fulfilled one of the long-standing aspirations of northern Ontarians – to have a medical school of their own.

NOSM will be watched closely by many people – policy makers, health care officials, medical educators, researchers, and, of course, Northern Ontario residents. Because the newest medical school in Canada was founded with so much hope and anticipation, one of the challenges facing NOSM is its ability to manage such high, sometimes unrealistic, expectations. Will the students of NOSM reflect the demographic, cultural, and linguistic diversities of Northern Ontario? Will NOSM graduates have comparable, if not better, academic performance than graduates from other medical schools? Will NOSM be able to train physicians who are willing to work in small or remote communities? Will NOSM graduates be competent rural physicians, able to handle complex medical problems in relative isolation? Will NOSM be able to produce physicians who have a uniquely northern perspective on health problems? Will the graduates be able to address not just individual health problems but also broader population health issues unique to rural or northern environments? Because the making of a physician is a long process, it will take years to determine the outcomes of the most daring and exciting experiment in Canadian medical education in many decades.

3

Learning Medicine in Rural and Remote Community Settings

ROGER STRASSER

INTRODUCTION

The establishment in 1889 of Johns Hopkins Hospital in Baltimore, Maryland, as a model teaching hospital, along with the publication of the Flexner Report on Medical Education in the United States and Canada in 1910, set the trend for medical education in the twentieth century (Papa and Harasym 1999). Flexner recommended that medical schools be university-based and that their education programs be grounded in scientific knowledge. This led to a model of medical education in which the first half of the undergraduate program is classroom-based, with a focus on the basic sciences, and the second half is clinically based. The teaching hospital provides the environment for learning clinical medicine grounded in the scientific method and research (Flexner 1910). By the latter half of the twentieth century, a growing concern that doctors were too focused on the "body machine" scientific model led to developments in problem-based learning and community-oriented medical education (Habbick and Leeder 1996).

The Northern Ontario School of Medicine (NOSM) is the first Canadian medical school of the twenty-first century. The NOSM model of medical education built on several educational developments during the last decade of the twentieth century, including problem-based learning (PBL), case-based learning (CBL), rural-based medical education, community-based medical education, the social accountability of medical education, and electronic distance education.

CASE-BASED LEARNING

Problem-based learning was introduced into medical education in the late 1960s and early 1970s by a group of pioneering new medical schools around the world, including that located at Canada's McMaster University. The essence of PBL is that students learn all their medicine in small groups through exploring a series of specially written, challenging, open-ended problems. In their pure form, PBL medical school programs have no separate courses or subjects and no forms of didactic teaching, such as lectures (Schmidt 1983). This cohesive, holistic approach takes integration in medical education beyond non-compartmentalized learning and organic systems-based curricula that were developed at the Western Reserve School of Medicine in the early 1950s (Papa and Harasym 1999). There are usually six to eight students in each PBL group, and they work as a team, developing their own learning objectives as a means of finding out about all aspects of medicine. The group facilitator is expected to encourage the self-directed learning process and to provide no specific medical expertise (Papa and Harasym 1999; Schmidt 1983).

Like PBL, CBL is a form of facilitated self-directed learning that occurs within small groups and that encourages teamwork among learners. A PBL problem would involve a very brief and concise (a paragraph or two) description of a case or condition for the students who are developing their own learning objectives. With regard to CBL, students are guided by broad learning objectives, and their cases involve complex, real-life scenarios that may run into many pages, emphasizing community and socio-demographic contexts (Kenny and Beagan 2004).

RURAL-BASED MEDICAL EDUCATION

Since the mid-1980s, research has shown that rural practitioners require a specific range of knowledge and skills. When compared to their metropolitan counterparts, rural practitioners provide a wider range of services and carry a higher level of clinical responsibility, and they do so in relative professional isolation (Hogenbirk et al. 2004). Rural family practice may be seen to have three broad components. The first component is broad, all round general practice/ family medicine. Like family practitioners in metropolitan areas, rural practitioners provide comprehensive continuing community-based care dealing with both acute and chronic illnesses. In fact, the rural practitioner is much more likely than is the urban practitioner to be providing all the medical services for individuals and families. The second component of rural practice is procedural care. Dealing with emergencies is generally an unavoidable part of rural practice. In communities where there is no hospital, emergencies come directly to the family practitioner's clinic. If there is a hospital in the town, the family practitioner is likely to be providing medical services there, including emergency services, as well as in-patient services covering anesthesia, surgery, obstetrics, internal medicine, pediatrics, geriatrics, and psychiatry. Where the community has other residential care, such as a nursing home and/or hostel, the family practitioner provides medical services to their residents (Rourke 2001; Strasser 1992; Strasser et al. 2000).

Rural family practitioners also provide community-level care, thus fulfilling a significant public health role. In some communities, this includes focusing on clean water, sanitation, food, and shelter. In addition, rural family physicians provide preventive care through immunization and health screening activities, which may be both clinic- and community-based. Also, rural practitioners often contribute to health promotion and community education activities, including through speaking to different community groups. There is evidence that rural people, unlike urban people, give more credence to health information received from their doctors than from any other source. This provides the opportunity for rural practitioners to bring about change in health-related behaviours at the community level.

Research into rural practice and, more broadly, into rural health led to the inclusion of specific rural-oriented curriculum content in rural-based family medicine residency programs (Hays and Gupta 2003; Strasser 2001; Working Group on Postgraduate Education for Rural Family Practice 1999). Medical education research shows that the rural setting provides all medical students and residents with the opportunity for high-quality clinical and educational experiences, including those on health care teams. This would indicate that all medical learners should undertake some clinical work in rural areas (Worley, Prideaux, et al. 2000).

In the United States, the Washington, Wyoming, Alaska, Montana, and Idaho (WWAMI) network started in 1970. Initially involving Washington, Alaska, Montana, and Idaho, this network linked the most rural states in the United States. Subsequently, Wyoming joined as well. WWAMI medical students undertake the first year of their four-year undergraduate education in their home state and then complete their second year at the University of Washington in Seattle. Years three and four are undertaken in a range of locations; for some students, this includes prolonged clinical attachments in rural primary care settings. In addition, there are a number of WWAMI residency programs that place particular emphasis on primary care and rural practice. The return rate of WWAMI graduates to rural and underserved areas is significantly higher than is that of graduates in other state medical schools (Ramsey et al. 2001).

Since the 1970s, other medical schools in the United States have included "rural tracks." These usually involve a selected group of rural-origin students undertaking some or all of their clinical learning in rural locations. Examples include the Rural Physician Associates Program (RPAP) of the University of Minnesota (Verby 1988), the Physician Shortage Area Program (PSAP) of Jefferson Medical College in Pennsylvania (Rabinowitz et al. 2001), and the Upper Peninsular Program in Michigan (Brazeau et al. 1990). In general, these programs report recruitment and retention rates in rural and underserved areas that are four to five times above the national average.

In addition to urban-based medical schools that provide rural clinical rotations, there is a growing list of medical schools that are established in rural communities and that focus on recruiting students from surrounding rural and remote areas. The University of Tromso Medical School in northern Norway was founded in 1968 and has been successful in graduating doctors who practise in that area. Eighty-two percent of Tromso graduates who grew up in northern Norway continue to practise in that region (Magnus and Tollan 1993). The Jichi Medical School, established in 1972, has also been successful, with the vast majority of its graduates practising in rural and remote parts of Japan (Inoue, Hirayama, and Igarishi 1997). The Zamboanga Medical School in the Philippines was opened in 1994 as a community-based school whose graduates were prepared to practise on Mindanao Island or in other rural parts of the Philippines. James Cook University School of Medicine in Townsville, Australia, was established in 1999, with a specific focus on rural, remote, and Aboriginal health (Hays, Stokes, and Veitch 2003).

In the mid-1990s, Flinders University in South Australia pioneered a form of rural community-based medical education in which a group of students completes its core clinical learning in rural family practice. Through the Parallel Rural Community Curriculum (PRCC), students undertake the third year of a four-year medical program based in family practice, and they live in one rural community for the entire year. The learning objectives for this third year are the same as those for third-year students in the city teaching hospital. They cover the major clinical disciplines in medicine (internal medicine, surgery, pediatrics, etc.); however, rather than learning these clinical disciplines in sequential blocks (known as clerkships rotations), the students learn them in tandem (Worley, Silagy et al. 2000). The PRCC has been studied closely and has been found to provide learning experiences that are equivalent to, if not better than, those provided by clinical learning in the metropolitan teaching hospital (Worley, Esterman et al. 2004). Specifically, PRCC students consistently outperform their city colleagues in the end-of-year examinations. In addition, PRCC students were found to have a higher level of confidence and competence within a broader range of clinical knowledge and skills than were their metropolitan counterparts (Worley, Strasser et al. 2004).

In general, evaluation of rural clinical attachments has demonstrated that the rural setting provides a high-quality clinical learning environment that is of potential value to all medical students. In particular, rural clinical education provides more "hands-on" experience for students, which means that they are exposed to a wider range of common health problems and develop greater procedural competence than do their urban counterparts. This is consistent with the findings that show that PRCC students achieve better examination results than do their colleagues in the metropolitan teaching hospital setting. Research into the Flinders PRCC suggests that the success of students who learn medicine in rural communities is based very much on student-teacher and student-student relationships as well as on student-community relationships across clinical, institutional, social, and personal dimensions (Worley et al. 2006). A key to improving learning involves paying attention to these relationships and ensuring that they are part of the curriculum.

COMMUNITY-BASED MEDICAL EDUCATION

Community-oriented medical education was developed in the late 1960s and 1970s largely by the same group of new medical schools that introduced problem-based learning into medical education. The intent was to have medical students learn not only about the biomedical and clinical scientific basis of patient problems but also about the community context and how it affects patients and their clinical problems (Habbick and Leeder 1996). This approach also provided the basis for establishing departments of family medicine and of clinical epidemiology/social and preventive medicine in these medical schools.

Community-based medical education developed out of community-oriented medical education in that students do not just learn about the community context in the classroom; they learn about it in different social and clinical environments. Specifically, clinical learning takes place in a wide range of community and health service settings, not only in large acute teaching hospitals (Howe and Ives 2001). Clinical learning sites include mental health services, long-term care facilities, and family practice clinics as well as hospitals and health services in remote, rural, and urban communities. Community-based medical education developed due to the recognition that a relatively small proportion of the population is cared for in large acute teaching hospitals and that trends in health care are towards greater community-based care, with acute hospitals focusing more on short-stay, high-technology interventions for rare or serious and often complex multisystem conditions (Green et al. 2001).

The development of community-based medical education in the 1980s and the 1990s provided the basis for suggestions that students would benefit from prolonged community-based learning, specifically in family practice, where they could learn the core clinical medicine known in North America as "clerkships" (Gibbs 2004). In the urban setting, this approach was developed at Cambridge University in England (Oswald and Jones 2001), and in rural family practice it became part of some "rural tracks" that were established by several US medical schools beginning in the 1970s (Ramsey et al. 2001; Verby 1988). As has been mentioned, it was the PRCC of Australia's Flinders University that provided the most comprehensive research evidence regarding the value rooted in rural family practice and community-based medical education (Worley, Silagy et al. 2000).

SOCIAL ACCOUNTABILITY OF MEDICAL EDUCATION

In 1994, the World Health Organization and the World Organization of Family Doctors co-sponsored a conference at the University of Western Ontario that focused on developing medical education that would meet community needs. Subsequently, the World Health Organization promoted the social accountability of medical schools as "the obligation to direct their education, research and service activities towards addressing the priority health concerns of the community, region and the nation that they have a mandate to serve" (Boelen 1995, S21). In 2001, the medical schools of Canada and Health Canada made a joint commitment to social accountability in the publication entitled *Social Accountability: A Vision for Canadian Medical Schools* (Health Canada 2001). When NOSM was incorporated in 2002, it became the first medical school in Canada whose establishment came with a social accountability mandate, in this case "to be responsive to the needs of the people and communities of Northern Ontario."

ELECTRONIC DISTANCE EDUCATION

Although distance education began in the eighteenth century, it was the development of the printing press and low-cost postal services in the nineteenth century that saw it expand to involve mass produced learning materials distributed to large numbers of learners at multiple locations. In the twentieth century, communication technology such as film, radio, television, and, most recently, the internet added to the range and scope, the complexity and flexibility, of distance education (Jeffries n.d.). For people in northern, rural, and remote areas, distance education provides access to educational opportunities that otherwise would be unavailable to them. In the 1980s, the Ontario government established Contact North, a provincial agency managing a wide-ranging northern educational network, to facilitate distance education, particularly in Northern Ontario, through the use of electronic communications.

More generally, the development of broadband communication information technology during the 1990s helped to reduce the isolation of rural living and also facilitated improvements in rural health care. Examples include teleradiology, which enables the transfer of digital X-rays and other medical imaging over large distances, as well as clinical telehealth services. In Northern Ontario, NORTH Network was established in 1999 to provide real-time health care using interactive video conference technologies. This clinical telehealth service has greatly reduced the need for people to travel in order to gain access to specialist care in rural and remote parts of Northern Ontario.

Combining electronic communications with distance education has enhanced flexible learning and improved opportunities for distributed medical education. With access to digital library resources and a growing range of educational resources available through the World Wide Web, medical students are able to pursue core learning while geographically dispersed. Electronic distance education gives students and residents the same access to curriculum materials, educational resources, specialist teachers, and other information as is available to their counterparts in large city teaching hospitals (Ruiz, Mintzer, and Leipzig 2006).

NORTHERN ONTARIO SCHOOL OF MEDICINE

Although the aspirations to establish a medical school in Northern Ontario stretch back over four decades, it was a combination of the educational developments mentioned above that made the NOSM model of distributed community-engaged medical education possible in the early twenty-first century. In addition, Northern Ontario had a strong track record of clinical education, beginning in the early 1970s with the Northwestern Ontario Medical Program (NOMP) and continuing with undergraduate and postgraduate medical education provided by both NOMP and the Northeastern Ontario Medical Education Corporation (NOMEC). In the early 1990s, family medicine residency programs were established in Northwestern Ontario through NOMP under the auspices of McMaster University, and in Northeastern Ontario through NOMEC in association with the University of Ottawa. Both these family medicine residency programs provided postgraduate medical education, using the preceptor model of one-on-one teaching-learning in clinical settings. These programs focused on preparing family medicine residents to practise in Northern Ontario and similar northern, rural, and remote areas. Both programs were very successful as, after fifteen years, over 60 percent of their graduates are practising in Northern Ontario (Strasser and Strasser 2007).

In addition, the Northern Academic Health Sciences Network (NAHSN) was established in 1997 as a pan-northern initiative linking NOMP and NOMEC. Funded by the Ontario government, NAHSN provided the framework for enhanced undergraduate and postgraduate specialty medical education rotations in Northern Ontario, plus clinical education in the rehabilitation sciences, inter-professional education, and "pipeline initiatives." The latter focused on encouraging Northern Ontario high school students, particularly Aboriginal and francophone students, to pursue health careers. All of these developments came together in a unique mix, which is the Northern Ontario School of Medicine.

Other factors that contributed to NOSM's being established in 2002 were essentially political. Northern Ontario had always been short of physicians and other health care providers; however, in the late 1990s, this shortage was felt nationwide. In this context, public and political attention was drawn to physician supply issues, and the possibility of establishing a new medical school was placed on the political agenda. In April 2001, the Ontario provincial government announced its decision to establish a new medical school in Northern Ontario.

The Northern Ontario School of Medicine was registered as a not-for-profit corporation in November 2002, with Lakehead and Laurentian universities as the members of the corporation. In the Letters Patent, which establish the corporation, the objects set out the school's social accountability mandate as: "providing under-graduate and postgraduate medical education programs that are innovative and responsive to the individual needs of students and to the healthcare needs of the people of Northern Ontario." The thirty-five NOSM board members are drawn from the two universities, the school, and community groups and organizations from across Northern Ontario.

In March 2005, the NOSM board approved the following Vision and Mission Statement: "The Northern Ontario School of Medicine is a pioneering faculty of medicine working to the highest international standards. Its overall mission is to educate skilled physicians and undertake health research suited to community needs. In fulfilling this mission NOSM will become a cornerstone of community health care in Northern Ontario" (see box 1).

NOSM's education and training programs are meant to span the lifecycle of a physician in Northern Ontario. This begins by offering programs that encourage Northern Ontario high school students to see themselves as possible future doctors and, therefore, to study hard and achieve the academic requirements needed to enter university and medical school in Northern Ontario. The NOSM selection

BOX 1: VISION & MISSION:
2005/06 – 2008/09

The Northern Ontario School of Medicine is a pioneering faculty of medicine working to the highest international standards. Its overall mission is to educate skilled physicians and undertake health research suited to community needs. In fulfilling this mission NOSM will become a cornerstone of community health care in Northern Ontario.

GUIDING PRINCIPLES

Our Students: NOSM will seek out qualified students who have a passion for living in, working in and serving Northern and rural communities. NOSM will develop physicians able to practice and engage in research anywhere in the world but who have a particular understanding of people in northern and remote settings.

Our Graduates: NOSM will graduate resourceful physicians who are successful in distant settings, have a preference for collaborative care and a greater capacity to serve their patients and communities with the available resources. While the context of the School will be northern, the application will be national and international.

Our School: NOSM, while preparing students for the full range of clinical disciplines in medicine, will focus on training general practitioners of medicine, family doctors and specialists, who remain generalists across their specialties. The School will foster an inter-professional approach to medical practice and research. It will value curiosity, inventiveness, integrity and be accountable in all aspects of its activities.

Our Faculty & Host Universities: NOSM will become another centre of academic excellence within Lakehead and Laurentian Universities. The School will be vigilant in the protection of academic freedom.

Our Employees: NOSM will treat staff with respect and, in accordance with its academic commitment, value honesty, integrity and openness in all dealings with its employees.

Our Communities: NOSM will pursue a culture of inclusiveness and responsiveness within the medical communities, the northern communities, the rural communities, and the Aboriginal and Francophone communities.

and admissions process favours applicants who come from Northern Ontario or similar rural/remote areas. Once admitted, students undertake an undergraduate medical program that has a strong emphasis on learning medicine in the Northern Ontario community context. Postgraduate programs provide residency training that targets practising in Northern Ontario or similar rural/remote areas. Once in practice, the school provides continuing education/professional development in order to support and maintain Northern Ontario physicians.

The curriculum for the undergraduate medical program was developed through a consultative process, which began with a curriculum workshop held in January 2003 and drew on the accreditation standards and curriculum resources of other medical schools. The January 2003 workshop, entitled "Getting Started in the North," was held in Sault Ste Marie and involved over 300 participants from all socio-geographic parts of Northern Ontario. To begin with, workshop participants were asked to identify the characteristics that physicians most needed if they were to practise in Northern Ontario. Responses provided a similar list of characteristics to that provided by the Educating Future Physicians for Ontario consultation of the 1990s (Neufeld et al. 1998). However, three characteristics stood out from all the rest: (1) a passion for living and working in the North, (2) the ability to be a team player and to contribute to the whole health team, and (3) sensitivity to diversity. Subsequently, consultative workshops were held with francophone and Aboriginal people as well as with health care providers across Northern Ontario.

In developing the NOSM undergraduate medical program, patient-centred medicine (PCM) was chosen as a core concept. PCM is a comprehensive clinical method with six interactive components, and it is supported by substantial and growing research evidence (Stewart et al. 2003). It links well to learner-centred education, which NOSM also chose as a core concept. NOSM's other core concepts are: "generalism" in health care; integration in health service delivery; interdisciplinarity (i.e., everyone on the health team, including specialists, acts as a consultant); and doctors as teachers and researchers. These core concepts are summed up in the six key academic principles that guide the development and delivery of all NOSM academic programs, including research (see box 2).

In order to ensure a holistic and cohesive curriculum, the NOSM curriculum offers no conventional courses or clerkship blocks; instead, the learning objectives are organized across four years in

BOX 2 ACADEMIC PRINCIPLES

The NOSM Academic Council has adopted the following key academic principles to guide the development and implementation of all NOSM academic activities and programs:

INTERPROFESSIONAL
The term interprofessional includes the key features of partnership, participation, collaboration, coordination and shared decision making. The term is applicable to all NOSM endeavors.

INTEGRATION
Integration in short, is the combination and interaction of individuals around common purposes and goals to create meaningful experiences for students, residents, faculty and staff.

COMMUNITY ORIENTED
Community orientation is the conceptual and pragmatic understanding of the dynamics of communities in the North and the creation of meaningful, enduring partnerships between all Northern Communities and NOSM.

DISTRIBUTED COMMUNITY ENGAGED
LEARNING
Distributed Community Engaged Learning is an instructional model that allows widely distributed human and instructional resources to be utilized independent of time and place in community partner locations across the North.

GENERALISM
Generalism is defined as a broad and holistic view and approach to activities, values and knowledge in educational, organizational and patient care activities.

DIVERSITY
Diversity encompasses a set of values that recognizes the richness of all cultures of Northern Ontario and the important ways they contribute to our lives.

the form of five themes: (1) northern and rural health, (2) personal and professional aspects of medical practice, (3) social and population health, (4) foundations of medicine, and (5) clinical skills in health care. Throughout the four years, classroom learning occurs mostly in small groups, with patient-centred case-based learning complemented by whole group sessions and clinical learning. Clinical placements occur in a diverse range of communities and clinical settings and are supported by high-quality electronic communications in the virtual learning environment. These include, in the third year, a full academic year of community-based medical education outside Sudbury and Thunder Bay.

With such a geographically vast area to cover, NOSM is heavily reliant on broadband communication information technology, which ensures that any space may become a teaching/learning space. Students are provided with a leased laptop computer and, wherever they are, they have the same access to information and educational resources as do their counterparts in urban teaching hospitals.

Through community-based medical education, NOSM students experience for themselves the diversity of communities and cultures in Northern Ontario, the different patterns of morbidity and mortality, the range of health service delivery models, and the challenges, rewards, and satisfactions of providing health care in Northern Ontario. Clinical learning takes place in over seventy different communities, not only in large acute hospitals but also in a range of health service settings, including mental health services, long-term care facilities, family practice clinics, rural community hospitals, and nursing stations in remote communities. During the third year of NOSM's four-year MD program, students have a prolonged clinical attachment that is based in family practice and involves living in one community (much like the PRCC at Flinders). During this "comprehensive community clerkship," the students become part of the health team and gain considerable "hands-on" clinical experience.

For NOSM, community engagement is consistent with the school's social accountability mandate and has a particular focus on collaborative relationships with Aboriginal communities and organizations, francophone communities and organizations, and rural and remote communities as well as the larger urban centres of Northern Ontario. These relationships are fostered through the Aboriginal Reference Group, the Francophone Reference Group, local NOSM

groups, and a vast network of formal affiliation agreements and
memoranda of understanding.

Like other medical schools in Canada, NOSM, through its residency programs, is responsible for postgraduate medical education.
Building on the successful family medicine residency programs in
the Northeast and the Northwest, NOSM's Family Medicine Residents of the Canadian Shield Program accepted its first residents in
July 2007. Through collaboration with McMaster University and
the University of Ottawa, NOSM is working towards offering accredited residency programs in the major general specialties of general internal medicine, general surgery, pediatrics, obstetrics/
gynecology, psychiatry, anesthesia, orthopedics, and community
medicine. This means that all NOSM MD graduates will have the opportunity to undertake residency training for family medicine and
the major general specialties within Northern Ontario.

Research is fundamental to improving health care and health outcomes; therefore, it is also essential to fulfilling NOSM's social accountability mandate. Building on existing health research
strengths, NOSM was successful in recruiting world-class scientists
to undertake research in its state-of-the-art laboratories. With funding from local, provincial, and federal governments, NOSM commissioned the report entitled *Creating a Sustainable Health Research
Industry in Northern Ontario*. This report offers thirteen recommendations, which provide not only a framework within which to
place Northern Ontario vis-à-vis the international health research
stage but also direction for NOSM research strategies. The primary
theme of NOSM research involves addressing questions that make a
difference to the health of the people and communities of Northern
Ontario. It should also be mentioned that NOSM has initiated annual northern health research conferences, which bring together
health researchers from all parts of Northern Ontario and beyond.

4

The Rural Physician and Medical Education

JOHN MULLOY

✳ The evening wind sighed in the spruce grove that surrounded the house as Michael lifted the steaming mug of tea to his lips. The ground, heavy with the fall rain, surrendered that almost chocolate odour so familiar in November. Snow was in the forecast. "That's unlikely," he thought out loud, "they're never right these days." The spindles of the porch railing offered little protection against the breeze but Michael barely noticed as his thoughts drifted.

"There must not be anywhere else on earth where a doctor can leave the operating room of a fifty-bed hospital at four in the afternoon and be fishing in the late afternoon sun in a canoe on the lake in front of his house. How is this kept such a secret?" he thought.

As beautiful as the moment was, however, Michael felt the uneasiness of a nagging concern. He had been feeling the beginnings of this concern for several months now but had preferred to push it away, as he would push the last piece of maple into the winter woodpile. Spring had come and gone without the arrival of the young physician and her husband. Michael and his eight colleagues felt that they had finally found the right person to join their group. She was the best prospect they had seen in the past six years – a family physician trained in anaesthesia who was willing to move into town. It was too good to be true. She was the right person with the right skills, liked by everyone and willing to move here. Everyone was relieved: "Finally, someone to help keep the surgical program running." It didn't happen. The mill didn't hire her husband as planned. Seems the price of pulp and paper was dropping, and, instead of hiring another engineer, the mill was announcing layoffs.

Michael had started to wonder if he would be able to retire as planned a year from now. Who would help care for his patients if he was to retire? In the past six years, three physicians had retired or moved away without finding their own replacements. Despite everyone's best efforts, doctors were hard to attract.

Almost six thousand people in a town, geographically isolated in Northern Ontario, were facing the prospect of increasing unemployment and shrinking access to medical care. By any analysis this was a terrible social situation – one with no single cause and obviously with no single solution.

No easy answers ever jumped out and presented themselves to Michael. "Ironic," he thought. This word often slammed into his consciousness. He was a surgeon in Northern Ontario who was willing to work but who had no possible way of administering an anaesthetic since the last anaesthetist had retired. A temporary supply of emergency locum physicians was the only thing that was keeping the town's surgeon from leaving too. Just like the winter woodpile, nothing had changed in months. Perhaps tonight's meeting with the medical school's representative might offer some hope. Michael removed his coat and went inside. Supper was ready. ✳

It was the resources that brought the workers to rural Northern Ontario during the first half of the twentieth century. First Nations communities had been here for centuries, but the mining operations and forestry industry brought an influx of families into Northern Ontario to provide the requisite labour. Municipal politicians across Northern Ontario and, for that matter, any part of rural Canada, might say: "The resources brought us here, but it is our resourcefulness that keeps us here."

In many ways, the same could be said about the health care workers who practised in these communities. As in many rural situations worldwide, clinical histories abound with details of physicians performing surgery or providing childbirth assistance at the family kitchen table. Excessive blood loss from emergency surgery was often met with blood donations from a member of the hospital staff or even from the physician her/himself. Resourcefulness is not limited to the improvisation of medical procedures and/or equipment but also often includes overcoming transportation barriers. Cross-country skis, canoes, and small float- or ski-equipped planes are essential tools for the rural physicians.

Companies quickly learned that keeping a healthy, happy, and productive workforce in isolated communities required that attention be paid to the health of the workers and their families. Doctors and nurses were even placed on corporate payrolls to ensure their presence in the community. Young medical graduates with minds full of ideas but bank accounts empty of savings often chose to work briefly for the companies to provide a short respite for themselves and their families in the period between medical school internship training and additional training in specialty residency programs. Under very difficult therapeutic conditions, inexperienced physicians performed incredible, even heroic medical acts while treating patients who were severely ill or suffering from catastrophic heavy industrial trauma. Tales of these acts became the stuff of folklore when these practitioners returned to specialty training programs in urban medical schools, and this distorted the true nature and rewards of rural northern practice.

While northern communities were growing in the mid 1900s, conditions were ripe for what resulted in decades of maldistribution of physicians in rural Ontario. Circumstances conspired to discourage young graduates from exploring the opportunities and adventures of rural practice. Northern communities enjoyed the services of a physician but only for the briefest period. Some still theorize that, paradoxically, this "corporate medical shuffle" functioned as a deterrent to a physician's establishing a permanent practice in these communities.

Some physicians, however, did come and happily stayed in many parts of Northern Ontario. For these people and their families, this meant enjoying all of the challenges and rewards of personal and professional careers, with daily recognition, interaction, and involvement with a community of patients becoming a way of life. Medical schools never really prepared these physicians for the boundary issues that arise when, for example, in seeking a home mortgage you must do so through a patient who works at the bank's loans office. Unique challenges arise when you are the only physician available to care for your secretary. How do you provide discipline to an employee if she/he is also your patient? How do you act as a physician to your own family when there is an emergency and the only other doctor in town is on vacation? These are vexing ethical questions for anyone, but for rural doctors they are a professional reality.

Those physicians who stayed in Northern Ontario quickly learned that they were not a renewable resource. Unlike the forest industry, which saw that new trees replaced those that were harvested, young doctors seemed not to be replacing doctors who were moving out of practice. Many communities were desperately short of physician services, and many factors, including family, religious, and/or cultural forces, were attracting physicians to the larger urban centres where they lived during their training programs. Communities quickly discovered that recruiting a physician often meant recruiting her or his spouse as well, both of whom had to be satisfied if they were to happily (and thus successfully) relocate to a new community.

The recruitment advantage enjoyed by communities involved in medical educational programs became self-evident. The cities with medical schools did not seem to suffer the same physician shortages as did those without them. During the mid-1900s, various physicians who trained in foreign medical schools were offered certification with the Royal College of Physicians of Canada if they agreed to a period of supervised practice in Ontario. Several of the larger northern communities hosted these supervised specialist candidates and, in fact, benefited from their retention after the period of supervision had ended.

Furthermore, many community physicians offered informal and "non-core" elective experiences to students from the medical schools from which they had graduated. Simply arranged, the former professor of medicine would receive a student's request to have a preceptor-based experience in a particular community, the professor would recall a graduate who had located to that community, the phone-call request would be made, and the student would be dispatched.

Overworked practitioners searching for new recruits could often spend months, if not years, enticing potential associates to their community. Locum or temporary work arrangements were often made for the new candidate, only to have that person eventually decline a permanent position. On the one hand, the locum technique, while frustrating, seemed to work, even if only inefficiently; on the other, it appeared that the preceptor-based technique was more natural and successful. In addition, the educational experiences that went along with the latter seemed to offer more satisfaction (albeit of an intangible nature) to the community preceptor. In some peculiar way, one's sense of self-validation, self-worth, and intellectual stimulation were all enhanced by teaching young students what it had taken years to learn in clinical practice. There was something truly "value-added" about work with visiting medical students: they were "extra work, but enjoyable to have around." In the words of Dr Len Kelly of Sioux Lookout, Ontario: "Many rural areas of Northern Ontario have a long tradition of teaching medical students. I came north as a medical student and returned as a clinician and teacher. Teaching is a vibrant part of rural medicine and most northern clinicians are very committed to it. Like anything else of value, passing it along is just the right thing to do. It is a part of the culture of rural medicine."

Coincident with the growing satisfaction with the entire rural community educational experience, in 1965 the Government of Ontario established a new medical school at McMaster University in Hamilton. There was some disappointment in communities across Northern Ontario as they had hoped a new school would be located in the northern part of the province. Notwithstanding this, key participants in the McMaster program were committed to the needs of the residents of Northern Ontario.

Dr John Evans, the McMaster school's first dean, and Dr J. Fraser Mustard, its second dean, were clearly visionaries and forward thinkers. They proposed and implemented a partnership arrangement with the communities of northwestern Ontario, whereby students from McMaster and all other southern medical schools would formally receive elective training experiences in Northern Ontario. Furthermore, the students from northwestern Ontario who applied to the medical school at McMaster would be given the same geographic weighting score as those students applying from Hamilton. The Northern Ontario Medical Program (NOMP) was created in 1970, and Dr John Augustine of Fort William (now Thunder Bay) was appointed as its first chair.

Not all practitioners embraced the initial academic partnership between a southern medical school and the communities of northwestern Ontario. According to Dr Augustine, "When the subject of NOMP and the alliance with the new avant-garde medical school was first discussed there were the usual nay-sayers with the recurrent theme of 'Why do we need a medical school to look over our shoulders? Some of us came up to the North to get away from their overbearing influence.' Or words to that effect." He also recalls the comment: "Once McMaster gets in here they will call all the shots." Further, he indicated that "the attitude of the more remote

practising physicians in such places as Dryden, Kenora, and Fort
Frances was actually more supportive, especially when improved
medical library services and actual visits from McMaster medical
faculty materialized."

Despite the vocal protestations of a few clinicians, there was
widespread enthusiasm among the northern practitioners, and clinical faculty were quickly recruited for the students desiring a NOMP
experience. Dr Augustine has many fine memories:

> Over a period of eighteen years I enjoyed the company of eighty-
> eight medical students in my practice of internal medicine. They
> were good company and in many cases an inspiration. Only one
> of these was a problem academically – and, wouldn't you know
> it, he was a local Thunder Bay lad in second year who later re-
> quired remedial help but did graduate with his peers. The bright-
> est of these eighty-eight students that came through my practice
> was a music student who changed courses and became a medical
> student. Does this say something about pre-med courses before
> entering medicine? A few of the medical students in NOMP came
> from other Canadian medical schools and a scattering from over-
> seas, including Scotland, England, and Switzerland. The medical
> teachers in NOMP generally had uplifting and broadening experi-
> ences with these young medical students. We also had residents in
> the general specialties at times.

Dr Augustine's reflections embody the spirit and attitudes of rural
and northern practitioners. Most of these people are strongly self-
reliant and have a keen sense of independence. However, most are
also acutely aware of the perils of professional isolation and admit
to liking the intellectual stimulation that is provided by academic
links to students and their teaching institutions. Most have mar-
velled in the joy and professional rewards that come with northern
and rural practice (although a few have only just survived professionally). Nevertheless, all know that they will not practise forever
and that they must plan for their own succession. This common
truth binds all northern practitioners to the objectives of rural, remote, northern, and community-based medical education.

In 1975, Dr Peter Neelands became the second chair of NOMP,
and, for almost twenty years, he guided the program. Looking back
at that time, Dr Neelands recalls the challenges of learning to juggle

the role of clinical preceptor while maintaining a busy practice: "For their part the students and residents brought to their mentors fresh critical thinking and ... [the ability] to access recent knowledge. Furthermore, the network connections with the universities that ensued became a fulfilling part of our lives. Our communities, our hospitals, and our spouses enjoyed and welcomed the new learners – many also with spouses – into our northern neighbourhoods."

Echoing the sentiments of other northern physicians, Dr Neelands states:

> The students coming to this environment learned how to make decisions without specialist backup on site. They gained confidence as they put their knowledge into practice at an early stage in their career. In many cases, as front-line workers, they were exposed to diseases or pathologies and learned how to handle situations that would have been relegated to others in the larger academic centres. In fact, many students and residents chose to follow their teachers into this kind of rural northern practice.

In his words:

> As chair of NOMP, I visited communities across the Northwest, began to set up the network, and recruited teaching doctors. As chairman I made certain that annual gatherings of the teachers occurred, thereby making it possible for them to express their own views about the program and the network. I felt a tremendous sense of satisfaction as we watched the network grow and receive positive feedback from the students, residents, and clinical teachers.

The first trainees in NOMP arrived in 1972, and, that year, eighteen medical students as well as thirty-eight postgraduate residents were placed for one month or more in the communities of northwestern Ontario. Dr Paul Humphries succeeded Dr Neelands as NOMP chair, and, in 1992, he guided the organization through the formation of the two-year family medicine residency program. Dr Humphries served a dual role in the Northwest in that he was both program director for Family Medicine North and chair of NOMP. In his words:

> Working to develop health care education in the region brought together an array of great people. Busy local doctors gave years

of service to teaching and to meetings in order to create and maintain an effective community faculty. Eccentric and politically daring administrators risked careers to challenge traditional bureaucracy. Students and residents threw themselves into pioneering projects and confirmed our commitment to this learning model with phenomenal clinical and academic performances.

In Thunder Bay, Family Medicine North (see below) received extraordinary efforts from Dr Neelands, Mr Peter Maurer, and Ms Susan Berry. Also providing limitless support was Ms Deloris McGirr, who was the "face" of NOMP for a decade.

The current NOMP chair, Dr Bill McCready, has published data showing that, by 1997, 2,355 trainees had participated in NOMP programs. He notes that:

Experiencing a NOMP placement was significantly associated with recruitment. This finding is consistent with the view that regional-based training leads to greater physician recruitment. Furthermore, of the individuals who experienced a NOMP placement, higher recruitment rates were found for postgraduates, undergraduates who came for multiple placements, and for those who came from certain universities. Rural experiences that are mandated may not have as large a payoff for recruitment as regionally focused initiatives that target training to those individuals who are raised in the region or who have an interest in northern and rural practice.

Dr McCready has witnessed the evolution of the northern practitioner from a rural or remote clinician into a community-based medical educator with a large clinical practice. He has witnessed the way in which, through their voluntary participation in the northern training programs, many overburdened, clinically driven physicians have transformed into student mentors and novice researchers. Like Dr Augustine, upon participating in the academic environment, he has enjoyed the broadening not only of his personal career but also of the careers of his colleagues.

According to Dr McCready:

While many clinicians came to northern Ontario to escape the world of academic medicine, the obligation to teach was never the reason they made that choice. Hence NOMP and NOMEC were able to provide teaching opportunities that many northern physicians embraced with enthusiasm. Teaching became a pleasure rather than an obligation. The volunteer nature of teaching also made certain that the two northern programs, by necessity, were extremely sensitive to the needs of their faculty. We, as teachers, then had the best of both worlds in that we maintained our independence while enjoying the challenge of teaching young physicians. The Northern Ontario School of Medicine has broadened the horizon for many of us, allowing clinicians to remain connected to their patients while pursuing an academic career that is uniquely northern.

Northeastern Ontario witnessed a similar formalization of community training experiences to that experienced in northwestern Ontario. In the mid- to late 1970s, an increasing number of medical students from Ontario medical schools were searching for community-based learning experiences in areas outside of the traditional academic teaching centres. NOMP was slowly becoming oversubscribed, and additional experiences were available in northeastern Ontario.

The University of Ottawa's medical school was experiencing some difficulty in achieving large-volume obstetrical clinical teaching cases for its rotating internship program. Expanded clinical capacity was needed, and Ottawa looked to Sudbury for a formal relationship between the medical school and the Department of Obstetrics at the Sudbury General Hospital. The parties held a series of meetings and formalized a one-month community rotation in obstetrics for rotating interns at the Ottawa Civic Hospital and the Ottawa General Hospital. Ottawa committed to twelve monthly rotations for one or two interns in order to provide a continuous presence on the obstetrical floor. The members of the Department of Obstetrics enjoyed some clinical respite, and the interns enjoyed an extraordinary clinical education.

In the early 1980s, with the growing popularity of these learning experiences, more students and residents were attempting to arrange community-based training experiences without a formal support program. Training was occurring via the informal network mentioned earlier as well as through the University of Ottawa's Community Outreach Program. With experienced faculty, and with solid evaluation data from multiple medical disciplines, two family medicine residents received approval to complete the entire second year of their two-year residency program in Sudbury.

Through the 1980s, word of the Thunder Bay/Sudbury experiences spread quickly among students and residents. The popularity of the learning opportunities created an increasing number of applicants. Evaluations included comments such as "Unfettered access to patients and their problems without having to stand back in the third row like at the medical schools"; "Outstanding teaching of practical patient management in the real world – not like in the big cities."

The rotations were so popular that students were competing for local preceptors. Several residents then applied for extended rotations across multiple disciplines in Sudbury, Timmins, and Sault Ste Marie, thereby making three- or four-month rotations ever more commonplace. Queen's University in Kingston built a solid relationship with the community preceptors in Timmins and established a major teaching presence on the James Bay coast at Moose Factory. The University of Toronto established programs in the Sioux Lookout Zone, and the University of Western Ontario had regular elective rotations in Sault Ste Marie. In many instances, eager faculty throughout the North were competing for residents and asking for a new student as soon as one had departed.

Throughout this period, all medical faculty gained pedagogical experience, and the university programs showed a record of solid evaluations for the academic rigour of the northern practitioners. There was a sort of mutual "self-awakening" to the fact that quality educational programs could, in fact, be delivered in areas far from a medical school and that busy community practitioners could not only provide quality patient care but could also become very effective teachers. The northern practitioners were proving their ability to the academic health science centres, and, more important, they were proving it to themselves.

Reflecting upon the expansion of clinical teaching across Northern Ontario, which would eventually lead to plans for a medical school, Dr Peter Hutten-Czapski of Haileybury, Ontario, comments: "Rural doctors, disillusioned [about] the prospects of having southern medical schools solve northern problems, felt a particular resonance for 'In the North, for the North, and by the North.' Buoyed by decades of success within northern academic programs preceptoring family medicine students and residents, the expansion proposals seemed eminently doable, despite the fact that few in the trenches had an appreciation for the magnitude of the enterprise and the changes that would occur."

With the looming introduction of the two-year family medicine residency in 1991, the departments of family medicine in Hamilton and Ottawa felt it was important to expose residents to community practice away from the academic centres. Their idea was to utilize the wealth of clinical teaching material in Northern Ontario. The doctors of the North believed that the next expansion of training should be entirely based in the northern parts of the province.

From 1989 to 1990, the group of clinical teachers in the Northeast and the physician teachers at NOMP in the Northwest, together with the support of the departments of family medicine in Ottawa and Hamilton, created a proposal to expand the intake of first-year family medicine residents by twelve at the University of Ottawa and by twelve at McMaster University. However, the northern proposal was that the expansion be based entirely in Northern Ontario. The existing northern electives programs would use their capacity and expertise to mount the entire two-year residency program expansion. The Ontario Ministry of Health appointed Dr Denis McCalla to chair an implementation advisory group to plan the expansion of the Ottawa and McMaster programs. The proposals were eventually approved, and, in 1990, Family Medicine North (FMN), based in Thunder Bay, and the Northeastern Ontario Family Medicine (NOMF) program, based in Sudbury, were born. Perhaps the most fortunate aspect of my career involved my being honoured by being named the first postgraduate program director of the NOFM program.

With solid academic evaluations and popular appeal, NOMF prepared rotations for the entry class of six students at each of the two northern hubs. Intake was planned at twelve residents, but we deliberately chose to start with a half cohort in order to ensure orderly development of the programs in Thunder Bay and Sudbury. From the outset, in order to meet the objectives of diverse student experience and broad faculty participation, the two programs were defined as decentralized.

Perhaps, from the outset, the biggest challenge was to convince the accreditation team of the College of Family Physicians of Canada that FMN and NOMF could meet the demands of the accreditation process within a non-traditional, community-preceptor, rural and remote residency model. As is required of all new programs, several accreditation visits occurred within the first two years of FMN and NOMF's existence.

A second major challenge was to ensure academic rigour in a popular program that involved overworked faculty serving a huge base of patients who were chronically underserviced. One can only compliment faculty members who gave endlessly of themselves to make the family medicine programs work. Without doubt, the overworked physician faculty dreamt that help would come if they could manage to "train to retain" the residents "in the North, for the North, and by the North"

In 1990, it was quite a novel idea to base an entire two-year family medicine residency program 300 miles away from the parent medical school. Many academics scoffed at the idea and predicted a rethinking of the approach once the residents faced their certification exams. In some circles, it was heresy to think that postgraduate medical education could occur five hundred miles away from a medical school. It was evident that a smaller, less formal program at Memorial University in Newfoundland was working well in Happy Valley-Goose Bay, Labrador, and the faculty believed strongly in the guidance of the Canadian College of Family Physicians.

Furthermore, the Northeast received immense support and guidance from Ottawa's dean of medicine, Dr John Seely, as well as from Dr John Forster and Dr Nick Busing in Ottawa. Mr Gerd duBois was recruited from Dalhousie University, Halifax, to act as the first program administrator in Sudbury. Continuous strong support also flowed from McMaster's chair of family medicine Dr Walter Rosser as well as from Dr Ron McCauley and Dr Allyn Walsh in Hamilton. Mr Jim Kramer was recruited from the University of Toronto to act as the administrator in Thunder Bay.

In the North, faculty would often muse that Ottawa and McMaster depended on us not to jeopardize their accreditations; occasionally, we would jokingly add that we also depended on them not to jeopardize *our* accreditations! In the event, Dr Paul Rainsbury and Dr Reg Perkins of the College of Family Physicians of Canada showed great faith in the efforts of northern faculty and accepted our innovative ideas for meeting existing standards for training programs.

I have often felt that the vision and support of Dean John Seely and Dr Walter Rosser truly empowered our efforts in Sudbury and Thunder Bay. They honestly believed we could accomplish our goals, and, furthermore, they could see that training physicians in areas where there was a shortage was a good thing to do.

At NOFM, the particularly dedicated efforts of Dr Brian Rowe, Dr Jane Cox, Dr Greg Mosdossy, and Dr Bill McMullen resulted in the creation of its academic program. This group was joined by Dr Jean Anawati of West Nipissing, Dr Al McLean of Sault Ste Marie, and Dr Eric Paquette of Timmins to engage in the construction of the NOFM program.

The governance structure in the Northeast was based on a not-for-profit corporation called the Northeastern Ontario Medical Education Corporation (NOMEC). Dr Bill McMullen served as the chair of NOMEC throughout its existence. A broad-based community representative board of directors helped guide the academic programs. Following the retirement of Mr duBois, the administrative team was headed by Miriam McDonald, who became chief executive officer. It was under Ms McDonald's direction that the major expansion and diversification of NOMEC programming occurred. She wrote proposals for the community development program and the Northeastern Ontario Postgraduate Specialty Program. And, through the digital information services of the Northern Ontario Virtual Library service, she ensured the relocation of medical library services into Northern Ontario. She also saw that third-year family medicine residency training was added to emergency medicine and anaesthesia.

NOMEC was founded with a northern accountability mandate aimed at recruiting and retaining health practitioners in all types of Northern Ontario communities. And it succeeded. In Ms McDonald's words:

> The feature that attracted our learners is our hands-on learning model offered in the unique environments of our northern communities. Our founding pioneers believed that training physicians alongside practising clinicians right in northern communities would convince them to stay and practise in these communities: they were right. Of the 170 NOFM graduates, 110 have remained in practice in Northern Ontario, and 40 percent are now clinical teachers themselves.

Dr McMullen, himself a seasoned faculty member, recalls some of the barriers to recruiting young physicians to the North: "It seems that often the difficulty faced by students is not a crisis of competence but rather a crisis of confidence. Exposure to community-based teaching experiences allows the students to prove for themselves that they truly have the ability to work outside of a major teaching community." Furthermore: "Residents from both large and small city backgrounds could feel confident to practise in rural and remote communities if they spent time training in those communities. As northern teachers we could do that for them. We could help them discover their abilities and the confidence to understand those abilities by showing them that they could do what we were doing every day. Things that they might never get to do in a southern teaching hospital."

NOFM and FMN matured to the point of maintaining twenty-four family medicine residents at each site, and many ideas for change came from these residents. They helped to build the very programs in which they were receiving their training and, in many ways, the current programs have been shaped by ideas that came from all of them. Everyone should admire the courage of the original six residents who came to NOFM and FMN. Faculty members repeatedly stated: "Our greatest inspiration came from the residents themselves. They were all truly magnificent people to be with."

Tracking studies of our graduates were conducted, and we were most pleased to see that the early numbers reflected our objectives. Clearly, our goal to train in the North, for the North, and by the North was succeeding, and FMN and NOFM were beginning to solve the physician shortage problems in Northern Ontario. The programs also demonstrated an ability to recruit francophone residents and residents from First Nations communities, who began to address the particularly acute shortages of physicians in these two key areas. Attempts were made to attract trainees who came from rural communities or those with a strong desire to practise in northern rural communities. And this strategy was clearly achieving results.

After ten years of operation, it seemed apparent that the essential foundation of a formal medical school had been put in place. Academic research was occurring, and faculty were asking for more residents than the existing programs were able to provide. As the northern model of decentralized community-based training demonstrated academic and recruitment success, other Canadian programs began to create similar programs in their own areas of influence. The committees of the College of Family Practitioners of Canada mandated that all academic programs include elements of community-based training to appropriately prepare residents for community practice. No longer were the Northern Ontario programs unique, and northern faculty realized that something more would be needed.

Increasingly, it seemed apparent that Canada should have a centre of excellence for northern, rural, and remote medical education. The geography demanded such a centre, and the population deserved it. It was time to move the faculty and the northern programs into a new home. It was time for a medical school. The Northern Ontario Medical School was about to be born.

PART TWO

The Content

5

Designing an Admissions Process for the Northern Ontario School of Medicine

JILL KONKIN

INTRODUCTION

This chapter describes the development of admissions policies and processes at the Northern Ontario School of Medicine (NOSM). Given that medical schools typically receive far more qualified applicants than they are able to accept, admissions policies and processes have functioned as important student selection tools, enabling the school to be more responsive to the needs of communities and to address physician recruitment issues in the region. The construction of NOSM's admissions process has been guided by the school's regional mandate, on the one hand, and by the available evidence regarding the effectiveness of different admissions procedures, on the other.

THE MEDICAL ADMISSIONS ENVIRONMENT IN CANADA

The decreasing number of Canadian medical school graduates choosing family medicine, along with the increasing shortage of physicians in rural communities, fuelled concern among both rural physicians, rural politicians, and rural community members regarding medical school admissions policies and processes. At the time of the development of NOSM's admissions process, a growing body of evidence indicated that it is possible to influence the mix of career choices among medical school graduates by changing admissions policies. Yet, little was changing in Canadian medical schools.

NOSM set out to develop an evidence-informed admissions process that would assist it in meeting its mandate. The task was made easier by the enthusiastic assistance of the admissions personnel, both faculty and administrative staff, from all six of the existing Ontario medical schools. The key innovations at the time of the development of the NOSM admissions process included: (1) the multiple mini-interview, which was developed at McMaster University; (2) the "bump-up" factor to the GPA scores of rural applicants, which was used at the University of Ottawa and the Quebec medical schools; (3) an evolving rurality index, which was being developed at the University of British Columbia to assist in recruiting students for that province's Northern Program (which commenced in 2004); and (4) the graduated weighting of GPA scores, which was being at the University of Ottawa.

THE MANDATE OF THE ADMISSIONS COMMITTEE

From the beginning of the development of the admissions policies and procedures for NOSM, the overarching goal was to reflect the demographics of Northern Ontario in the classroom. This meant that the admissions policies and procedures needed to recruit candidates who would be more likely to meet the needs of the communities of Northern Ontario, in particular the need for family physicians and generalist specialists who would stay and practise in these communities. NOSM's social accountability goals made it imperative that applicants from the communities of Northern Ontario, including a significant number of francophone and Aboriginal people, be in the majority in the charter class. The second imperative was to ensure that those applicants chosen for the charter class be capable of successfully graduating from the program.

THE EVIDENCE

What evidence regarding admissions policy is available in the literature? In the broader picture of medical education, research into admissions policies and procedures had been increasing over the fifteen years prior to the development of NOSM. Important elements of such admissions policy include:

- MCAT and GPA scores
- premedical coursework

- applicant background and demographics
- interviews

Evidence from all of these areas was used to inform the development of NOSM's admissions policies.[1]

MCAT and GPA scores

While many studies have indicated the use of the Medical College Admission Test (MCAT) scores for predicting the academic achievement of medical students (Mitchell, Hayne, and Koenig 1994), there is no evidence to validate this test either for Aboriginal Canadians or for francophone Canadians. It also should be noted that, at the time of the development of the admissions policies and procedures, there were no MCAT writing centres in Northern Ontario. The MCAT is an expensive test, made more expensive by the preparatory courses and materials that test takers feel is necessary to ensure better scores. Adding travel and accommodation costs to this could become a significant burden for those potential applicants studying or working in Northern Ontario. For these two reasons alone, it was decided that NOSM would not use the MCAT as one of the elements of the application cycle. At the time, neither McMaster nor the University of Ottawa used the MCAT to screen applicants, nor did any of the Quebec medical schools, except McGill. There is new evidence that the MCAT may be a better measure of academic performance than the undergraduate GPA (Julian 2005). However, there continue to be issues relating to cost, access to testing sites, and the validity of the test for NOSM target groups.

Undergraduate grade point average (GPA) is another predictor for performance on medical school and licensing examinations. The Admissions Committee chose to use 3.0 on the 4.0 scoring system as the minimum GPA requirement for application. There was little evidence in the literature at the time regarding the minimum necessary GPA to predict success on medical school assessments, though discussions with officials at several other medical schools indicated that many thought that at 2.8 students were likely to have some academic difficulties. Since the time of the implementation of the

---

1 Most of the citations in this section were the ones used at the time of the development of the policies. However, where a newer article improves the evidence, this is cited instead.

admissions process at NOSM, there has been some evidence published that 3.0 is a reasonable cut-off for undergraduate GPA (Albanese, Farrell, and Dottl 2005).

Premedical coursework

The content of required premedical course work is another area that was reviewed. Most Canadian medical schools continue to require certain courses, mainly sciences, before they will consider a student's application. There is little evidence that students who have taken undergraduate science courses prior to medical school have a significant advantage over those who have not (Brieger 1999). Certain courses (i.e., biochemistry and anatomy/histology) may improve test scores in the early undergraduate medical school years in those specific fields (Caplan et al. 1996).

Applicant background and demographics

Evidence regarding the premedical school characteristics of applicants that predict for family medicine and, in particular, rural practice was very important in the development of NOSM's admissions policies. The school's social accountability mandate was to serve the communities of Northern Ontario, and some of the outcome measures of this will be the numbers of graduates who choose family medicine, generalist specialties, and rural practice.

Studies do show that rural origin medical students are more likely than their urban peers to choose to practise in communities of similar size to those in which they grew up. Students of rural origin are also more likely to choose family medicine. As for the characteristics of the latter, the evidence indicates that these include female gender, a tendency to give oneself to one's community (Owen, Hayden, and Connors 2002), rural origin, and career plans to be a primary care physician at the time of admission (Rabinowitz et al. 2001). It has been shown that a program that, through special admissions policies, recruited medical students from rural backgrounds who expressed an intention to practise family medicine in rural and underserviced areas was successful in producing family physicians (five times more likely than the regular admissions program) and, in particular, rural family physicians (three times more likely) (Rabinowitz 1988). In a more contemporary Canadian study, the likelihood of rural origin students' choosing rural practice was 2.5 times as great as was the likelihood of their urban colleagues' doing so (Woloschuk and Tarrant 2004).

The Society of Rural Physicians of Canada Task Force on Admissions, which was available long before a summary was published (Rourke et al. 2005), helped to inform the admissions policy development. Recommendations of the Task Force included:

- ensuring that rural physicians and rural community members are represented on admissions committees;
- including rural physicians and rural community members as interviewers;
- developing strategies to increase the numbers of rural origin applicants to medical school;
- improving financial assistance to rural origin students in need; and
- developing a strategy/policy for rural admissions with a "rural adjustment factor."

Interviews

A literature review of interviewing processes at medical school determined that the reliability and validity of the predominant style of interviews, either one-on-one or panel-style, were being questioned (Kreiter et al. 2004). In the process of examining new possibilities, the multiple mini-interview process developed at McMaster (Eva et al. 2004) fit the needs of NOSM not only due to its increased reliability and validity but also due to its possible ability to level the playing field for applicants with varying abilities for self-promotion.

COMMUNITY GOALS

It was clear from the curriculum workshop held in Sault Ste Marie in January 2003, the Aboriginal curriculum workshop held with the Wauzhushk Onigum First Nation in June 2003, and the francophone symposium of May 2005 that the people of Northern Ontario expected to see the youth of the region well represented in their medical school.

An important message from the Aboriginal communities was that they wanted admissions policies that not only treated their youth fairly but that also would not be seen as lowering the standards in order to admit them to NOSM. The broad description of "Aboriginal" that appears in the Canadian Constitution (see below) was adopted to guide the determination of eligibility of applicants for the Aboriginal admissions stream.

The francophone community was clear that it expected significant numbers of franco-Ontarians in the charter class. However, in early discussions, the definition of who was francophone was quite wide open, and there was a significant push to consider anyone who was bilingual as being in this category. Over time, a more culturally based description of "francophone" was developed. The Aboriginal Reference Group and the Francophone Reference Group provided ongoing input into the policies and procedures of the medical school, including the admissions policies.

Community members were engaged in the admissions process at several levels. The initial consultations in Sault Ste Marie and with the Wauzhushk Onigum First Nation laid the groundwork. At both consultations, the report of the project known as Educating Future Physicians for Ontario (EFPO) figured prominently in the discussions (Neufeld et al. 1998). The key expectation that the medical school class would mirror the demographics of Northern Ontario was espoused in these consultations. The Admissions Committee and the Aboriginal Admissions Subcommittee recruited public members to sit as full members. Interviewers for the multiple mini-interview were a mix of NOSM faculty, Lakehead and Laurentian faculty, and members of the public. As well, the continuing participation of the Aboriginal Reference Group and the Francophone Reference Group provided helpful advice in the ongoing development of the admissions policies and processes.

ONTARIO EXPERIENCE: ONTARIO MEDICAL SCHOOL ADMISSIONS COMMITTEES AND THE ONTARIO MEDICAL SCHOOL ADMISSIONS SERVICE

From the outset, the individuals involved in admissions at other medical schools in Ontario (and, for that matter, elsewhere in Canada) were more than willing to discuss the policies and procedures of their own admissions processes. Admissions deans and chairs of admissions committees willingly found the time both for phone interviews and for face-to-face meetings. The same was true of the administrative heads for admissions in Ontario medical schools, who were very open to assisting with the logistics, both steps and timing, necessary to support the admissions process.

All medical school admissions in Ontario are channelled through a central body, the Ontario Medical School Application Service (OMSAS). Individuals at OMSAS were also very helpful and supportive during the development and implementation of the admissions policies and procedures for NOSM's charter class. Working with the Information Technology Unit at NOSM, the OMSAS staff ensured that NOSM was able to obtain most of the applications data from them electronically, starting in the first admissions cycle. Everyone shared their experiences and any evidence they had gathered for their own admissions processes. A genuine interest was shown in how a new medical school might be able to initiate new policies that other admissions committees might be interested in initiating at their own medical schools – polices that could take months to years to negotiate on their own.

The Admissions Committee

The composition of the committee that oversees the process of student selection is key to determining how admissions policies are enacted in practice. The NOSM Admissions Committee was formally constituted in early 2004, with a broadly representative membership. The twenty-one members of the committee were as follows:

- associate dean, admissions and student affairs (chair)
- medical students (2) – to be implemented once the Charter Class was in place
- medical sciences faculty members (NOSM) (2)
- clinical sciences faculty members (NOSM) (2)
- human sciences faculty members (NOSM) (2)
- faculty at large (NOSM) (1)
- clinical faculty at large (NOSM) (2)
- Lakehead University faculty (1)
- Laurentian University faculty (1)
- rural/remote NOSM faculty (2)
- Northern Ontario community members (2)
- Ontario Medical Association (Representative must be a clinician practising in Northern Ontario) (1)
- Aboriginal faculty member (NOSM) (1)

- francophone faculty member (NOSM) (1)
- senior admissions officer, non-voting

This mix of members allowed for a significant role for individuals outside of the full-time medical school milieu. The members of the Inaugural Admissions Committee were situated throughout Northern Ontario in two time zones. Individuals from rural communities were at the table, as were representatives of the two key partner communities: the Aboriginal and the francophone communities.

Meetings were held by teleconference, though it had been anticipated that there would be one or two face-to-face meetings per year. In the first two years of operation, only the subcommittee charged with the final detailed review of files met face-to-face. There was a consensus on the Admissions Committee that the group was effective and efficient as a virtual committee. This is an important message for all medical schools: it is possible to include people on the Admissions Committee who are distant from the metropolitan centre in which the medical school is situated without requiring them to travel to the city for meetings.

The Process

While the development and ratification of the terms of reference and membership of the Admissions Committee was under way, two working groups were set up to begin the admissions policy development: one for the overall admissions process and one for the Aboriginal admissions stream. These working groups were replaced in February 2004 by the Admissions Committee and the Aboriginal Admissions Subcommittee.

The Terms of Reference for the Admissions Committee passed by the Interim Academic Council on 26 February 2004 include:

> The Admissions Committee is charged with selecting the most suitable candidates to fill the designated number of positions available in any given year from the pool of applicants that apply to the school in that year. This committee has the delegated authority of the Academic Council to admit or decline to admit students, following guidelines and procedures approved by the Academic Council.

The committee will provide advice on all matters related to admissions to the undergraduate medical program, ... [will] receive reports from the Associate Dean, Admissions and Student Affairs, and ... [will] approve admissions policies.

The Admissions Committee met frequently through the early months of 2004 to review the evidence and to develop the policies for the admissions process at NOSM. An express goal of the NOSM admissions process was to "increase the number of entrants who come from rural, remote and northern urban backgrounds as well as applicants who are Aboriginal and franco-Ontarian." The Interim Academic Council further requested that the "Admissions Committee ... attempt to reflect the demographics of northern Ontario in the selection of the medical school class." The Academic Council document also requested that the Admissions Committee develop a selection process that is "open, transparent and equitable" as well as "evidence-based."

The Admissions Committee developed information (including the application form) for OMSAS to include in its website. All applications to Ontario's medical schools are handled centrally by OMSAS, and, by the time that NOSM joined, all applications were handled online.

The Policies

The Office of Admissions and Student Affairs developed policy papers on all of the key areas for admissions policies, incorporating what evidence there was at the time in order to facilitate the policy decision-making process.

The Admissions Committee was committed to fulfilling its mandate to reflect the demographics of Northern Ontario. To this end, it was necessary to examine identified barriers to admission of rural/remote origin applicants, Aboriginal applicants, and franco-Ontarian applicants.

Decisions regarding the prerequisites for application included:

- four-year undergraduate university degree (to be completed no later than June of the year of the offer of admission);
- no specific course prerequisites, though a recommendation that applicants with degrees in sciences should include courses in arts/

humanities/social sciences, while those with arts majors should include science courses in their degrees;

- MCAT not required; and
- minimum GPA for admission of 3.0 on the 4.0 scale.

The Admissions Committee decided not to include first-year marks in the calculation of GPA, the reason being that it wanted to avoid disadvantaging rural and remote origin applicants whose adjustment to the move to attend university might adversely affect their first-year standing. As well, the committee adopted a weighted formula, which allowed for increasing weight for the yearly GPA as applicants progressed through their undergraduate degree.

Quebec medical schools initiated a GPA "bump-up" as their rural adjustment factor – something that had been adopted by at least one Ontario medical school. However, the NOSM Admissions Committee determined that it would rather develop a scoring system based on the size of community from which an applicant came and the length of time she or he had lived there rather than "bumping–up" her/his GPA. This method would give an advantage to applicants from rural/ remote and northern urban communities while still allowing NOSM to follow the real GPA scores in its outcomes evaluations. The Admissions Committee developed a point system based on the size of community or communities in which an applicant had lived, the length of time she/he had lived there, and the distance of that community from a major urban centre. This was the NOSM "rural adjustment factor," as recommended by the Rourke Rural Admissions Task Force. Unlike other English-speaking Canadian medical schools, NOSM processed all applications from applicants meeting the minimum requirements (four-year undergraduate degree and 3.0 out of 4.0 GPA).

Messages given to potential applicants clearly indicated that there would be an advantage for those from specified backgrounds, as evidenced in the information developed for the OMSAS website:

The goal of the School's Admissions Committee is to reflect the demographics of Northern Ontario in its medical school class profile. Applicants who grew up in the communities of Northern Ontario, Aboriginal applicants and Franco-Ontarian applicants will all receive extra points on the Admissions Questionnaire. The Admissions Committee will choose students from a broad range of backgrounds who are capable of succeeding in the Medical Program. The School is focussing on family medicine and the generalist specialties of medicine (general internal medicine, general surgery, paediatrics, obstetrics and gynaecology, psychiatry), although the Medical Program will prepare students for postgraduate training in any field of medicine. The School is encouraging applications from students with a strong interest in and aptitude for studying and practicing medicine in rural, remote and northern urban communities. The Admissions Committee will be looking for highly motivated students who are self-directed and who will thrive in a small group case-based, distributed learning environment.

While there were some questions as to the fairness of this policy, mostly from parents of prospective medical school applicants who lived in the metropolitan centres of southern Ontario, it was widely accepted as an important strategy for a medical school with a very explicit social accountability mandate. Human rights professionals were consulted during the development of the admissions process. In Ontario, it is still possible to give an advantage to historically disadvantaged groups in processes such as admissions policies for medical school.

Consideration was given to using some form of non-cognitive psychometric testing, for example the Personality Qualities Assessment (Lumsden et al. 2005). There was little in the literature at that time, though medical schools in the United Kingdom and Australia were at various stages of piloting and/or implementing this sort of assessment. There were also some concerns about possible human rights issues that might be involved in the implementation of such testing. It was decided that this would not be part of the first admissions cycle but that it would be reconsidered at a later date.

Given the historical and severe underrepresentation of Aboriginal people in the medical profession throughout Canada, it was determined that there should be a dedicated Aboriginal admissions stream. The Admission Committee formed the Aboriginal Admissions Subcommittee, which was given the responsibility of making recommendations regarding this stream.

THE ABORIGINAL ADMISSIONS SUBCOMMITTEE

This subcommittee consisted of the following members:

- Aboriginal faculty member of the Admissions Committee (chair)
- practising Aboriginal physician

- director, Aboriginal affairs (NOSM)
- Aboriginal resident or medical student
- representative of an Aboriginal educational organization
- Aboriginal community member
- associate dean, admissions and student affairs

The initial Aboriginal Admissions Subcommittee was fortunate to recruit two practising Aboriginal physicians from Northern Ontario as well as an Aboriginal family medicine resident. All members of the inaugural Aboriginal Admissions Subcommittee were Aboriginal except for the associate dean. The chair of the subcommittee, one of the Aboriginal physicians, was also a member of the Admissions Committee.

The Process

The Aboriginal Admissions Subcommittee was charged with reviewing all candidates in the Aboriginal admissions stream who met the minimum requirements (GPA 3.0 or more; undergraduate university degree) and with recommending to the Admissions Committee those candidates who should receive an interview. Once the interviews were completed, the subcommittee reviewed the files of all interviewed candidates and recommended to the Admissions Committee those who should be considered.

The Aboriginal Admissions Subcommittee also developed preadmission workshops to which applicants interested in the Aboriginal stream could come for general information regarding the application process, including the multiple mini-interview and information about the NOSM Medical Program. Applicants and potential applicants could contact the Aboriginal physician members of the subcommittee by phone and/or e-mail in order to receive information and support.

The Policies

The Aboriginal Admissions Subcommittee worked to develop an open, transparent, and fair system for determining the eligibility of candidates for the Aboriginal admissions stream. The Constitution's definition of "Aboriginal" was adopted, which includes First Nations (status and non-status), Inuit, and Métis. Applicants were asked to provide some evidence of Aboriginal origin and a letter from an Aboriginal organization supporting their application. The process was to be as inclusive as possible, while ensuring that applicants had some connection to the Aboriginal community (in its broadest sense) and/or Aboriginal culture. Applicants in this stream were required to meet the same minimum requirements as were those in the general application stream (i.e., GPA 3.0 or greater, four-year university degree). The subcommittee members decided to use the same scoring system that had been developed for the general application pool to inform their process.

THE FIRST ADMISSIONS CYCLE

Information Technology and the Database

The members of NOSM's Information Technology Unit were instrumental in developing a user-friendly database for admissions, including online accessibility of all applications that facilitated secure, online application scoring. This system was designed from the ground up to meet the needs of NOSM's admissions process. All functions related to determining the ranking of applicants – both to determine who would be invited for interviews and to determine the final ranking list to be reviewed by the Admissions Committee – was managed through the database. It also allowed for the scheduling of both interviewers and interviewees.

Ontario Medical School Application Service

OMSAS personnel, the associate dean, admissions and student affairs, the senior admissions officer, and NOSM Information Technology Unit personnel worked together to ensure that the OMSAS online database downloads would be compatible with the NOSM database so that information could flow seamlessly between the two organizations. NOSM was one of the first Ontario medical schools to have a completely online admissions process. The ability to download information directly from OMSAS onto the NOSM database was of significant benefit to the process.

Applications Processing

Members of the Admissions Committee as well as NOSM faculty members not on the committee read through all eligible applications, which, in the first year (2005), amounted to 2,098 of the original 2,156 applications. Some of the applications did not meet the minimum requirements and so were disqualified. Each application was read and scored separately by two readers, and then the scores were averaged. All application readers either attended a preparatory workshop or were oriented to the work on a one-on-one basis by the associate dean.

The Admissions Committee developed scoring criteria in advance, and these included criteria for the autobiographical sketch as well as for the short-answer questions on the application form. They highlighted qualities such as self-reliance, self-directedness, and preparedness for work and life in Northern Ontario. The scoring criteria were informed by the University of British Columbia's Rural and Remote Suitability Score (Bates, Frinton, and Voaklander 2005) as well as by the evidence regarding characteristics that might make an individual more likely to choose a career in family medicine.

The scoring to determine the interviewee list was based on GPA (one-third), application score (one-third), and context score (one third). The context score was used to consider the community/communities of origin and the length of time the applicants had lived there.

Interviewing

NOSM adopted the multiple mini-interview (MMI) style of medical school interviews, which was developed at McMaster University. Members of the McMaster Admissions Committee and the admissions administrative staff provided significant information and support for the implementation of this interview process at NOSM.

The question writing and general logistics of the interview process were delegated to the MMI Subcommittee of the Admissions Committee. One of the initial concerns regarding this form of interview was the need for a facility with many small offices in close proximity to each other. One of the large medical clinics in Thunder Bay graciously offered its space for the two days of interviews held in that city. Sudbury proved more challenging as an adequate outside facility could not be found. The Sudbury interviews, held in March 2005, were conducted on two floors of the Willet Green Building, a large multi-use building that had housed the NOSM development team.

Individuals interested in serving as interviewers were invited to apply. The response to the advertisements – at NOSM, at the Northwestern Ontario Medical Program, at the Northeastern Ontario Medical Education Corporation, from the faculties of both Lakehead and Laurentian universities, and from the public at large – was impressive. All potential interviewers were required to attend an orientation workshop of about two and one-half hours, held both in Sudbury and Thunder Bay. The workshop was also given by videoconference so that individuals in communities outside of these two cities could participate. NOSM staff members most graciously volunteered to work on the weekends of the interviews to support the logistics of the MMI. Interviewers met in the morning of their interview day for the second of two orientation sessions.

After much discussion, it was decided that all interviews would be conducted in English, even when the interviewer and interviewee were French speaking. It was agreed that this policy would be reviewed in subsequent years. Four hundred applicants were interviewed over two weekends – two days in Thunder Bay and two in Sudbury.

Choosing the Charter Class

Once the interviews were complete, the final ranking list and waiting list were determined using the database calculation (i.e., all scores throughout the process were entered into the admissions database and calculations were performed on it). The application score and interview score were weighted 50:50. All Aboriginal applicants' files were reviewed by the Aboriginal Admissions Subcommittee. A list of applicants recommended for offer letters was developed and forwarded to the Admissions Committee.

The Admissions Committee mandated a subcommittee to review all of the files of applicants on both the letter of offer list (both general pool and Aboriginal pool) and the waiting list. Checks on references given in the autobiographical sketch, part of the online application, were completed before this subcommittee met.

Once the letters of offer were sent out, the database assisted in keeping track of acceptances. After some discussion, it was decided to regularly inform those on the waiting list of their own ranking and to update them regarding movement on the list.

The Admissions Committee had set a three-year period to meet the targets reflecting Northern Ontario demographics. These were

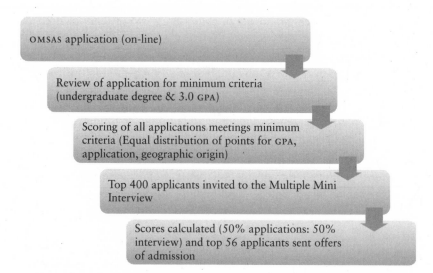

Figure 5.1: The Admission Cycle

met in the first year, with 12 percent of those sent letters of offer coming from the Aboriginal stream and 17 percent being franco-phone (30 percent were bilingual). More than 80 percent of the charter class had spent a significant part of their lives in communities in Northern Ontario.

The first admissions cycle was considered to have been a success. All new systems hit some potholes along the way, but the policies proved sound and the procedures were robust enough to allow for last minute logistical corrections without having an adverse impact on the integrity of the admissions policies and processes themselves.

THE SECOND ADMISSIONS CYCLE

Given the success of the first admissions cycle, few changes were needed in the second. These included minor refinements to the criteria for context scoring (to improve their clarity), database changes (to improve its already user-friendly interface and to incorporate some technical lessons learned in the first admissions process), and improvements to the compatibility between the NOSM and OMSAS databases. In the second cycle, student representatives from the charter class were added to the Admissions Committee and were in-volved in the interviews.

A study (Tilleczek et al. 2006) of interviewers, interviewees, and NOSM officials conducted at the time of the MMI interviews in Spring 2005 and immediately thereafter determined that all three groups felt that the multiple mini-interview was a fair procedure. Virtually all of the interviewees saw the process in a positive light, describing it as "fun," "student-centred," and "challenging." Most interviewers were also very positive. There had been some logistical difficulties at the Sudbury site with scheduling interviewers, and some interviewers saw this as a significant issue. Changes in the interviewer notification process were planned for the second admissions cycle.

There was further refinement of the means by which the Admissions Committee determined whether or not those who indicated they were bilingual in French and English were able to communicate in French. The initial plan had been to have a special station in the interview cycle for francophone applicants that would be conducted in French. Given logistical difficulties, it was decided that, in the first year, this would be replaced by asking candidates to write a short response to a written question. It was made clear to applicants that it was language, rather than content, that would be reviewed. For the second year's admission process, the written test was changed to an oral test.

The results of the second admissions cycle (2006) were similar to those of the first cycle in terms of mirroring the demographics of Northern Ontario.

The NOSM Admissions Committee is committed to a yearly evaluation of the admissions policies and processes. Some of the most important data will not be available until after 2009, once the charter class members have chosen their residency programs and then chosen the communities in which they will practise.

SOME LESSONS LEARNED

The experience of the Northern Ontario School of Medicine serves to confirm that it is possible to build an admissions system to enable previously underrepresented groups to be successful in becoming medical students. Starting with a clear understanding of the desired outcomes and using evidence-informed policy development and decision making allowed NOSM to build an innovative system to meet the expectations and needs of the communities it served as well as a fair, open, and transparent system for the applicants.

Steps to ensuring that the admissions policies of a medical school contribute to its fulfilling its social mandate include the following:

- Ask the community what principles it would like to see guide the admissions policies and use these as the basis for the medical school's policies.
- Clearly articulate the desired outcomes of the admissions process.
- Be acquainted with the evidence regarding admissions policies and processes and use this to make evidence-informed decisions.
- Collaborate with admissions colleagues from other Canadian medical schools.
- Ensure broad representation on the Admissions Committee.
- Involve community members in the interviews.
- Develop databases to assist the process and to track Outcomes.
- Add to the evidence with rigorous evaluation and study of your faculty's admissions process and outcomes.

While admissions policies play a role in predicting the career choices of medical students, undergraduate curriculum and experiences are significant factors as well. It is important to ensure congruence between admissions policies, the curriculum, and the overall mission of the medical school. NOSM is committed to doing this.

6

Building a New Curriculum for NOSM

JOEL LANPHEAR

It takes a village to train a doctor.
> Dr Dan Hunt, former vice-dean academic affairs, NOSM, 2005

The historical, political, economic, and geographic forces that have contributed to the creation of the Northern Ontario School of Medicine (NOSM) are described in other chapters. As Fisher and Levine (1996) have noted, medical school curricula tend to have patterns shaped by both internal and external forces. It is the purpose of this chapter to present the unique NOSM curriculum and to identify the processes, events, concepts, and decisions that led to its creation.

THE BACKGROUND FOR A NEW MEDICAL CURRICULUM

The foundation for what has become the NOSM curriculum is its educational social accountability mandate: "Providing undergraduate and postgraduate medical education programs that are innovative and responsive to the individual needs of students and to the health care needs of the people of Northern Ontario" (NOSM 2002b). In order to meet this mandate, curriculum planners, physicians, medical educators, and administrators had a variety of curricular models to consider when creating the NOSM blueprint. Fisher and Levine (1996), Papa and Harasym (1999), and Toohey (2002) have identified and agree upon the strengths and weaknesses of a variety of medical curriculum models.

Perhaps the best known is the discipline content based model, popular in the 1950s, in which specific subjects are taught separately based upon the principle that each has its own logic and is best learned as a separate discipline organized along departmental lines. The primary historical advantage of this model had to do with the research productivity of academic departments. Its obvious disadvantages are that, for the first two years, it separates medical science from clinical experiences and gives little attention either to the sequencing of basic science courses or to curricular experiences that provide students with the opportunity to bring together the content of separate courses. Finally, courses offered in specific disciplines tend to take on a life of their own, with little oversight on the part of the medical school as a whole.

A second medical curriculum model, which also emerged in the 1950s, is the organ systems model, in which the theme of each unit of instruction concerns a human organ system. This approach to integrating the medical (and sometimes clinical) sciences into organ system blocks was promising as body system faculty teams were created to develop course materials and presentations.

The organ systems model was heavily influenced by the behavioural theorists, who held that learning could and should be specified in terms of performance. Thus, organ systems developed extensive lists of objectives that included both "terminal" and short-term "enabling" objectives for each module and course. The best examples are those created at Southern Illinois University School of Medicine (1976).

The continued existence of departmental influences on specific content and the focus on faculty integration of teaching rather than on student integration of learning was a disadvantage of the organ systems model. Additionally, the complexity of integrating medical science and clinical science sometimes led to the oversimplification of material. However, perhaps its greatest flaw was its failure to present medical learning within an appropriate context – the patient.

In the 1970s, Dr Howard Barrows at McMaster University in Hamilton pioneered the problem-based learning (PBL) model (Barrows and Tamblyn 1980). This model, based upon small group learning that utilized commonly presenting patient problems, "contextualized" the learning of medical science and clinical science through the use of patient cases. Each small group, with a faculty facilitator who was responsible only for process issues and for suggesting new directions for obvious errors, was influenced by new learning theories from cognitive science research and, to some extent, by concepts from experiential learning. In other words, medical students were to play a role in determining their learning needs, to specify learning objectives, and to be held responsible for integrating content within the context of patient problem cases. The PBL and organ systems models have been largely adopted by North American and international medical schools. The PBL model does, however, have shortcomings. Among these is the assumption that the diagnostic process is generalizable to all medical problems. In a landmark publication, Elstein, Schulman, and Sprafka (1978) found that clinical reasoning is problem-specific; that is, correct diagnosis is knowledge-, disease-, and case-specific. Historically, with long hospital stays and high numbers of patients being common, medical students enhanced these diagnostic skills in the "clinical years" of the medical curriculum. Another criticism of the PBL approach is that student-generated objectives may not be comprehensive enough without expert input. Finally, the PBL approach has been criticized because it presents a specific problem or diagnosis, and this means that students tend to reason "backwards" to initial data and symptoms. Research indicates that expert physicians derive differential diagnoses from data and symptoms, ruling out hypotheses as information becomes clear about any specific case.

In the 1990s, the University of Calgary's Faculty of Medicine (Mandin et al. 1995) proposed the clinical presentation curriculum model. Drawing upon cognitive psychology research, and with a primary care curricular orientation, the clinical presentation model was based upon 120 common presentations with six possible aetiologies for a total of 720 disease categories. The basis of this model was a series of targeted strategies, or a decision tree (referred to as "schemata" in cognitive psychology research). Each clinical presentation includes a schemata review and lectures, and it finishes with a small group PBL case. This model presents a structure for forward clinical reasoning based upon an appropriate medical science and clinical information base.

The purpose of this discussion is to inform the reader of the "state of the art" of medical curricula as the planners for NOSM began their deliberations. Susan Toohey (2002, 66) posed the question, "Does one approach always dominate?" Professor Ronald Harden (1989) proposed the concept of the "mixed educational economy" in an attempt to develop optimal learning experiences for medical learners. The section that follows addresses how the NOSM curriculum was shaped by the processes and information available at the time.

THE NOSM MODEL: THE EARLY YEARS, 2000–03

In January 2000, a liaison council for the Northern Ontario Rural Medical School (NORMS) was formed with broad representation from physicians, the faculty and administrators of Laurentian and Lakehead universities, and hospital administrators. The report of the Liaison Council (NOSM 2000) was presented to the Expert Panel on Health Professional Human Resources.

The NORMS report set out the major parameters for the design of a new school, which was built to meet the cultural and geographical needs of the North and was to seek accreditation as a stand-alone school with campuses in Sudbury and Thunder Bay. It would have a distinct admissions process, its own curriculum, and its own degree-granting status. It would have a distributed learning model, with students working in small groups in clinical contexts throughout the North. Its curriculum would integrate basic science and clinical education, and learning would be problem-based and systems organized. The aim was for a high quality of medical education that, because of its northern context, could not be duplicated by medical education based in the south. The report provided an early blueprint and direction for much of what has become the NOSM model.

A second panel of medical education experts presented a report entitled "Proposal for the Curriculum of the Northern Ontario Medical School" to the Ontario Institute for Studies in Education (NOSM 2003a). It argued for innovation in medical education in order to address the shortcomings of current practice and to incorporate concepts of modern cognitive learning theory. In addition to the model outlined in the NORMS report, it addressed the assessment of student performance. It was proposed that a system of progress testing be employed to assess the acquisition of content in formative and summative fashion. Objective structured clinical examinations (OSCE) were proposed as a method to assess clinical skills and competence.

The assessment of the process dimension of learning was addressed by suggesting peer, self-, and mentor review as well as the use of a reflective journal. The assessment of professionalism was also included as an important assessment modality.

THE BUSINESS PLAN

In August 2002, a business plan was presented to the NOMS Implementation Management Committee (NOSM 2002a). The plan recognized the curricular model set forth in preceding documents and, for the first time, emphasized the importance of blended learning solutions and environments that would support synchronous and asynchronous learning. It mentioned interactive learning modules, self-assessment, smart classrooms, video conferencing, and interactive learning via online technologies. It also included, as its preferred option, a model with campuses in Thunder Bay and Sudbury.

In addition to a comprehensive staffing plan and fiscal implications, the plan included two components closely tied to the curriculum: the Health Information Resource Centre (HIRC) concept and preliminary proposals for the educational buildings on the Lakehead and Laurentian campuses.

The HIRC document focused on the need for a team of user-centred information professionals, technology support for learning and writing, the creation of multimedia courseware, and the synthesis of information services with information technology. It went on to note the availability and importance of commercial web-based products for course delivery via blackboard. The business plan also included the physical facility requirements for two purpose-built educational buildings. The current impact of the business plan on high-level management in NOSM remains enormous, whether in relation to organizational plan, budgetary thought, physical facilities, or conceptual models.

COMMUNITY WORKSHOPS

True to the design to be socially accountable in meeting the needs of the North, a series of community workshops was held between 2003 and 2006 to obtain stakeholder input into the curriculum and its various components.

Curriculum workshops

The first of these workshops, "Getting Started in the North," was reported in a document entitled "A Flying Start: Report of the NOMS Curriculum Workshop January 16–18, 2003." It was held in

Sault Ste Marie, included over 300 participants (NOSM 2003b), and invited the engagement of Northern Ontario communities in the development of NOSM. In particular, it provided a vehicle for community influence on what educational content would be suitable for physicians who would work in Northern Ontario. To this end, it established working groups to continue to develop curriculum resource materials. The report summarized the workshop outcomes as points of awareness, including the type of knowledge, skills, and attitudes appropriate to Northern Ontario communities.

Aboriginal workshop

A workshop focused on Aboriginal interests was held from 10 to 12 June 2003 and was entitled "Follow Your Dreams." Its report, based on the input of 131 attendees, included three recommendations that affected future curriculum development.

1 the need for NOMS (faculty, staff, programs, etc.) to acknowledge and respect Aboriginal history, traditions, and cultures (e.g., by consulting with elders);
2 a detailing of the expertise and resources in Aboriginal communities (e.g., traditional healing), which could assist in the growth and development of NOMS; and
3 suggested opportunities for collaboration and partnerships that would be to the mutual benefit of Aboriginal communities and NOMS (e.g., the development of pre-medicine or access programs for Aboriginal youth)

Other recommendations included Aboriginal representation on various committees and the establishment of an Aboriginal reference group.

Assessment

The first detailed discussion of the assessment of student performance occurred at a workshop on student assessment held on 21 July 2003 in Thunder Bay. It was from this workshop that the philosophy and guiding principles of NOSM student assessment emerged, as reported in NOSM (2005a).

Consistent with a learner-centred approach, assessment is primarily for the benefit of the students themselves. It is performance-based, with a strong emphasis on continuous feedback. In line with NOSM's mission and values, assessment covers a full range of behaviours and aims for consistency across different teaching sites.

The final outcome of assessment of the NOMS MD program will be pass or fail. Throughout the program, students will be given feedback on their own performance, and outstanding performance will be recognized through prizes and honours. The intention is to celebrate achievements based on a broad range of criteria, which may include the votes of fellow students. There will be transparency in the final assessment, including information provided on behalf of the student/graduate to the Canadian Resident Matching Service.

Curriculum Development

The Curriculum Development Working Group was created in 2002, and it received input from workshop recommendations and seminal documents in order to begin work on the NOSM curriculum. On 8 December 2003, this group formed the nucleus of the Undergraduate Medical Education Committee, as recorded in its minutes of that date (NOSM 2005a).

The impending Liaison Committee on Medical Education/Committee on Accreditation of Canadian Medical Schools (LCME/CACMS) site visit of March 2004, which required a November 2003 database submission, prompted the leadership to create the Accredited MD Program Work Group (AMDG) (NOSM 2003c). It was this group that codified the major curricular components discussed and developed by the earlier Curriculum Development Work Group. These were later approved by the Undergraduate Medical Education Committee and are reflected in the subsequent curriculum. Important philosophical tenets and frameworks of medicine and medical education include: patient-centred medicine, generalism in medicine and health care, interdisciplinary cooperation, integrated health service delivery models, and physicians as teachers.

Finally, the four course themes were identified: (1) personal and professional aspects of medical practice, (2) social and population health, (3) foundations of medicine, and (4) clinical skills in health care. At this time, northern and rural health was envisioned not as a separate theme but, rather, as permeating the entire curriculum. Within a month, northern and rural health became the fifth course theme. The AMDG met in subsequent retreats (July 2003 to March 2004) and further refined the curricular concepts. A virtual learning environment concept was added, and curriculum content was specified as basic medical sciences, behavioural sciences, clinical sciences, and humanities and social sciences.

It was during this time period that the notion of "curricular threads" was introduced (it is interesting to compare these with the "curricular threads" of 2005 [see below under section entitled "The NOSM Curriculum"). These are:

- Aboriginal health
- addiction
- cancer
- chronic and elderly care
- injury
- occupational health
- research

The key characteristics of NOSM case-based learning were articulated as complex real life scenarios, structured guided learning, and informed tutors/facilitators. These characteristics clearly identified the NOSM curriculum as a case-based model that would structure learning and eventually create tutor and student guides. The concept of organ systems was also introduced at this time.

It is during these AMDG retreats that we hear the first mention of curricular phases. It was agreed that phase 1 would be years 1 and 2, phase 2 would be year 3, and phase 3 would be year 4. A preliminary curriculum management structure was also proposed, and the notion of the module as a discrete learning period was developed. Thus, the concept of the case-based module (CBM) was born. A weekly delivery model was also developed, which included student-generated issues (SGI), case-based learning (CBL), topic-oriented sessions (TOSs), whole group sessions (WGSs), and clinical teaching sessions (now the structured clinical skills [SCS] sessions). Community learning sessions (CLS) were added later. Thus was born "NOSM Speak" – the creation and use of new letter abbreviations for NOSM learning activities. With the submission of the LCME database in November 2003, and the inaugural meeting of the Undergraduate Medication Education

Committee in December 2003, the work of both the ADMG and the Curriculum Development Working Group was complete. Without the work of these two groups and the faculty and staff who provided leadership at this critical juncture, it is unlikely that initial conditional accreditation could have been achieved.

THE NOSM MODEL: PILOT TESTS, ACCREDITATION, APPOINTMENTS, AND IMPLEMENTATION, 2004–06

The period from January 2004 to September 2006 witnessed three LCME/CACMS site visits (two limited and one secretariat visit). In addition, curriculum pilot tests were run in February and May 2004, and a pilot test of the Aboriginal CBM 106 was run from 6 to 24 June 2005. The year 2004 saw the appointment of nine full-time faculty; a vice-dean for academic activities; a vice-dean for professional activities; and associate deans for research, undergraduate medical education, and postgraduate planning, respectively. A division head for human sciences joined already appointed division heads for basic medical sciences and clinical sciences. A symposium for francophones in Northern Ontario and a follow-up Aboriginal workshop were also held. The purpose-built medical school buildings on the Laurentian and Lakehead campuses were completed on time. To a greater or lesser degree, each of these events affected the final development and implementation of the curriculum that greeted the charter class of students in August 2005.

TESTING THE CURRICULUM

Two pilot projects in February and May 2004, and a third in June 2005 (a pilot of the Aboriginal module), provided valuable information on the efficacy of the proposed curricular structure, content, delivery model, e-learning environment, and related proposals.

In February, a total of fifty-two students, three groups on the Lakehead campus and four on the Laurentian campus, were engaged in a one-week pilot test of one case from Module 102: "Burnt Ridge." For the February pilot, paper-based student and tutor guides were provided, and tutors were given a document entitled "Information on the NOMS Curriculum for New Tutors," which provided a broad context for understanding the entire curricular structure. The

Summary Report, dated February 2004, indicated that CBLs, TOSs, and WGSs were employed (NOSM 2004). Overall, student and faculty evaluations confirmed that the cases were realistic, that the session organization was generally appropriate, and that the web platform supported the teacher-guided discovery model employed. It was also observed that a longer pilot project should be employed in order to evaluate content. In discussions with individuals directly involved in both the February and May 2004 pilots, it appeared that the learning materials for the former were paper-based. This is not hard to imagine as many of the faculty tutors had been students at institutions in which it was the norm for problem-based learning sessions to be paper-based (and where other resources were also paper-based). In one sense, the week-long pilot became a test for how to create a pilot.

The May 2004 pilot included fifty students in the same configuration as the February group (but with no student overlap). The project comprised a three-week pilot of a CBM focused on the respiratory system. The pilot included most components of a CBM, including CBLs, TOSs, and WGSs. In an effort to evaluate the outcomes (particularly facilitator impact) in a systematic fashion, a literature review led to the creation of an observation tool. Curriculum and instructional designers observed the facilitated groups.

Following the recommendations that came forward from the pilot projects on campus as well as the Aboriginal Pilot Project, an electronic learning environment and platform was developed in-house, which provided for modular schedules, objectives, module overviews, and student/facilitator guides for each module. Thus, a full online curriculum was created in time for implementation of the new curriculum in the Fall of 2005. On the Sudbury and Thunder Bay campuses, smart classrooms were developed so that WGSs could be delivered by faculty from either site in each of the first two years of the curriculum and could therefore be distributed across the North using fibre-optic connectivity. The Laurentian and Lakehead locations and all facilities in the buildings are connected via Ontario Research and Education Network (ORION). Students in the integrated community experiences (ICEs) on the reserves are connected via K-et, the Aboriginal network. In year 3 and beyond, it was planned that the students would be connected at all sites via the network known as Smart Systems for Health Agencies. At the time of writing, plans were under way to create a unified NOSM system. In addition, small group rooms were developed for both the TOS and CBL sessions, which, through the use of a wi-fi network, included smartboards and connectivity throughout the purpose-built buildings. As CBMS 106, 108, and 110 were developed, so was connectivity between all of the sites. This was done via video cable and telecommunication links so that, in keeping with NOSM's definition of distributed community-engaged learning (DCEL), the curriculum would continue to be delivered in the same way in each campus, wherever it might be located. DCEL is defined as: "An instructional model that allows widely distributed human and instructional resources to be utilized independent of time and place in community partner locations across the North."

As part of the students' fee structure, each person received a fully loaded laptop upon which to access online curriculum materials or those materials that had been preloaded with curriculum support materials and information. At the time of writing, plans were under way to provide personal digital assistants to medical students at the end of year 2 for use in documenting clinical encounters in years 3 and 4. Additionally, as part of the fee structure, students received new laptops at the end of year 2.

Thus, the plan to provide connectivity between students and locations across the North was met, and provisions were made to expand it in the years to come. These design components have created an electronic learning environment that can be accessed anywhere e-mail exists and that is the primary source of all learning information for NOSM students.

ABORIGINAL PILOT

It was just over a year later that a pilot project for the Aboriginal experience in phase 1, year 1 (CBM 106) was conducted for three weeks, 6 to 24 June 2005 (NOSM 2005b). Eight Aboriginal communities were selected from volunteer partner communities across Northern Ontario, and two students were located in each community for two weeks following a one-week orientation in Sudbury. Afterwards, each student went through a one-week debriefing session, also in Sudbury. The students were elective medical students from universities in Ontario and Manitoba.

Fifteen students participated in the pilot project and received elective credit. They were medical students who had just completed year 1 of medical school and four final-year nursing students. There were eight students from the University of Western Ontario, one each from the universities of Manitoba and Toronto, one from Queen's, and four from Lakehead.

The pilot revealed a number of issues primarily related to the need for better communication between the school and the communities involved regarding the expectations of each. Some communities have more programming in place and more experienced individuals to serve as coordinators than do others. Students need to be prepared for the challenges of isolated communities. More careful forward planning could make the process smoother.

ACCREDITATION PROCESS: THE IMPACT OF ACCREDITATION

The process of obtaining and maintaining accreditation through the LCME and CACMS has been pivotal in the creation of NOSM and is essential for its survival. Through the site visitation process, using published external standards, NOSM has responded to the concerns of the accrediting bodies and has developed a truly unique curriculum that meets rigorous international standards. Curriculum-centred concerns related to sufficient faculty and staff, student evaluation, and assessment of student professionalism were met by the rigorous recruitment of outstanding faculty, administration, and staff. The assessment of a variety of student performance dimensions, including professionalism, has been addressed, as has a student appeals process. Concerns about the teaching and learning of the contemporary content of traditional science disciplines in an integrated case-based curriculum were addressed by dissecting each set of content objectives and setting them within disciplinary blocks. After its final visit in September 2006, the committee issued a report that was very positive and that indicated that NOSM was eligible for a site visit for full accreditation in the fall of 2008.

ORGANIZING TO SUPPORT THE CURRICULUM

The 2002 business plan proposed an organizational structure that included a teaching department that would house the heads of ten clinical and medical science areas. It also proposed an associate dean for undergraduate medical education with coordinators for years 1 to 4, a clerkship coordinator, and a medical education director. In addition, there were offices of e-curriculum, technology, and library services, all of which would have a large impact on the curriculum.

As the school developed, the organizational structure supporting the curriculum moved from a project office model to work groups and committees. By January 2004, the Undergraduate Medical Education Committee was formed (NOSM 2003c). Its subcommittees included phase 1, phase 2, and student assessment and program evaluation. Reports were received from the divisions of human sciences, medical sciences, and clinical sciences. Theme work groups were formed, and theme coordinators were named for each of the five curriculum course themes and were represented in each phase committee. It was becoming clear that taking an integrated curriculum from a conceptual model to an operational model was a difficult task.

As the phase and course committees worked towards the implementation of the curriculum in the spring and summer of 2005, it became clear that another organizational adjustment was necessary. The curriculum was organized around three phases (phase 1 = years 1 and 2; phase 2 = year 3; phase 3 = year 4) and was delivered, at least in years 1 and 2, through eleven CBMs of approximately six weeks duration. It was recognized that learners would need a "go to person" if they had questions about content or process in any given module and that they would need to manage the weekly module coordination sessions. Thus, module coordinators were appointed to oversee the delivery of each of the modules and to provide a liaison between faculty and students. They are expected to be active in collecting information regarding the progress of the module and, although they have no authority to alter curriculum, to coordinate modifications as deemed necessary. At this time, module work groups were created for each of the eleven modules, with an identified phase coordinator lead person and including representation from each of the course theme committees to establish specific module objectives.

The organizational structure in place by September 2005, shown in Figure 6.1, has remained relatively unchanged at the time of writing.

THE NOSM CURRICULUM

The curriculum that was in place for the inaugural class (E-2005) was true to NOSM's social accountability mandate, had met the criteria of the accrediting bodies, and had been approved by the two university senates.

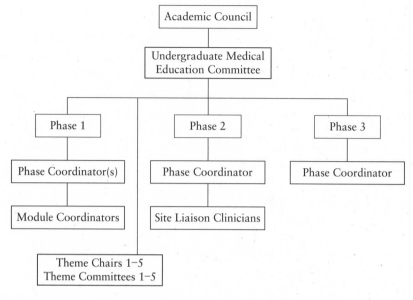

Figure 6.1: Organizational structure

The curriculum content is centred on five course themes:

1 northern and rural health
2 personal and professional aspects of medical practice
3 social and population health
4 foundations of medicine
5 clinical skills in health care

These course themes are enhanced by a focus on the seven competencies described in CanMeds 2005, which are:

- medical expert
- collaborator
- manager
- health advocate
- scholar
- professional
- communicator

In addition, a series of curricular "threads" run through the four-year curriculum. They are:

Organization/Delivery of Medical Education at NOSM

Phase 1		Phase 2	Phase 3	Residency	Continuing Medical Educaion/Professional Development
Year 1	Year 2	Year 3	Year 4	Years 5, 6 and Beyond	Lifelong
101	107	Comprehensive Community Clerkship	Clerkship & Electives	Individual Specialty Choice	Professional Development
102	108				
103	109				Continuing Medical Edication
104	110		Licensure Examination		
105	111				
106	Electives				
Case Based Modules					

Figure 6.2

- Aboriginal health
- interprofessional education and work
- health effect of social problems
- WSIB concepts/curriculum
- dementia project
- gender issues
- CMPA patient safety curriculum

Figure 6.2 depicts the delivery of the NOSM curriculum as a continuum.

THE CURRICULUM: A PHILOSOPHY AND AN APPROACH

The curriculum employs a case-based approach to student learning. The emphasis is on self-directed learning, and the role of faculty tutors is to facilitate this. In years 1 and 2, this model is employed with the CBLs and the TOSs. In year 3, virtual academic rounds are utilized to bring small groups of learners together to discuss cases from their personal clinical experiences. Objectives and learning tasks are provided to guide study and to indicate the depth of understanding required for successful completion of the module. However, the curriculum demands significant self-directed work and study on the part of the individual student.

As noted earlier, the NOSM model, influenced by the Report of the Liaison Council to the Expert Panel and the report of the Ontario

Institute for Studies in Education as well as input from community consultations, included a strong interprofessional emphasis. Most modules include health care providers from a wide variety of professions. In addition, a large number of facilitators come from these professions, including nurse practitioners, physiotherapists, social workers, and occupational therapists.

Throughout phase 1 and phase 2 of NOSM's undergraduate medical education program, students are provided with numerous opportunities to recognize, value, and experience interprofessionalism and the role that both community-based services and health care professionals have in supporting the health of individuals and the community. In keeping with the six identified academic principles and the social accountability mandate, the NOSM curriculum was intentionally designed to foster these opportunities and to encourage students to deepen their understanding of the community and the populations that NOSM serves.

During phase 1 of the MD program, each medical student attends one three-hour CLS in each week of ten of the eleven CBLs. Specific learning objectives for each of the themes of the undergraduate curriculum have been aligned with the CLS placements. Students use the CLS experience as an opportunity to consolidate their learning, focusing on the specific site in which they are placed. They are responsible for developing their own personalized learning plan, which is to be reflective of each of the clinical/community settings in which they are placed.

To provide students with the opportunity to better understand the range of services as well as health care providers and community workers, the CBLs are broadly grouped into three areas, each of which the student is to attend:

1 physician settings (family practice, specialists offices);
2 interprofessional health care settings (medical laboratories, diagnostic imaging laboratories, paramedic services, diabetes education clinics, cardiac rehabilitation clinics, etc.); and
3 community and social services settings (mental health agencies, addiction services, halfway houses, soup kitchens, women's shelters, etc.).

During the phase 2 comprehensive community clerkship (CCC), NOSM students attend two- to three-hour specialty enhancement sessions (SES) on a weekly basis. The intent of these sessions is to enable the student to gain experience in the various health care settings of their future patients.

Students participate in a variety of planned learning activities in order to strengthen their understanding of resources and services available in the community and to broaden their perspectives on culture, interprofessional teams, and health and social service delivery in northern and rural communities. In fulfilling the overall objectives of SES and meeting their personal learning needs, students are encouraged to engage in self-directed learning, reflective learning, and peer interactions.

During the clinical experiences encountered in SES during the CCC, students should be able to:

- observe and practise interviewing and clinical skills as appropriate to each setting;
- describe the practice and administration of each environment;
- describe interprofessional aspects of each setting; and
- describe how the clinic or organization interacts with other health care providers, organizations, and so on.

Ultimately, the distribution of these sessions among hospital, clinic, and community organizations is determined by the student's site coordinating preceptor and depends on the student's progress in meeting the learning objectives. The SESs associated with each discipline are spread over the entire year in order to allow for continuity of patient care and clinical experience.

These SESs are broadly grouped into three types of setting: hospital-based care, community-based care, and health care support organizations. Examples include:

- hospital-based care sessions: specialist clinics, operating room/surgical assist, radiology, laboratory, pathology, pharmacy, gastroenterology, HIV/AIDS clinics, crisis intervention, eating disorders, rehabilitation, etc.;
- Community-based care sessions: specialist clinic, physiotherapy, children's treatment centre, breast screening clinic, nursing homes, public health unit, diabetes education, cardiac rehabilitation, etc.; and
- health care support organizations: sexual assault treatment programs, women's shelters, mental health programs, addiction treatment programs, group homes, child and family services, senior services, etc.

Module		System focus
CBM 101 CBM 102 CBM 103 CBM 104 CBM 105 CBM 106	Phase 1 Year 1	Review/introduction Cardiovascular/respiratory system Gastrointestinal system Central nervous system/peripheral nervous system Endocrine system Musculo skeletal system
CBM 107 CBM 108 CBM 109 CBM 110 CBM 111	Phase 1 Year 2	Reproductive system Renal system Haematology/immunology Neurological/behaviour End of life issues

* Yellow denotes an ICE away from the Lakehead and Laurentian campuses.

Figure 6.3: Case-based modules

The Phase 1 curriculum is divided into eleven CBMs. Six of these occur in year 1 and five occur in year 2 of the program. CBM 101 is four weeks in duration, while the remaining modules are six weeks. All information about the CBM is available online and is provided in increments to the students as needed for their learning activities. This material, along with other scheduled learning activities and content information, guides student learning throughout phase 1. Each CBM has a body system emphasis, as outlined in figure 6.3.

In years 1 and 2 there are five distinct types of learning opportunities at NOSM: large group sessions, small group facilitated sessions, structured clinical skills sessions, laboratory sessions, and community learning sessions.

Large Group Sessions

MODULE COORDINATION SESSIONS (MCSS)

Each week begins with a one-hour facilitated session during which students are encouraged to raise any concerns about the instructional content of the learning process. The session provides an opportunity for dialogue between students and faculty.

WHOLE GROUP SESSIONS (WGSS)

These sessions are usually three hours in length and are scheduled once per week, as determined by the instructional demands of the curriculum. In a WGS, the class is instructed as a whole by a faculty member. The instructional format includes traditional lectures, demonstrations, and large group tutorial activities. These sessions are simultaneously video-conferenced between campus locations.

Small Group Sessions

CASE-BASED LEARNING (CBL)

Each week students meet with a facilitator in groups of no more than eight for a two-hour session. Through a model of guided discovery, which is designed to support self-directed research, students consider a complex case that directs the learning for the module. Each module reflects six weeks of study and explores instructional content related to the five course themes. Prepared objectives guide student learning during CBL sessions.

TOPIC-ORIENTED SESSIONS (TOSS)

These two-hour facilitated sessions occur two or three times each week. The TOS focus is on an individual patient whom students have met through the module case. Using a problem-based learning format, students identify learning issues, develop a strategy to acquire the necessary knowledge, and share that knowledge through independent research. As the week progresses, information is revealed about the patient until the objectives related to these sessions have been fully explored.

Structured Clinical Skills Sessions (SCSs)

These weekly three-hour sessions focus on instruction and practice in patient/doctor communication and physical examination skills. Students meet in small groups with a clinical instructor and practise their interviewing and examination skills with simulated and standardized patients. The objective of these sessions is to explore the knowledge, skills, and attitudes defined by theme 5 of the curriculum (i.e., clinical skills).

Laboratory Sessions (LAB)

These three-hour sessions occur four times in every six-week module. In each LAB session, students initially meet as an entire group for a WGS. Students are then required to meet in small groups to focus and work through case studies based on learning objectives outlined and explained in the WGS. For each module, the LAB sessions focus on four sets of learning objectives related to basic anatomy and histology, pathology, diagnostic imaging, and clinical/ diagnostic skills.

Community Learning Sessions (CLSs)

Each week there is one three-hour session dedicated to providing students with a wide range of community-based clinical experiences. Observing and interacting with patients under the guidance of a preceptor, students visit patients at their homes, at hospitals, at long-term care centres, at doctors' offices, at pharmacies, at rehab centres, at nursing homes, or at other health service providers or organizations. These experiences involve all five course themes and provide a focus for interprofessional learning.

Distributed Tutorial Sessions (DTSs)

A DTS is developed by a faculty member and is related to specific learning objectives. It is conducted via electronic means, either synchronously or asynchronously. A DTS is analogous to the weekly WGS for on-campus modules but incorporates instructional methods appropriate to distributed or distance education models. The DTS is usually implemented in the ICE modules CBM 106, 108, and 110.

SELF-DIRECTED LEARNING CYCLE

Diagram 6.4 and its accompanying narrative describe the cycle of self-directed learning as a part of the TOSs and CBLs. The tent diagram is a visual analogy for the integration of the various student-learning activities in the NOSM curriculum.

While CBM 105 has a specific francophone emphasis and CBM 106 is an ICE on site in an Aboriginal community, the curriculum, through its cases, reflects francophone and Aboriginal content. Francophone physicians and patients are included in modules 101–05 and 107–11. Similarly, Aboriginal patients and health care providers are featured throughout in modules 101, 102, 106, and 107–111.

The students' own investigation is supported by weekly whole group sessions. The students at both campuses are linked by videoconference during these sessions. Facilitators are faculty who are content experts.

During clinical skills sessions, students will receive instruction in communication skills, interviewing and history-taking, and a range of other clinical skills. Students will work with standardized and volunteer patients. Many clinical skills are further supported by labs. Community learning experiences are provided to augment the learning in each module.

Figure 6.4 Self-directed learning cycle

Table 6.1
Typical week schedule in phase 1 (years 1 and 2)

Week X	Monday	Tuesday	Wednesday	Thursday	Friday
9 – 10	Module coordination session (MCS)	Community learning session (CLS)	Whole group session (WGS)	Structured clinical session (SCS)	Lab
10 – 11	Case- based learning session (CBL)				
11 – 12			Personal study		
12 – 1	Lunch	Lunch with student affairs	Lunch	Lunch	Lunch
1 – 2	Topic-oriented session (TOS)	Student affairs opportunity (1 – 2:30)	Personal study	Topic-oriented session (TOS)	Personal study
2 – 3					
3 – 4	Personal study			Personal study	

In addition to the modules on the Laurentian and Lakehead campuses, there are three six-week ICEs in phase 1 modules. They are CBM 106 in year 1 (Aboriginal), and modules 108 and 110 (Remote/Rural). It is important to note that learning experiences in all five course themes continue during these ICEs. In many important ways, ICE modules 106, 108, and 110 are similar to the other phase 1 modules; however, they also differ in several important ways. The first two weeks are spent on the home campus with a concentrated orientation, WGSs and LABs, which are difficult to deliver in the various community settings. This also allows time for students to focus on their respective community and clinical activities

The Phase 2 Curriculum

The phase 2 (year 3) curriculum varies significantly from traditional Canadian year 3 clerkships, in which students learn the major clinical disciplines in an urban teaching hospital in fixed sequential blocks known as rotations. Based on the Parallel Rural Community Curriculum (PRCC) pioneered at Flinders University in Australia (Worley et al. 2000), NOSM students are exposed to the clinical disciplines as they encounter cases in the context of rural family practices. NOSM's year 3 is referred to as the comprehensive community clerkship (CCC), a longitudinal, eight-month experience. In April 2005, two Australian physician educators who had developed the PRCC, Dr Paul Worley and Dr Lucie Walters, began consultation with NOSM regarding the CCC. Their experiences and successes in an area with similar needs to those of Northern Ontario formed the genesis of NOSM's third-year clerkship.

The phase 2 (year 3) CCC at NOSM provides students with clinical experiences away from the main campuses at Sudbury and Thunder Bay. Students, who are assigned in pairs to primary care practice settings, live and learn as small groups of up to eight learners in one Northern Ontario community for an eight-month period. The communities of Kenora, Sioux Lookout, Fort Frances, Timmins, North Bay, Sault Ste Marie, Parry Sound, Bracebridge, Huntsville, and Temiskaming Shores were chosen to host CCC learners. Subsequently, Dryden and Kapuskasing also became CCC communities.

The aim of the phase 2 curriculum is to provide academic and professionally relevant learning opportunities that, through small group sessions and clinical practice, exemplify reflective learning and comprehensive interprofessional care. Furthermore, opportunities to care for patients in a safe and efficient manner are enhanced by the clerkship's prolonged duration, which promotes continuity of care. The students increase their knowledge of medical care through clinical encounters and through the socio-cultural context in which the patients and their families cope and adapt to their health care needs. This social and intellectual process is encouraged through continuous interaction with community-based faculty members.

The ccc experience enhances the nosm learner's personal and professional development. Additionally, the nature of the course work and the learner-centred environment promotes critical thinking and life-long learning skills. The ccc provides an opportunity to enhance knowledge, skills, and attitudes conducive to an understanding of medical practice in remote, rural, and/or underserved communities. Learners observe the skills and attributes of health professionals in stimulating environments, furthering their consideration of career choices, including with regard to clinical practice and research.

As in the first two years, the five course themes continue through the phase 2 (year 3) clerkship. Additionally, theme 5 (clinical skills) is subdivided into:

- child health
- women's health
- internal medicine
- mental health
- family medicine
- surgery

Rather than specific sequential rotations in each of the disciplines, students have parallel exposure to these areas of medicine.

Although the community-based faculty member provides direction for the student with regard to achieving her/his learning goals, ultimately it is the responsibility of the learner to maintain a high level of motivation and a self-directed approach to learning. Much of this learning is opportunistic, and, wherever possible, students are encouraged to engage in, and navigate through, specific learning objectives.

As the learning is family-focused, the students identify families early in the year and, through informed consent processes, follow

Table 6.2

Activity	Duration
Orientation	2 Weeks
Comprehensive community clerkship	14 Weeks
Holiday break	3 Weeks
Comprehensive community clerkship	16 Weeks
Review and OSCE	2 Weeks

them through an illness/wellness continuum. Under the community preceptor's guidance, students examine a range of psychosocial and multicultural contexts in which the family interacts with other members of the health care team and health-related organizations and services.

This experience forms the basis of personal research and reflection exercises that are rich in experiential data and that extend beyond the boundaries of clinical medicine. It is expected that some of these experiences will enhance the students' clinical practice and influence how they behave as physicians.

Students are encouraged to take ownership of their learning as they begin to *think* and *act* as *critically reflective practitioners* – an attribute central to safe and rewarding medical practice. Students are given opportunities to work in partnership with patients and their families, with appropriate supervision and support. To this end, it is anticipated that they will develop and practice patient- and family-centred care.

DESCRIPTION OF PHASE 2 INSTRUCTIONAL SESSIONS

In year 3, phase 2, there are two distinct types of learning opportunities during the CCC: (1) explanatory sessions, which provide didactic instruction specific to the core clinical disciplines, and (2) experiential sessions, which provide clinical experiences in a variety of settings.

Explanatory Sessions

DISCIPLINE-FOCUSED SESSIONS (DFSS)
These sessions are three hours in length and are scheduled as determined by the instructional demands of the curriculum. In a DFS, the

class is instructed by NOSM faculty. The instructional format includes traditional lectures that review key concepts and issues related to the objectives attached to the cases that are discussed and presented in small group discussions.

VIRTUAL ACADEMIC ROUNDS (VARS)

In groups of eight, students meet twice weekly with a facilitator for two three-hour sessions. Through a model of guided discovery, students identify learning issues, develop a strategy to acquire the necessary knowledge, and share the knowledge gained through independent research by considering cases identified from their clinical experiences in the community. Each case discussion is divided into two 1.5–hour segments. Early in the week, in the first 1.5–hour segment, the case is presented and the objectives are reviewed. The objectives are then discussed and presented in a subsequent 1.5–hour session later in the week. The sessions explore specific objectives, which have been selected to guide discussions related to the student's case presentations. The objectives of the discussion are related to all five course themes.

Experiential Sessions

PRIMARY CARE SESSIONS (PCSS)

On a weekly basis, five half-day sessions provide opportunities to develop and refine the students' communication and physical examination skills and management approaches under the supervision of experienced clinicians. Students participate in the care of two to four patients per half-day session. Using available resources, including electronic texts and evidence-based materials, students conduct independent research regarding their patients and utilize their findings as part of the clinical encounter reviews they discuss with their faculty members. Supervising faculty members also review the students' findings and suggested management plans.

SPECIALTY ENHANCEMENT SESSIONS (SESS)

Each week's schedule includes two three-hour sessions dedicated to providing students with a wide range of clinical experiences related to the six core disciplines of family medicine, surgery, internal medicine, mental health, child health, and women's health. Students examine patients and assist with the management of their illnesses or conditions under the guidance of health care professionals. These sessions include participating in surgical assistance, specialty clinics, physicians' offices, and a variety of hospital and community-based programs related to the core clinical disciplines. These experiences explore the content of all five course themes and provide an opportunity for interprofessional learning.

IN-PATIENT ROUNDS, ER, AND OBSTETRICAL CARE SESSIONS

Students are to participate in the daily care of in-patients as directed by their site coordinating teacher. Emphasis is placed on continuity of care. The student participates in the patient's admission and subsequently follows up on the patient in the community. Emergency room and obstetrical care sessions are assigned by the site coordinating teacher, and student participation in the care of patients is overseen by a faculty member.

Logging Clinical Encounters

While not all the specialist services may be present at each individual CCC site, students nevertheless have the advantage of encountering patients over time and in different stages of care and, therefore, experiencing the realities of continuity of care. Students observe and record their learning opportunities, which arise from personal interaction with patients, families, and communities, in an electronic log. Benchmarks for specific numbers and types of clinical encounters and clinical procedures have been established by the Phase 2 Committee. The electronic logs of individual students are reviewed on a regular basis in order to help students achieve their objectives.

Orientation to the Comprehensive Community Clerkship (CCC)

Year 3 includes an initial orientation period to ensure that students are familiar with particular skills, roles, and procedures prior to entering the clinical environment. The orientation also provides outlines of the roles, responsibilities, and expectations of students during the clerkship period. While many of the hands-on aspects of the orientation are conducted at the clinical sites, supplemental material is provided by means of DFSs.

Once students are at their sites, they are oriented to the clinics and hospitals in which they will be learning in order to facilitate

Table 6.3
Year 3 CCC weekly schedule

TIME	Monday	Tuesday	Wednesday	Thursday	Friday	W/E
8 – 9	In-patient	In-patient	In-patient	In-patient	In-patient	OB/ER
9 – 12	Virtual academic rounds (VAR)	Primary care session (PCS)	Primary care session (PCS)	Virtual academic rounds (VAR)	Specialty enhancement session (SES)	OB/ER
12 – 1			Lunch Break			
1 – 5	Primary care session (PCS)	Primary care session (PCS)	Specialty enhancement session (SES)	Primary care session (PCS)	Self study	OB/ER
7 – 11		OB/ER consults				OB/ER

their integration into the work environment. Introductions are made to the faculty members with whom they are to work, and to the health care and administrative staff, in order to help make them feel like part of the team. It is felt that the social aspects of this experience are important because the learning environment encompasses much more than readings and formal instruction. Students make career and practice location decisions based upon the relationships they develop with physicians and other health professionals while learning in clinical environments. They learn to care for patients from observing patient-physician interactions and from informal interactions with staff and community members.

Thus, by the fall and early winter of 2006, phase 2 CCC was well on its way to implementation. It remained to solidify community readiness, to provide faculty development opportunities, and to help students become more comfortable with the communities and faculty that would affect their training and shape their future lives.

In May 2006, a phase 3 planning committee was struck, its purpose being to begin the process of developing a blueprint for year 4. It was headed by the phase 3 coordinator and also included the founding dean, vice-deans, associate dean UME, and the phase 2 coordinator. In May 2006, the Academic Council had approved a series of academic principles to guide all NOSM endeavours. These were the basis for the planning endeavour and are as follows:

- interprofessional (includes the key features of partnership, participation, collaboration, coordination, and shared decision making);
- integration (the combination and interaction of individuals around common purposes and goals to create meaningful experiences for students, residents, faculty, and staff);
- community orientation (the conceptual and pragmatic understanding of the dynamics of communities in the North and the creation of meaningful, enduring partnerships between all northern communities and NOSM);
- distributed community-engaged learning (an instructional model that allows widely distributed human and instructional resources to be utilized independently of time and place in community partner locations across the North);
- Generalism (a holistic approach to activities, values, and knowledge in educational, organizational, and patient care activities); and
- Diversity (a set of values that recognizes the richness of all cultures of Northern Ontario and the important ways they contribute to our lives).

The preliminary planning document included the following rationale and program design considerations.

The overriding purpose of the phase 3 curriculum is to provide students with an integrated exposure to the various specialities and subspecialties that will enable them to meet the graduation requirements of the Medical Council of Canada. It will allow students to observe, learn, and participate in the care of patients whose problems are being addressed by specialists in various disciplines, to provide care within a secondary- or tertiary-care institution, and to experience the continuum of care that seriously ill patients receive in the North. It will provide students with an opportunity to consider various specialities that they may pursue as career choices in their postgraduate years. Through electives, it will also allow students the opportunity to experience medicine in settings outside the traditional geographic area taught by NOSM. It will provide important background knowledge, which will allow students to graduate and transition into the first year of their post-graduate residency.

Students entering phase 3 (year 4) of the curriculum will have successfully completed a longitudinal thirty-two-week clerkship attached to a primary care practice and will have followed patients from that practice to in-patient care settings. In this context they will have learned a great deal about internal medicine, women's health, surgery, mental health, and children's health within a primary care setting. The numbers of patients and depth of patient care interaction will be documented via an electronic log. Given the extensive longitudinal experience of students in phase 2 (year 3), it is important to be clear on how phase 3 (year 4) experiences are envisioned. The guiding principles for phase 3 design include:

1 There will be a focus on the sharpening of management approaches to acute problems most often requiring hospitalization.
2 There will be a continuing focus on diagnosis and treatment models in Northern Ontario.
3 New knowledge and skills will be developed through WGS and TOS (in the latter case students will present topic-oriented cases).
4 There will be a focus on continuity of care through the development of a small cohort of patients in each discipline rotation.
5 Emergency room shifts will provide one source of patient cohorts (one shift per week).
6 Students will take calls.
7 Students will work with individual community faculty.
8 Students will be required to document a specified standard of numbers and types of patients in phase 3.
9 Scheduling of curricular experiences will be on discipline-specific rotation for four weeks each (internal medicine, women's health, children's health, mental health, and surgery).

By September 2006, the Phase 3 Committee had been constituted and was working towards creating a more comprehensive phase 3 syllabus. As planning progresses, student experiences in phase 2 will no doubt be significant in finalizing the year 4 curriculum.

The reality of a medical school with a curriculum for and delivered in the North was the result of many events and the endeavours of many individuals. When the inaugural medical student class entered in the fall of 2005, it was introduced and oriented to a set of curricular experiences that reflected the blueprint developed in the preceding years. In an effort to meet the needs of Northern Ontario, this blueprint draws upon the best thinking of medical educators, physicians, administrators, and the public.

Although the curriculum plan has met all external accreditation standards to date, it must still face challenges from student critics, faculty, community stakeholders, and its own design. One fact is certain: the curriculum will change and evolve in response to these challenges as NOSM moves towards it ultimate test in the quality of its graduates.

SOME LESSONS LEARNED

Pilot Projects

Pilot projects are invaluable for testing component parts of a curricular design or for testing how a series of components fit together into the larger curricular scheme and flow. They are, however, time-consuming and difficult to mount, particularly when faculty and staff are occupied in trying to develop the very materials and processes that will be in the test.

Nevertheless, the three NOSM pilot tests described in this chapter led directly to the development of the e-learning platform that continues to be employed to this day. In addition, the pilots provided information on organization, logistics, and working with communities that, had it been lacking, would have resulted in significant problems during implementation. The advantages gained far outweigh costs and disruptions to ongoing development.

When You've Seen One Community ...

At the time of writing, NOSM is engaged with over seventy different communities across the North, which are being used as "classrooms" for our students and residents. While it may be possible to generalize about population demographics, it would be a mistake to think that any two communities are the "same." In addition to obvious cultural and linguistic differences, each community deals with its issues in unique and creative ways. For instance, in one community the best internet access is located after hours at the parking area for the Ace Hardware Store. Medical practice patterns, hours, and community resources are all variable, depending on the community. This has led to the conclusion that "if you've seen one community, you've seen one community." It is both dangerous and foolhardy to make assumptions about communities in the North.

Engage and Re-Engage

Not only are communities unique in how they deal with a variety of issues, but they are also changeable. The loss or addition of one health care professional, a change in political leadership, or changes in local economies can have a profound impact on any community, but particularly on small communities (where the balance can be easily tipped). There is no substitute for personal contact in communities in which face-to-face daily interactions are the rule. It is important that e-mail-driven organizations, faculty, and administrators communicate in ways appropriate to the culture of the community in question.

For these reasons, it is vitally important, albeit time-consuming, to re-engage with community faculty leaders and health professionals. The program evaluation information provided by personal contacts creates a sense of involvement, collegiality, and professional engagement that is critical to program survival in these community campuses.

The Value of Curriculum Blueprint

A curriculum blueprint that specifies educational program goals, values, principles, and processes is an invaluable tool in the creation and maintenance of educational programs. Based upon the best evidence from educational research and practice, a blueprint provides at least two distinct advantages. First, it provides a reminder of, and a sense conscience about, the curriculum vision. In other words, when practical issues of budget, organizational change, or student/faculty/public unrest challenge the curricular model, the blueprint, which has been approved by the Academic Council, faculty senates, and so on, provides a clear reminder of the program's approved direction. Second, a blueprint, in conjunction with minutes from meetings, provides a source of institutional memory that reminds newer faculty and staff of why decisions were made and actions taken.

7

The Students

GEOFFREY TESSON, HOI CHEU, AND RAYMOND PONG

INTRODUCTION

The intent of this chapter is twofold: first, to capture the reflections of the first wave of NOSM students who embarked on this new venture and, second, to give concrete expression to the demographic data of NOSM's admissions process. We do the latter by examining the ways in which some of the students expressed their aspirations. Their comments illuminate the realities that lie behind the categories commonly used to select them and can provide important insights into the effectiveness not only of this program but also of rural medical education in general.

Our discussion is based on a number of different data sources. The first is a multi-year longitudinal tracking study conducted by the Centre for Rural and Northern Health Research (CRaNHR) at Laurentian University in order to ascertain the response of NOSM students to the program and, eventually, to study where they practise upon graduation. In this study, each cohort of students is tracked over a number of years through mail and/or web-based surveys. In this chapter, we use data from the first and second cohorts of students. The surveys are supplemented by in-depth interviews of a subsample of the students in order to gain a better understanding of such complex issues as decision making and changes in career plans. The interviews were conducted by Dr H. Cheu and transcribed by CRaNHR research staff. Another important source of student comment is the footage of the documentary film, *High Hopes: The Northern Ontario School of Medicine*, shot in 2005 by

Dr Cheu during NOSM's inaugural year. Data from the Admissions Office regarding the demographic breakdown of the student body is also presented.

The two interview sources, the film and the tracking study, while related, differ significantly from one another. The film was shot for the purposes of archiving and celebrating the school's grand opening. Dr Cheu was selected because of his position as a professor of film production. As a result of the documentary filmmaking process, he had the chance to hear the students telling their stories without feeling that they were being "studied." After the completion of *High Hopes*, CRaNHR invited Dr Cheu to conduct the interviews for the Multi-year Tracking Study.

In this chapter, stories from both projects are used to form a simulated landscape upon which the researchers map the ecology of northern medical education. It is important, however, to recognize the difference between the contexts of the two projects. With regard to sociological research, the film might be regarded as an obtrusive medium because the students were conscious of the fact that it would be publicly screened. Interestingly, however, the film footage contains more emotional and narrative content than do the transcripts. This is because the students were telling their stories instead of just answering structured questions. For their part, the transcripts reflect more thoughts and ideas than does the film. This is because the interview protocol was designed to extract such information. The basic premises of Dr Cheu's film interview come from literary theory, particularly from the assumption that humanity is a "symbolic species" (Deacon 1997) or a "story species" (Gold 2002). He does not treat his participants as subjects who offer "data" for researchers to observe and extract and, therefore, does not try to standardize questions and maintain objectivity; rather, he applies active listening techniques to encourage participants to tell their stories. Clearly, he is aware that storytelling is one way of communicating knowledge.

In this chapter, the stories from *High Hopes* are quoted directly and the students are identified (the film has gone through a strict consent process and is now a public document). In accordance with Research Ethics Board approval, materials from the Multi-year Tracking Study are used without identifying the speaker; synthesis, paraphrasing, or omission in cases of direct quotation apply in order to protect confidentiality. The student commentaries are framed within the context of the demographic data from the Admissions Office and the quantitative results of the questionnaire survey.

THE ISSUES

For the purpose of framing the discussion, we identify four core issues relating to the strategic goals of the NOSM admissions process:

1 *northern and rural background* as a factor predisposing students to northern practice;
2 *the social composition* of the student body in relation to the social composition of the region ;
3 the ability of NOSM to attract the kinds of students it wants in sufficient quantities (*if we build it, will they come?*); and
4 the orientation of students to primary care or more specialized disciplines (*family medicine or specialization?*).

Northern and Rural Background

It seems plausible enough to explain as a natural affinity the propensity of students from northern and rural backgrounds, upon graduation, to return to the North to work (Talley 1990). Certainly, this affinity seems a much better basis for drawing doctors to rural practice than incentive payments, which have been notably ineffective. But what does "natural affinity" mean in practice? What features of rural life exert an influence over young people's life plans, and how are these issues expressed in their commentaries and their questionnaire responses?

THE DATA
In the first three years of NOSM's operation, admissions data show that the proportion of students entering the school from northern or rural backgrounds is uniformly high, increasing from 80 percent in 2005 to 91 percent in 2007. Table 7.1 shows responses to questions about practice location from the first three cohorts in the tracking study. Those opting for Northern Ontario locations range from 63 percent in 2005 to 90 percent in 2006. When asked about the preferred size of community for their practice location, substantial numbers express a preference for communities with a population under 50,000 (36 percent in 2007, 62 percent in 2006).

Table 7.1
Practice preferences from tracking study for the 2005, 2006, and 2007 cohorts

	Cohort		
	2005	2006	2007
Preferred type of practice[†]			
Solo	2.0%	6.5%	3.8%
Small group	24.5%	31.1%	37.7%
Large group	6.1%	4.3%	5.7%
Multidisciplinary	18.4%	45.7%	41.5%
Preferred practice location[†]			
Ontario-Northeast	40.8%	56.5%	45.3%
Ontario-Northwest	22.9%	34.8%	30.2%
Ontario-South	6.3%	4.4%	5.7%
Others	16.3%	17.4%	18.9%
Size of practice community preferred[††]			
Under 5,000	15.4%	27.9%	10.4%
5,000–50,000	35.4%	34.4%	25.4%
50,000–500,000	41.5%	37.7%	58.2%
Over 500,000	7.7%	0.0%	6.0%
Size of practice community not preferred[†††]			
Under 5,000	27.3%	20.8%	27.4%
5,000–50,000	3.0%	0.0%	2.7%
50,000–500,000	7.6%	1.9%	0.0%
Over 500,000	62.1%	77.4%	69.9%

[†] Percentages based on the number of respondents who selected "Strongly inclined to select" for a given category.

[††] Percentages based on the number of "strongly inclined to select" responses for each variable divided by the total number of "strongly inclined to select" responses for this question. Some respondents selected more than one category.

[†††] Percentages based on the number of "strongly inclined to avoid" responses for each variable divided by the total number of "strongly inclined to avoid" responses for this question. Some individuals selected more than one category.

Among the factors that respondents cited as influencing their future practice location, family connections (*Influence of spouse/partner; Proximity to extended family/relatives*), followed by an appreciation of the nature of northern and rural practice (*Medical needs in community; Opportunity for a variety of medical experience*), emerged as the most important. In answer to a question tapping into their beliefs about rural practice, rural lifestyle (*There are things I enjoy doing in rural areas*), professional employment (*There are good opportunities for employment in rural areas*), and variety (*Working in a rural area provides more opportunity to practise a variety of skills*) were the predominant responses.

As expected, students who have chosen to apply to NOSM have positive attitudes towards rural practice; however, it is encouraging to see this natural affinity for rural living associated with the perception that such settings can also provide rewarding career opportunities.

THE INTERVIEWS

NOSM's admissions policy gives a substantial advantage to applicants with extensive northern and/or rural experience. When we see a student body that, though very diverse and complex, demonstrates a common interest in northern and/or rural practice, the reasonable conclusion is that this policy works. Nevertheless, it may be misleading to give all the credit to the admissions criteria. Some of the students were admitted to more established medical schools with more proven systems and yet *chose* to be a part of NOSM's charter class, fully cognizant that the newly formed program would experience glitches. Some students also said that they would not have applied to medical school if there had not been a northern school. Many of them even revealed that they were inspired to become physicians when they learned that a medical school was being established in Northern Ontario. In these cases, there is certainly a natural affinity, enough to indicate that many of these students had already made up their minds to practise in the North before they applied.

This affinity is expressed in four different levels of involvement: personal, familial, communal, and socio-political. On a personal level, students express an interest in the rural lifestyle. Many are attracted to the natural habitat of the North, constantly emphasizing their love for outdoor activities such as fishing, hiking, boating, and tree planting. On a familial level, students often enjoyed a good childhood with their families and wanted to stay close to them (by "close," they usually meant within a day's drive). Most of the students grew up in smaller cities or rural/remote areas, and they appreciated the lifestyle offered by these communities, feeling safe within them and connected to them. As one of them explained:

As a child I grew up in a very rural community, not in the Far North, but it was a village outside of [a northern city] ... I

enjoyed my childhood ... Eventually, I moved to southern Ontario to study like many people do, but I had a great childhood
and experience with my family, so after university, I tree planted
in northern environments all across Canada for five years. I just
really enjoy the North for many reasons: the natural environment, the people, et cetera. I have some very positive experiences
in rural communities that I think really influenced my desire to
practise [medicine in these communities].

Unique in its own way yet similar to many others, the preceding
personal history demonstrates that the different levels of interest in
practising rural medicine are always interrelated.

Nevertheless, it is not necessarily a positive experience that draws
students to rural medicine. A moving part of *High Hopes* involves
the story of Lana Potts, an Aboriginal student from a reserve in
Alberta. Potts had a broken family. Her mother died in a car acci-
dent, and her father was not there for them. She was exposed to
drugs and alcohol at a young age and had to raise her siblings in un-
favourable conditions. But her belief in education and the strength
she gathered from the traditions of her people helped her to realize
that she had to "put faith back to life." Potts saw hope in her people's eyes when they learned that she had applied to medical school.
They understood the implications of this: a possibility that had previously been unknown to them was now available. Right after she
received her letter of acceptance, Potts said: "That means the kids
who live down the street can eat now ... because I know I will give
back to my community more than they have ever given me."

Like Potts, many NOSM students exhibit a strong sense of social
responsibility. For example, in *High Hopes*, we meet a cultural an-
thropology student (Stephanie Giroux) who worked in Third World
development in Africa before attending NOSM; a biochemist (Dr
Philip Berardi) who applied to the school because he wanted to improve the cancer care system; a lawyer (Tracy Ross) who aban-
doned a potentially higher-earning profession in the corporate
world because nothing was more important to her than saving lives
and promoting health; a herbalist (Jessica Moretti) who wanted to
bridge the gap between natural medicines and Western medicine.
These students are thinking actively about how they can contribute
to making a difference; they are activists in the constructive sense of
the word or, as Alexandre Anawati (an outspoken student who is

enthusiastic about cultural awareness in medical education) would put it, they are "health advocates." Dr Cheu titled the film *High Hopes* not just because NOSM promises to bring hope to rural communities but also because hope is what one feels when confronted with the sense of social responsibility expressed by these students. Many chose NOSM because they were adventurous, and they identify their desire for social change and improvement with NOSM's experimental premises. As one student, who had been accepted by other schools but preferred NOSM's community orientation, reveals: "I found it very exciting to be part of the first class and to help shape the future of the school."

Social Composition

A recent survey of the social composition of Canadian medical students shows a significant bias towards urban, white, upper middle-class backgrounds (Dhalla et al. 2002). One way to increase the number of doctors willing to practise in underserved areas is to ensure that the social composition of graduating medical students reflects that of the area they are expected to serve (Bowman 2007). In the US context, minority physicians are much more likely than are their counterparts to opt to practise in underserved areas, so increasing the proportion of minority groups graduating from medical school is viewed as an effective way of meeting the needs of underserved areas (AAMC 2005). Given this, NOSM has adopted a strategy of seeking a student body whose socio-cultural composition reflects that of Northern Ontario, which has a substantial number of Aboriginal and francophone communities.

THE DATA

The proportion of Aboriginal and francophone students admitted to NOSM closely reflects their demographic representation in Northern Ontario. Aboriginal students made up 11 percent of the 2005 intake and 10 percent of the population of Northern Ontario; while francophone students made up 18 percent of the intake and 19 percent of the population of Northern Ontario. As far as educational background is concerned, NOSM students tend to come from families with above average education. The 2005 survey shows that nearly 70 percent of NOSM students had fathers who had completed their postsecondary education and only 8 percent had fathers who had not graduated from high school. The comparative figures for the population of Northern Ontario in 2001/02 cited in chapter 2 indicate that 43 percent completed postsecondary education and that 33 percent had not completed high school. In this respect, NOSM students do not mirror the social composition of Northern Ontario but, rather, are more reflective of the upper middle-class bias found by Dhalla et al. (2002). One other important divergence from the demographic profile of Northern Ontario is reflected in the high proportion of female NOSM students (71 percent in the first cohort), even though the process of selection is "gender blind." This does, however, reflect a general trend towards increasing female participation in Canadian medical school admissions (AFMC 2007).

THE INTERVIEWS

Since social accountability is paramount for NOSM, the student selection emphasizes diversity: that is, the school seeks students who reflect the social and cultural composition of the North. Although NOSM specifically identifies the Aboriginal and the francophone communities, along with the mainstream English component, in its educational program, this does not mean that it does not attract other minorities as well. The curriculum's goal is to provide the students with enough knowledge to adapt to different circumstances. With a wide variety of ethnic origins (Asian, African, Arab, South American, etc.), and with some coming from families of mixed cultures and languages, the student population actually reflects the social accountability mandate far more than is implied in NOSM's francophone-Aboriginal emphasis.

Yet, of course, "social composition" involves issues far deeper than skin colour and language. Goyce Kakegamic, deputy grand chief of the Nishnawbe-Aski Nation, states: "Sometimes Canada takes pride as one of the best countries to live, and yet when this same standard that the United Nations uses applies to the First Nations and other rural communities, our country may be more like a Third World. The lack of appropriate health care will be one of the key factors" (NOSM 2005). The social reality of rural medicine in Northern Ontario is tied to that region's socio-historical context, and this includes poverty, racism, gender inequality, domestic violence, and a general lack of access to higher education and health care facilities – all of which intertwine with issues relating to mental health, substance abuse, diet, and so on. Understanding a patient's social context is, therefore, as important as knowing her/his medical history.

The social composition of NOSM students can be analyzed in terms of their socio-economic backgrounds. And, when social and economic factors are taken into consideration, cultural boundaries begin to break down. During the Multi-year Tracking Study, a student revealed that she was inspired to become a physician by the knowledge that her grandmother had been one of the first women awarded a medical degree in Ireland and had practised in Nigeria during the Second World War. Alexandre Anawati, whose father is a physician from Egypt and whose mother is a francophone nurse, has other siblings going to other medical schools. When, in *High Hopes*, a Nigerian student introduces himself by saying, "My name is Oluwole Aveni; I grew up in Kapuskasing, Ontario," the people in the audience often smile, delighted that multiculturalism has moved deep into Canada's small towns. As the story unfolds, we learn that Aveni is the son of a general surgeon who immigrated to Kapuskasing in 1987. In terms of race, he may belong to a minority, but in terms of socio-economic factors, he is one of several students whose parents are in the medical profession. He was brought up in a middle-class family and was exposed to the medical profession very early.

However, a family background in medicine does not mean that a child will be pushed to become a doctor. Alexandre's father insisted that he did not encourage his children to go into medicine. He did, however, encourage them to develop a strong sense of social responsibility and to think constantly about how they could contribute to the community. With the examples of his parents, Alex and his siblings chose to become doctors. Doctors' families tend to produce doctors not only due to resources but also due to the social values they pass down from generation to generation.

There is also a group of students that consists of people who are already professionals and are certified in such fields as midwifery, nursing, speech pathology, physiotherapy, counselling, and social work. This group seems to be extremely committed to northern and rural practice, and, in the interviews, a number of its members indicated that it was practising in rural and remote areas that led them to enter NOSM. Working in a health care-related profession sometimes helps people to see the seriousness of the doctor shortage, with the result that they decide to become qualified themselves. Of course, "rural" experiences are not limited to the North. Originally from southern Ontario, one student experienced rural medicine while working as a missionary abroad:

When I was working in Africa, I worked with a home-based nursing organization and it struck me how they could do so much with so little. But there was this point where they couldn't do anything else. They had no doctor who would come ... they had one nurse ... and even the nurse's knowledge about HIV and AIDS was very limited to treat these patients. Then when I went to India, I was working in an AIDS hospice and was again struck with how little they could do for these patients without having medical training ... I knew my life was being steered in a different direction, and I realized it was medicine.

Also, some students, like Lana Potts (a nurse), had not considered medical school a possibility until they found out about NOSM. Because of their professional backgrounds, despite their cultural and racial differences, these students already belong to the medical culture.

Some students had difficult backgrounds that seemed to bind them strongly to their families and communities. Consider the following excerpt from the Multi-year Tracking Study:

My parents come from a very impoverished background – my dad is from Croatia and my mom is from Poland. When they were growing up, there wasn't always enough food ... They completed high school in their respective counties and came here. My mom's always stayed home with us and my dad worked ... as a machine operator. It wasn't a job that really challenged him or a job that he enjoyed. They made a lot of sacrifices so that my brother and I could have a good education, and they always instilled in us how important it was to get educated, to work hard and give back to [the] community. So that factored certainly into my decision to come into medicine. The fact that I've never had extended family factored into my decision to stay at NOSM because my family is very important to me.

In many ways, especially with regard to the value of education and the desire to give back to one's community, this story recalls Lana Potts's story, albeit from a different historico-political and cultural context. In the students' stories, what we see is a complex interplay between self-determination and social circumstances.

If we build it, will they come?

NOSM planners were preoccupied with whether the school would draw the same number and quality of student applications as the established schools. Universities in general and medical schools in particular are beset with issues of prestige because, rightly or wrongly, how a program is perceived externally reflects on its academic credibility. High rates of application are one indicator of prestige.

THE DATA

Any anxiety about the ability of NOSM to attract the necessary numbers of high-quality students has certainly been allayed. The students did come, and they came in droves. In 2005, there were 2,095 applicants for fifty-six places, which is equivalent to thirty-seven applicants for each available place – the highest ratio of applicants per place for all Canadian medical schools in that year.[1] A similar rate of application has continued in the two subsequent years, with 2,050 applicants in 2006 and 2,274 in 2007. This high level of application demonstrates that meeting the social goal of having a class that reflects the socio-cultural composition of Northern Ontario can be achieved without any compromise in academic standards. Although what is motivating this demand is not entirely clear, the students' commentaries provide us with valuable insights into what attracted them to NOSM's program.

THE INTERVIEWS

The high number of applicants indicates that there is no shortage of quality students, and, based on our study, the students faithfully reflect the social composition of northern and rural Canada. This confirms the value of NOSM's admissions process. First, the decision to allow students with a good general GPA to apply, with no requirement for MCAT results or an undergraduate degree in science,

---

1 The comparison is made based on data provided by the Association of Faculties of Medicine of Canada (2007), tables 12 and 80.

definitely has a significant impact on the diversity of the student body. Since many rural communities have limited access to different areas of education, the MCAT requirement often functions as a barrier: "A big attraction for me," one student pointed out, "was not having to go and write an MCAT and go back to take more courses." This student is one of many who has a degree in nursing and whose experience enables her to contribute a lot to the classroom. Along with medical knowledge, she also sees communication skills and the ability to understand human interaction as essential qualities of a good physician.

The admissions process also succeeds in finding those rural students who have the desire to "give back to community." Dr Jill Konkin, the associate dean of admissions and student affairs, explains that the admissions process was carefully set up so that a rural applicant's lack of access to establishments in bigger cities would be minimized. For example, in order to find students with a high sense of social responsibility, medical schools always ask applicants to list their volunteer work. According to Dr Konkin:

> Rural kids are on the same continuum as urban kids: some kids do a lot, some do nothing, and then there is a whole range in between. But what is available to rural kids is different in that, if you look at volunteerism in urban communities, it has become task-oriented. You go somewhere, you sign in, you tick off your name, there you are for an hour – somebody else does all the organizing. In a farming community, for instance, the neighbour gets very sick and I run the farm for him for two months. That is a huge part of my community and volunteering, but that's not a tick on a sheet that someone keeps. It isn't often things that applicants think of putting on their biographical sketch, where they list all the volunteering activities. If you look at our application, one of the questions we ask is how you are involved in your community, which is how we allow applicants to tell us about things they might not list as volunteering activities.

With all the "health advocates" admitted to the school, this attention to detail in the design of the application process seems to be working tremendously well. It has resulted in high-quality applicants and an impressive selection.

Table 7.2
Preferred specialization from entry surveys for the 2005, 2006, and 2007 cohorts

	Cohort		
	2005	2006	2007
Preferred specialization[†]			
Anesthesiology	12.5%	6.8%	7.5%
Emergency medicine (family practice)	51.0%	55.6%	37.7%
Family medicine	62.5%	62.2%	54.7%
General surgery	8.2%	15.2%	20.8%
Internal medicine	22.4%	6.7%	13.2%
OB/GYN	6.1%	15.6%	35.8%
Pediatrics	14.3%	31.1%	24.5%
Psychiatry	10.4%	6.8%	7.5%
Public health/community health	12.2%	17.8%	17.0%

[†]Percentages based on the number of respondents who selected "Strongly inclined to select" for a given category.

Family Medicine or Other Specialization

One of the most important needs in Northern Ontario, as in other regions of Canada, is for primary care physicians, and yet family medicine has been declining as an option for Canadian medical students in comparison with more specialized branches of medicine (Wright et al. 2004). The expectation is that NOSM students will be encouraged by their immersion in northern and rural clinical settings to adopt a more favourable view of family medicine.

THE DATA

Some of the students with whom we talked had already formed a clear view of their future career path, but others were more circumspect. How they talk about their future plans is of considerable interest to future planners, and, in listening to them, we can get some sense of what it is that engages their interest in rural practice. And this might help us counter the pressures that draw most of them into specialty disciplines.

Tracking study results show a clear preference for family medicine, emergency medicine, and the general specialties. Well over half of the students in all three years chose family medicine or a combination of family practice and emergency medicine.

Respondents were asked about the factors that were important with regard to their determining their choice of medical specialty. Those most frequently cited as extremely important were: *Compatibility with my personality* (49 percent), *Diagnostic challenge/intellectual content of the specialty* (31 percent), *Emphasis on primary care* (27 percent), *Emphasis on continuity of care* (24 percent), *Having close personal relationships with patients* (24 percent), and *Opportunity to deal with varied medical conditions* (24 percent).

THE INTERVIEWS

Almost all the students interviewed were happy with NOSM's program; they felt that they had received a high-quality and innovative medical education. When asked what they most liked and do not like about NOSM, there were far more positive than negative responses. Many faculty members were praised for their commitment to teaching. The students liked small groups and experiential learning, and they also enjoyed having a practicum in phase 1 of the program. There are complaints that the mechanical methods of evaluation are not able to reflect the actual learning experience. There are also problems with the arrangement of placements – of particular concern was the feeling that some community placements were too long and that there was not much to learn. Some students wished for a more flexible schedule for people with children or other commitments, but most generally agreed that such issues are temporary problems that will be found in any new program. Most of them also believed that the Student Society does a good job of taking their concerns to the school's authority. So there is an overall level of satisfaction with the new medical school.

There is, however, a difference between the students and the school regarding the issue of speciality. NOSM emphasizes primary care; however, during the process of their medical education, students are also exposed to a variety of possible specialities, and this can create a dilemma:

When I got into medical school, I was going to be a family doctor no matter what 'cause I had no idea that there were even options to be a specialist in the North. I knew I wanted to stay in the north, so then I thought, OK. Well, now I would really like to do dermatology. I did an elective in the summer and I really liked it. But the problem is it's very hard to get in … and you can't train in

Northern Ontario. You have to go to [the major metropolitan cit-
ies] and it's a five-year residency. So that would take me away
from Northern Ontario for five years in the time that I'm going
[to] want to be getting married and starting a family. That's a key
time that's taking me away from Northern Ontario, and I'm
afraid maybe that I wouldn't come back.

Conversely, another student, who had planned to take oncology
or internal medicine, decided to go for family medicine: "I have a
cancer research background, so something like oncology or internal
medicine would have been specialities ... I was maybe thinking
about ... urology, because I was working on prostate cancer ... But
since coming here, and I'm sure NOSM will love this, they have definitely sold me on family medicine."

When one investigates, one finds that the students who are interested in specialities are not so much concerned with the fact that
they provide higher pay than does general practice as they are with
personal interest, job fulfilment, and lifestyle. Students also recognize that there is a need for specialists. As a student who is also a
physiotherapist expressed it:

There is a deficit of family medicine. Say ... in Sudbury that the
community can handle one hundred family docs and they might
be short of forty – I get that. But you know what? Sudbury might
also have a need for ten psychiatrists and they only got three.
There is a proportionally larger deficit in specialists ... so I think
it's important not to hang our hats on family medicine because
that's the greatest deficit. In raw numbers absolutely it's a great
deficit; in proportion, however, it would be fair to say that there's
just as much a lack of specialists as well.

Dr Daniel Hunt, NOSM's vice-dean, explained in an interview that
sending students to urban areas for specialities may not be a bad
idea. People go to the cities for special treatments, so it is good to
have specialists who understand the delivery of health care in rural
and remote areas. Many will come back to northern cities. After all,
medical education should not be bounded by geographical borders.
It is NOSM's vision, and it is shared by its students, that its graduates will have a wide range of skills that will serve them in both

urban and rural environments. As Chief Archie Meekis (a community partner from Deer Lake) says at the end of *High Hopes*: "I want [our students] to be able to work anywhere in the world – for humanity."

CONCLUSION

The evident enthusiasm of the first groups of students for the NOSM program and its related health care goals is highly encouraging. There is nothing definitive about this: only the long-term tracking of graduates undertaken by the Centre for Rural and Northern Health Research will show whether or not the youthful idealism of these students eventually translates into firm commitments to practise in the communities that provided the context of their education. Still, it is a very positive sign.

What has enabled NOSM to meet its admissions targets is the exceptionally high number of applications. This has meant that the school has been able to meet its recruitment targets for students of northern and rural background, to have a class whose social composition reflects that of Northern Ontario, and to maintain a high academic standard. Not only does this mean that there is a strong likelihood that these students will stay in the North to practise, but it is also a concrete expression of NOSM's social accountability mandate. The students' commitment to careers in family medicine also seems substantial, and, where they envisage other specialties, their choices are entirely consonant with the needs of northern and rural practice.

There were also unanticipated findings. The admissions process did a good job of ensuring the solid representation of Aboriginal and francophone populations. And, in meeting this need, it also managed to attract a broad range of cultural diversity. Clearly a good thing. Furthermore, the interviews revealed a refreshingly high level of social engagement and student idealism. Of course, they are the first generation of students in a new school, and it is natural that they should be excited about this. Also, the conditions under which the interviews were conducted might be expected to elicit more positive responses than what might have been the case with private dialogues. Nevertheless, public perceptions of young people often focus on their preoccupation with material satisfaction and downplay the widespread evidence of their desire to give something back to their communities (Yates and Youniss 1999). The whole point of NOSM's creation is to attract those students who would be most likely to direct their talents and energies back to their communities. The evidence so far is that it has accomplished this goal to a degree far greater than its designers had dared hoped.

8

Governance and Organization

ARNIE ABERMAN AND DOROTHY WRIGHT

INTRODUCTION

In this chapter, we address two key organizational features of the Northern Ontario School of Medicine: (1) its governance structure and (2) its establishment as a quasi-autonomous organization (with its own faculty and administrative staff) that is also inextricably linked to its two host universities. We describe how NOSM's governance structure was designed to enable it to serve as the single Faculty of Medicine for two independent universities – Lakehead and Laurentian. Implementing this structure and recruiting faculty and staff to run the new school posed some special and unique challenges.

FACULTIES OF MEDICINE

In Canada, medical schools are organized as academic units (usually called faculties) within universities, and they are no different than other faculties (e.g., law, arts, engineering, etc). They are not legal entities. Although usually the leader of a much bigger unit, the dean of medicine's official authority is no different than that of other deans, and she/he usually reports, as do other deans, to the chief academic officer (vice-president academic or provost). Although there may be separate additional funding from the provincial ministries of health to teaching hospitals and/or clinical faculty (in Ontario such funding is referred to as the Clinical Education Budget), faculties of medicine receive their operating budgets from the parent university, as do other faculties. Because of the unique and important status of teaching hospitals in the academic mission, in some universities the dean of the Faculty of Medicine may also have a vice-provost/vice-president appointment and report to the university president with respect to relations with teaching hospitals and other community health facilities whose medical (and other health profession) staff have academic appointments and who participate in clinical teaching and, increasingly, in research programs.

Undergraduate education programs in medicine (not the medical school) are jointly accredited by the Committee on Accreditation of Canadian Medical Schools (CACMS) – a joint committee of the Canadian Medical Association (CMA) and the Association of Faculties of Medicine of Canada (AFMC) – and the American (Liaison Committee on Medical Education (LCME). The LCME is jointly sponsored by the Association of American Medical Colleges (AAMC) and the American Medical Association (AMA).

Like other faculties, faculties of medicine have no degree-granting authority: that belongs to the parent university. In Canadian universities, academic authority resides in the university senate (in universities with bicameral governance) or is delegated by the university board to the senate or senate-like committee (in universities with unicameral governance). A university senate is a committee with a majority representation of elected faculty members and with variable membership of non-academic staff, students, and the university board. It has the authority to control, regulate, and determine the educational policy of the university (to confer degrees, to conduct examinations, to approve the courses of study, to determine admissions qualifications). Thus, all academic policies of faculties of medicine have to be approved by the university senate.

HOW NOSM CAME TO BE LINKED TO TWO UNIVERSITIES

NOSM, unlike all other Canadian and American medical schools, "belongs" to two separate universities – Lakehead University in Thunder Bay and Laurentian University in Sudbury. This unique feature resulted in NOSM's structure being different from that of other Canadian and American medical schools.

In July 1999, Robert McKendry, a professor of medicine at the University of Ottawa, was appointed by the Ontario minister of health and long-term care as a fact finder commissioner to "provide advice on the scope and nature of physician supply, mix and distribution issues." (McKendry 1999) Among its many recommendations, the resulting McKendry Report (McKendry 1999, 79) suggested that "Ontario consider the advisability of creating a new medical school in rural medicine with a specific mission to attract students who are interested in working in the province's small, rural and remote communities." The school was to build on programs already in place at Lakehead and Laurentian as well as the existing postgraduate medicine programs and elective undergraduate rotations organized by the Northeastern Ontario Medical Education Corporation (NOMEC) (under the governance of the University of Ottawa) and by the Northwestern Ontario Medical Program (NOMP) (under the governance of McMaster University).

At the same time as appointing the fact finder, the minister of health and long-term care also made a commitment to establish an expert panel (chaired by Peter George, president of McMaster University) to undertake longer-term planning for Ontario's physician workforce. One of the reports submitted to this Expert Panel was entitled *A Northern Rural Medical School*, and it was presented in June 2000 by the Northern and Rural Medical School (NORMS) Liaison Council (an ad hoc committee consisting of key players in NOMEC and NOMP, prominent Northern Ontario physicians, and senior academic administrators from Lakehead and Laurentian as well as community leaders) (NORMS Liaison Council 2000). This was a detailed proposal for the establishment of a new decentralized multi-campus medical school, the Northern Rural Medical School, based at Laurentian and Lakehead universities.

The report of the Expert Panel, known as the George Report and submitted in May 2001, did not accept the proposal to establish a new medical school in the North, saying it would "take time for the different regions of the province to develop the capacity to deliver medical education independently" (Ontario 2001, 6). Instead, the panel recommended expanding the existing clinical education campuses, each of which was affiliated with a medical school in Thunder Bay and Sudbury, respectively. This report was, understandably, disappointing to those who were advocating a new medical school. However, it did not deter those who continued, on multiple levels, to lobby for a new medical school.

On 17 May 2001, the provincial government announced, as an initiative in response to the George Report (but going beyond its recommendations), that a new northern medical school would be established, with the "main site" at Laurentian University and a "clinical education campus" at Lakehead University (Ontario 2001). This (traditional one-university medical school) model, with Laurentian as the main host of the medical school and Lakehead playing a secondary role, had not been promoted (at least openly) by any group and quickly proved to be divisive. Not surprisingly, the press conference announcing the new medical school was held in Sudbury. The press release quoted a pleased president of Laurentian; there was no quote from anyone at Lakehead.

THE IMPLEMENTATION PROCESS

The next major event in the development of NOMS occurred on 25 October 2001, when Ontario premier Michael Harris announced the creation of the Implementation Management Committee (IMC) to develop a business plan for NOMS. The IMC was to be chaired by Sudbury mayor Jim Gordon. Other members were Councillor Linda Cunningham of Kirkland Lake, Councillor Rene Larson of Thunder Bay, and Dr Geoffrey Tesson, a senior academic administrator from Laurentian University with expertise in health issues. A fifth place on the IMC was held vacant for the dean of the medical school whenever he or she was appointed. A senior member of Mayor Gordon's staff was appointed as IMC general manager. One of the first actions of the IMC was to appoint the consulting firm of Price waterhouseCoopers to assist it in developing the business plan. PricewaterhouseCoopers promptly engaged the services of Dr Arnie Aberman, the ex-dean of the Faculty of Medicine of the University of Toronto, as a consultant on the project. In January 2002, Dr Aberman was appointed consulting dean of the proposed medical school and joined the IMC as its fifth member. It was anticipated that Dr Aberman would step down as consulting dean and as member of the IMC when the founding dean was appointed.

The IMC quickly learned that the recommended configuration (based in Laurentian University/Sudbury) of the proposed medical school was problematic. The key players in Northwestern Ontario – Lakehead University, physicians, and community groups – were unwilling to play a secondary role. On 15 January 2002, the *Thunder Bay Chronicle-Journal* ("NAN Leads Fresh Call for Full Med School) reported on a 14 January meeting convened by the Nishnawbe Aski Nation to convince the province to reverse the decision that made

Laurentian the medical school's main campus. At the meeting, Lakehead president Fred Gilbert and Thunder Bay mayor Ken Boshcoff, among others, were quoted as urging the Ontario government to return to the original plan to create a northern medical school that would be developed jointly by Lakehead and Laurentian, each of which would have equal status. The IMC learned that, without participation by Northwest Ontario physicians and hospitals (40 percent of the existing medical education programs were taking place in Northwest Ontario), it would be very difficult, if not impossible, to mount a program for the planned number of medical students. Laurentian University also made it clear that it had no objection to an equal partnership with Lakehead University. The IMC made these views known to the Ministry of Health and Long-term Care, and, on 10 May 2002, in the Ontario government's throne speech, it was announced that the medical school would have "full" campuses in Sudbury and Thunder Bay and that Lakehead and Laurentian would be joint hosts.

The IMC then considered, among many issues, the proposed organization of this "two-host-universities" medical school. There was no medical school in Canada or the United States with two parent universities, so there was no precedent upon which to rely. The conventional structure of having both Lakehead and Laurentian create separate faculties of medicine did not seem to be workable. How would we construct the desired integrated single Faculty of Medicine with two separate faculties? Each faculty would have to be identical, with the same faculty members, the same department structure, and the same academic leadership in place. Such a model would, it seemed to the IMC, create intractable administrative challenges, not to say destroy any ability for the faculty, administrative staff, and students to feel that there truly was only one medical school. The coordination problems in such a model would be insurmountable. And the IMC thought that there would be great difficulty in complying with several CACMS/LCME accreditation standards with each university having its own separate faculty of medicine and separate undergraduate medical education programs.

A DIFFERENT KIND OF MODEL

While all this was going on, Arnie Aberman (one of the authors of this chapter) happened to be reading a book on the merger of two of Harvard University's teaching hospitals – Brigham and Women's Hospital and Massachusetts General Hospital – which took place in 1993–94 (Kastor 2001). Although the problem that the leaders of these hospitals confronted (i.e., how to structure the merger) was certainly not identical to the issue with which NOSM was faced, the solution that they came up with seemed to be applicable. Briefly, they created a new not-for-profit corporation known as NEWCO whose members[1] had been members of the Brigham and Women's Hospital and Massachusetts General Hospital (each of which is a not-for-profit corporation). Then all the members of the Brigham and Women's Hospital and Massachusetts General Hospital resigned their positions and were replaced by NEWCO, which was now the sole member of both hospitals. As the sole member, NEWCO now had the ability to appoint the board of directors of both hospitals and, thereby, exert control over these, on paper, independent entities.

Using this model, the IMC proposed the following structure, which, in fact, has been put into place at NOSM. NOSM would be incorporated as a not-for-profit corporation with Lakehead University and Laurentian University as the sole voting members, thus ensuring their control of the school. Both Lakehead and Laurentian would pass the necessary resolutions to make NOSM the Faculty of Medicine for both universities. Then all academic staff, administrative staff, and academic leaders appointed to NOSM would also be appointed to each university and, thus, would be identical for both universities. Of course, a not-for-profit corporation is not in itself an unusual structure in either Ontario or Canada: it is commonly used for charities, professional organizations, NGOs, and, indeed, universities. However, it is a unique structure for a medical school, which is usually a division within a parent university rather than a separate entity. Furthermore, unlike Ontario universities, which are created by an act of the Ontario Legislature and are chartered as educational institutions, NOSM was simply incorporated under the Corporations Act of Ontario and was not chartered as an academic institution. It would use the academic structures of both parent universities (who alone

1 Members are to not-for-profit corporations what shareholders are to for-profit companies, the main difference being that each member has one vote and that they do not own the company (although they do control it, in accordance with its by-laws).

can grant the MD degree), with their two senates appointing a joint senate committee to confer academic status upon it and to oversee its academic programs, just as they oversee the academic programs of other faculties.[2]

In Canada, a not-for-profit corporation may or may not have charitable status. If a not-for-profit corporation chooses to apply for charitable status and the application is approved by the Canada Revenue Agency, then donations receive favourable tax treatment. However, there are additional regulations governing charities, and these may complicate the operation of a medical school. Accordingly, NOSM chose not to apply for charitable status. Consideration will be given to creating a separate charitable foundation to receive donations to support NOSM and its programs.

NOSM's bylaws were drafted to reflect this structure. The dean of the Faculty of Medicine is also NOSM's CEO. Membership of NOSM's Board of Directors includes an equal number from Lakehead and Laurentian, respectively. In addition, there are community members on the board who represent NOSM's many stakeholders. The bylaw is a public document and is readily available. The NOSM board, like the boards of all universities with a bicameral structure of governance, is responsible for the government, conduct, management, and control of the school and its property, revenues, expenditures, business, and affairs. The board also has all powers necessary or convenient to perform its duties and to achieve NOSM's purposes. However, academic matters are reserved to the joint senate committee. The bylaws specifically state that the rotating chair of the board is to be the president of either Lakehead or Laurentian. The dean, as CEO, reports to the chair of the board. It should again be emphasized that, academically, NOSM acts like all other faculties and reports to the senate.

This structure, although in a sense forced on NOSM because of the two host universities, has certain advantages. First, unlike all other medical schools, NOSM is a legal entity, which means that it can enter into contracts. Unlike all other Canadian medical schools, NOSM has a corporate board and, at least theoretically, can be responsive to the changing environment without having to go through

---

2 The IMC subsequently learned that Algoma College, affiliated with Laurentian University, is also a not-for-profit corporation without degree-granting authority and that it receives its academic status through Laurentian.

a university bureaucracy, which, understandably, has to consider all other faculties in its decision making. Having a board with community representatives, NOSM can be closer to the communities that it, in a sense, serves since clinical service is an inextricable a part of a medical school's mission. Second, the provincial government can have a direct relationship – both financial and non-financial – with NOSM. Again, this differentiates NOSM from all other Ontario medical schools. Of course, there is another side of this independent status – namely, the possibility that NOSM could become alienated from its parent universities. Such a development would be a threat to its academic identification. As well, a community board may be tempted to interfere with the academic freedom of the academic staff to vigorously challenge accepted views, and the universities will have to be vigilant in protecting this right of their faculty. As usual, more than what is down on paper, it will be the relationships among the leaders of the three institutions (Lakehead, Laurentian, and NOSM) that will be crucial in managing any conflicts that may arise. Only time will tell whether this structure will serve NOSM well, but it is off to a promising start.

FROM DESIGNING TO BUILDING: THE CHALLENGES OF IMPLEMENTATION

While the governance model of a separate non-profit corporation with the two host universities as members provided specific benefits to all three parties, the reality of what it would take to translate this model into a fully operational medical school was significantly underestimated.

Role, responsibility, and accountability of the three parties

The IMC Business Plan provided sound recommendations regarding "what" should be done. However, given an environment that included an expectation gap for all three parties, conflicting interpretations of the impact of the governance model, and the unique cultures, experiences, and priorities of the host universities, there was a degree of mistrust regarding "how" to make this work. It quickly became apparent that collaboration, compromise, flexibility, creativity, and commitment to best practices, as well as lessons learned from other medical schools and the host universities, would be critical to successful implementation. The opportunities to benefit from the experiences of others in the academic, health, public, and private sectors in administrative development were available to the NOSM leadership when it was attempting to implement the first new medical school in Canada in over thirty years.

Time was not on our side, given the initial mandate to accept the first class of students in 2004, nor was there an established relationship with a single host university. Concurrently, the major components of academic and administrative infrastructure, curriculum design, and development based on community engagement needed to move forward rapidly.

An initial agreement on principles and framework was necessary to provide the context within which to proceed. The document entitled *Principles and Framework for Working Arrangements Involving Lakehead University, Laurentian University, and the Northern Ontario Medical School* (NOSM 2002) provided guiding parameters:

PRINCIPLES

As the two Universities and NOMS proceed with establishing working relationships, these are to be guided by the following principles:

- the arrangements are to be established in ways which maximize the benefits to the Universities as well as to the Medical School
- there should be no unnecessary duplication
- new structures and processes should seek to maximize efficiency and effectiveness
- opportunities should be taken for innovation and creativity in addressing administrative and academic issues

The model's designers expected that the host universities would have the capacity to provide the support required for the start-up and the ongoing operations of an accredited, fully operational medical school.

One medical school for Northern Ontario

In some respects there was a dissonance between the governance model of one school for Northern Ontario and the expectation that two independent competing organizations with distinct cultures, policies, and protocols would come together to support one medical school.

For two provincially funded small universities in Northern Ontario, the fiscal constraints of the mid-1990s had resulted in lean operations, with significant reductions to academic and administrative support functions. The capacity of either university to undertake increased workloads to support the start-up activities and unique needs of a medical school was minimal. Early implementation placed significant reliance on both universities for support in human resources, financial processing, technology, and the provision of facilities. In spite of limited capacity, best efforts were made to assist the management of the school on an interim basis while the infrastructure was implemented. With funding and a dean in place, the priority was to hire a team of skilled academic and administrative staff to develop the school's functions.

HUMAN RESOURCES: THE RECRUITMENT CHALLENGE

An enthusiastic project team at Laurentian University, led by Dr Geoff Tesson, greeted the dean. While Lakehead University had provided input to the NOSM plan, there was no dedicated individual at that site. The dean hired Dorothy Wright as a project development officer. While this small but energetic team continued to deal with logistical issues, the recruitment of experienced academic and administrative leadership needed to proceed quickly.

Search consultants were engaged to develop position descriptions and to recruit key positions, starting with campus (vice) deans for each campus, chief administrative officers, associate deans of undergraduate medical education, admissions and student affairs, and research . National and international searches were conducted, and interview teams included representatives from the host universities and other medical schools. Community input was sought from the attendees at the public presentations made by the campus and associate dean candidates. While many talented individuals were identified, the reality of joining a medical school that was a non-profit corporation in the process of organizing and seeking accreditation in Northern Ontario presented challenges to many who came from traditional medical school environments. Initially, the opportunity to participate in the development of a new model of education resulted in successful recruitment.

However, for some positions, and for a number of reasons, success was temporary. The senior academic administrative positions were filled with physicians, which is traditional in established medical schools. But, at NOSM, these physicians had to face challenges that differed from those to which they were accustomed. These included ambiguity regarding roles, functions, and reporting relationships as well as, given the time commitment required by a developing school, limited opportunities to practise and participate in research and patient care.

When the school faced turnover in senior levels during the initial recruitment, many physicians and experienced academics assisted the dean. Three individuals who provided transitional leadership were Dr Arnie Aberman, who acted as campus dean west; Dr Tom Scott, interim campus dean east and associate dean of undergraduate medical education; and Dr David Boyle, executive director, project development. Their commitment, guidance, mentorship, and hard work assisted in moving NOSM forward.

Having learned some lessons in the initial phases, the recruitment strategies required review and clarity regarding some fundamental issues. Initially, the staff and the dean were "employed by" and "paid" through the respective host university in which they were geographically located. A decision about employment was required for the long term.

Who should be the employer of the faculty and staff of NOSM?

The presidents of the two host universities commissioned a study engaging two former senior academic administrators – Dr Hermann Falter and Dr John Whitfield – as the leads. The task was to provide an outline of alternative strategies for the appointment of faculty and staff to the Northern Ontario Medical School. Such strategies should allow the universities and NOSM to share the common goals of assuring: (1) the rapid and successful development of NOSM programs and (2) long-term harmonious and cooperative interaction between the universities and NOSM. A report was issued in April 2003 recommending that the school be the employer of all academic and administrative staff, and that conditions of employment for academic staff not vary greatly with regard to those set out in existing faculty collective agreements at the two host universities (NOSM 2003).

The implications of this report were significant. As the employer, NOSM reviewed strategies and options to develop the human resources policies, protocols, and systems. These systems included, to name just a few, position descriptions, recruitment, selection, employment contracts, compensation plans, training, personnel files, and performance management. What transitional strategies would be employed during the building phase so that progress could continue?

Several strategies were employed to address transitional and ongoing human resource requirements, starting with a set of human resource principles based on transparency, fairness, and competencies, along with benchmarking with the host universities. NOSM continued to use search consultants for senior academic administrative positions, expanding the areas of search and reinforcing the qualifications, which included tolerance for ambiguity, high energy, and experience working in a distributed environment.

An experienced human resource consultant, Ms Sheila Tyndall, was engaged to establish the human resource unit, including recruitment of the human resource staff, development of policies and protocols, compensation plans, and service agreements. This unit would be primarily responsible for supporting all non-academic staff recruitment. Collaboration leading to the establishment of agreements with the host universities to second staff to the medical school and provide operational support through payroll services, technology, expenditure processing, and purchasing were critical.

Attracting the Academic Staff and Clinical Faculty

Two well-established medical education organizations, the Northwestern Ontario Medical Program (NOMP) and the Northeastern Ontario Medical Education Corporation (NOMEC), provided staff to assist in faculty development activities and encouraged physicians to assist in curriculum planning and development. In addition, these organizations provided NOSM with paymaster services, using the compensation practices accepted by the Northern Ontario physicians, an area unfamiliar to the host universities. With the assistance of the experienced clinical education administrators of NOMP and NOMEC, NOSM was able to engage physicians across Northern Ontario as faculty. Many of the physicians teaching in NOSM's medical education program today participated in the programs of NOMP and/or NOMEC.

The host universities, hospitals, and public health units also assisted the development of NOSM through their support of secondments of experienced academic staff and researchers to the school.

The participation of vice-presidents, academic; deans; and allied health staff of the host universities on the Interim Academic Council was important in the development of academic policies pertaining to faculty appointment, promotion, and tenure.

The priority was to get the academic staff in place. Would NOSM be able to do this? How could it support an academic research when its laboratory facilities were not yet constructed? Would its academic staff have appointments at the host universities?

Working with an interim campus dean (an experienced medical school academic administrator), division heads for medical and human sciences (two experienced academics seconded from the host universities) conducted extensive searches for academic staff. They were successful in repatriating medical and human science staff to Northern Ontario from the United States, the United Kingdom, and other parts of Canada. Bright, talented young researchers and academic staff joined the division heads and associate deans in the monumental task of developing curriculum content. Incentives to assist in the enhancement of their respective research careers were offered, as were opportunities to work with other talented researchers at the cancer centres of the large regional hospitals in Sudbury and Thunder Bay.

The challenges faced by NOSM in attracting clinical faculty, including allied health professionals, to participate in interprofessional education are not unlike those faced by communities, hospitals, and public health organizations in Northern Ontario. Collaboration with partners to determine common human resource needs and to develop strategies to attract allied health professionals to communities has been effected through various mechanisms.

Both NOMP and NOMEC had various programs that were directed towards increasing the number of allied health professionals in Northern Ontario communities. When these organizations were integrated into NOSM, the latter assumed responsibility for the continued support of community-based program initiatives. One such program was the Community Development Officer (CDO) Program, which had initially been set up to support communities with regard to the recruitment and retention of physicians. However, these development officers, who worked closely with communities, also assisted in tracking requirements for allied health practitioners. They represented communities and promoted Northern Ontario as a place to live and practise, aligning the needs and wants of practitioners with those of the communities. Following up with prospects and partners as well as facilitating community orientation was part of their ongoing role. The CDO Program provided opportunities to better address the common human resources priorities of the different communities.

Similarly, NOSM, on behalf of McMaster University, is continuing to administer the Northern Studies Stream Program, which places physiotherapy and occupational therapy students in northern communities for training. In 2006, working cooperatively with the Dietitians of Canada, NOSM established the Northern Ontario Dietetic Internship Program, which provides internship opportunities in four northern communities. This program is intended to develop the unique skills required to meet the growing demand for health professionals in Northern Ontario. Graduates of these programs provide potential future preceptors and clinical faculty.

In actively engaging physiotherapists, dietitians, occupational therapists, pharmacists, speech pathologists, nurses, and other allied health professionals in various roles, NOSM has provided the opportunity for many to work with their professional colleagues. Marketing these opportunities and providing training in small communities requires the cooperation, flexibility, and support of community and public health organizations, hospitals, clinics, and the school. And it also requires moving away from traditional employment relationships.

With the support of their primary employer, who has entered into agreements with NOSM, many allied health professionals are participating in the school and committing various amounts of time to it. However, given the few resources and increasing needs in the North, there is the danger that health service organizations will compete with each other for the same resources and that this will negatively affect health outcomes. Thus, creative arrangements for attracting, sharing, and supporting scarce human resources are critical.

The employment of academic staff and clinicians by a non-profit corporation required the establishment of faculty compensation plans as well as terms and conditions of employment unique to academic staff. Determinations of compensation levels for academic rank and comparability to the host universities were issues to be resolved within the recommendations of the April 2003 report commissioned by the host universities.

What should clinicians be paid for extensive involvement in NOSM? While NOMP and NOMEC had compensation guidelines for preceptor work, NOSM required extensive time from many of the physicians in academic administrative positions. Unlike other medical schools, NOSM does not have practice plans or clinical departments attached to large teaching hospitals (which provide some funds to compensate physicians who are participating in academic activities). At this time, the challenge of physician compensation for academic activities is a work in progress.

Freedom to Choose Location: Recruitment Strategy

The challenges extended beyond recruitment activities to include determination of campus location for various academic administrators and staff. NOSM, based on a distributed model with sites connected by technology, provides flexibility with regard to the location of some of the senior academic administrative positions.

For those unfamiliar with managing and working across distributed sites, NOSM was a challenge. However, as a distributed education model whose students and faculty would be geographically dispersed and connected through technology, it was critical that all staff embrace and work within this model.

Initially, with the exception of technology and e-learning unit leads (which were to be located at the same campus), there was much flexibility regarding location. As NOSM's structure evolved, location decisions were made in order to better align geographic distribution with need. And it was recognized that positions, particularly academic leadership positions, could be distributed more broadly across Northern Ontario.

With this recruitment strategy, it was recognized that traditional management styles and top-down hierarchical communication methodologies had to be adjusted. The establishment of an environment within which expectations and priorities were clear, within which individuals were empowered to act and encouraged to question and critique, was critical to maintaining the passion and commitment of those who worked tirelessly to meet the endless challenges.

The Formation of the Northern Ontario School of Medicine Faculty Association

In Canada, every medical school has at least one association representing the academic staff for purposes of collective bargaining. In

February 2005, faculty, librarians, and professional academic staff founded the Northern Ontario School of Medicine Faculty Association (NOSMFA). The first president was Dr Brian Ross (associate professor, medical sciences). Usually, in Canada, a faculty association represents academic staff in both the medical school and the rest of the university; however, this does not hold true in NOSM's case. Since NOSM is the medical school of two universities, its governance structure resulted in its being a separate employer, thereby necessitating a separate faculty association. For the academic staff, the foundation of their association was part and parcel of their ongoing activities in helping to found a successful new medical school. In part, for example, faculty were motivated by a desire to secure terms of employment that were commensurate with conditions elsewhere, thereby ensuring the recruitment and retention of academic staff colleagues. NOSMFA immediately applied for and was granted affiliation with the appropriate national organization – the Canadian Association of University Teachers (CAUT) – and sought recognition from NOSM. In December 2005, a subgroup of the association, consisting of the full-time faculty, librarians, student affairs officers, and curriculum instructional designers, submitted a request to the Ontario Labour Relations Board for certification as a trade union. This request was granted once a successful vote was taken of the possible membership.

NOSMFA's first bargaining unit included approximately twenty-five members, and, as with other, newer, faculty associations in Canada, its membership was broad, including professional academic staff as well as faculty and librarians. The next step involved negotiating a new collective agreement.

Dr John Cowan, a renowned medical scientist and principal of the Royal Military College, accepted the role of chief negotiator for NOSM's first collective agreement. With the support of a relatively inexperienced team, Dr Marc Blayney, vice-dean, professional activities (a pediatrician by profession); Dr Garry Ferroni, division head, medical sciences (a microbiology professor and researcher); Dr Nancy Lightfoot, division head, human sciences (epidemiologist and researcher, cancer centre); and Dorothy Wright, chief administrative officer (chartered accountant, with a senior administrator background), the negotiations started in March 2006. NOSMFA was represented by the chief negotiator, Dr Geoff Hudson (assistant professor, human sciences); Dr Zacharias Suntres (associate professor, medical sciences); Dr Marion Maar (assistant professor, human sciences); and Laura Csontos (student affairs officer). CAUT provided NOSMFA with professional assistance.

After many long days and nights, the negotiations concluded with the signing of the tentative agreement on 1 December 2006. They were collegial, and neither party saw the need for third party mediation, arbitration, or job action. Both the Board of Directors and the faculty association membership ratified the agreement.

NOSMFA, with a membership of twenty-three, comprises the only unionized faculty and staff within the school. NOSM employs over 200 individuals and over 700 clinical faculty distributed across Northern Ontario. This is a far cry from the initial few of 2002.

Bringing the Team Together: Administrative Support

Many bridges needed to be built in order to create one medical school. Many of its initial staff members were involved in administrative support and were keen to do a good job; however, this often entailed looking for the established procedures and protocols that were simply non-existent in a developing organization. The standard rule was: "where NOSM does not have a protocol or policy, it will follow the policies of the host universities." This was an interim measure used while NOSM developed protocols to align the policies of the two host universities, factoring in environmental changes and efficiencies often recommended by the staff of other medical schools and/or managers in the host universities. NOSM was in an enviable position in that it could capitalize on the experience and case literature regarding best practices in organizational development.

In bringing the team together, it was recognized that academic and administrative leaders would rely on administrative support staff with regard to policies, protocols, and procedures. Much of the literature indicates that individuals who have control over various aspects of their work perform better than those who do not. Applying the principles of empowerment and teamwork, the NOSM leadership challenged the administrative support staff to prepare NOSM's administrative procedures. The geographically dispersed administrative support team worked together to accomplish this task, forming relationships that would assist in ongoing communication and training as NOSM expanded. The team was also responsible for continuing to review and recommend changes in and improvements to the processes it developed.

This team, while invisible to many, conducted NOSM's day-to-day activities (e.g., answering phones, arranging meetings, taking minutes, etc.). The lesson that any developing organization should take from this is: do not underestimate the benefits of a strong administrative team. And, if the administrative support team could work across the various geographical sites, would we expect any less from NOSM's leaders?

Funding: The Enabler

The Province of Ontario accepted a business proposal that resulted in $95 million being committed to the capital construction and development of NOSM. All funds are received directly by the non-profit corporation. In accordance with the principle of avoiding unnecessary duplication, NOSM engaged both host universities to provide financial services at their respective campuses. The school compensated the universities for all services, often by paying for additional staff plus operating expenses.

This interim measure, however, was not without challenges, including differing policies and protocols as well as timeliness. And this created issues that ranged from inconsistencies in salary rates, reimbursement amounts, and purchasing policies to undue delays in activities critical to the rapid progress of NOSM's development. The unique nature of some of the school's expenditures (such as physician stipends) required system adjustments, and this created confusion and additional demands on university staff. Regular financial reports to the various ministries and the board were compromised, with records being split between two universities. Inconsistent policies and protocols between sites did not support the existence of "one medical school" for Northern Ontario. This needed to be addressed, and systems needed to be aligned to support the school.

While the host universities made strong efforts to accommodate NOSM, they were reeling from the effects of fiscal constraints, and this resulted in staffing realignments in many administrative areas. In the face of increased research grants and institutional program expansion initiatives, Laurentian and Lakehead needed the full-time dedication of their financial management teams and staff in order to meet their priorities. As a result, neither university submitted a proposal to provide the requisite aligned system for NOSM. Consequently, NOSM implemented an integrated administrative system that was used by both host universities and that benefited from their collective experience and recommendations.

The benefit of NOSM's having its own financial system is that it has been designed to support specific medical school requirements and funding sources. Synergies are achieved within one integrated budget framework. Traditional medical schools are required to use various systems (some of which are determined by their host universities) in order to attain funding from the Ministry of Training, Colleges and Universities. Other medical school-specific funding from the Ministry of Health is normally found outside the university finance system and is often received directly by the Faculty of Medicine. Downloads from the university system and a combination of information from other internal faculty systems are required to provide a true financial picture of the faculties' activities. In NOSM's case, all financial information is recorded in one system, allowing for the consolidated financial report and the allocation of support services across all programs regardless of the funding source.

As the full amount of any funding is received directly by NOSM, there is no direct university administrative charge, as there is with other traditional medical schools. Effective management of cash flows and investment of excess cash for short periods of time increase the funds available for specific school priorities. Traditionally, these activities and funds would rest with the university. The ability to take on new initiatives that affect financial administrative processes is enhanced by virtue of the flexibility provided by NOSM's having its own financial system.

Service contracts continue with both host universities with regard to collecting tuition, administering student accounts, and managing and tracking bursary funds. Some research grants are also managed by the host university research offices, including the processing of respective research expenditures. The universities provide the enrolment reports, which NOSM submits directly to the Ministry of Training, Colleges and Universities in support of the enrolment-driven operational funding that is provided to it directly.

The ongoing challenge is to monitor the reasonableness of the charges for the support services provided by the host universities and to manage NOSM's administrative support costs within its program funding. There are guidelines for medical schools, and NOSM must continue to work within them in order to determine the cost-effectiveness of the existing administrative structure.

While the development funding has enabled NOSM to progress, the responsibility for prudent use of public funds demands effective and efficient processes. The support of the host universities and the Finance and Audit Committee's monitoring both contribute to NOSM's success in this area.

Ubiquitous Technology: The Goal

Given the advancements Lakehead had achieved with the smart classroom infrastructure of its Advanced Technology and Academic Centre, the IMC recommended that NOSM's technology and e-learning units be located at the Thunder Bay campus.

Given that, initially, NOSM had no technology staff, the directors of technology of both Lakehead and Laurentian provided the school with assistance. Through service agreements and secondments of technology staff, NOSM was able to move forward in developing its initial plans for the technology infrastructure, the first priority being to link the two sites as one school. An interim lead seconded from Lakehead assisted with the hiring of technicians, the purchase and installation of video conferencing equipment, and the establishment of a common e-mail system and public website.

In line with the principles set out by the IMC, NOSM's technology infrastructure resides within the systems of the host universities. NOSM is part of Laurentian University's e-mail system. This was essential in order to "quick start" the project and to support distance communication. Evolving program needs and increased volumes have compromised the integration of Lakehead's and Laurentian's respective technology systems. Incompatibilities of infrastructure designs and equipment, and a failure in any one of the three systems, affects NOSM's requirement for a reliable technology platform. Drawing on the smart classroom technology at Lakehead, NOSM has been able to implement this technology in the lecture theatres of both campuses.

Under NOSM's distributed model of education, technology infrastructure must extend beyond the two campuses and into the communities in which students and residents will work and learn. Reliable connectivity in rural and remote northern communities, including Aboriginal sites, is required. NOSM achieved its objective by forming partnership agreements with organizations that are connected to and serving these communities. With partners such as Contact North, Ontario Telemedicine Network (formerly North Network), and Keewaytinook Okimakanak Health Services, NOSM has accomplished this task. Working with these partners, NOSM attained additional funding to expand connectivity in remote areas of Northern Ontario.

Sustainability of the technology on a long-term basis is critical to NOSM's meeting its mandate. Efforts to address this issue include the implementation of technology standards regarding the equipment and software that the school can reasonably be expected to support. To enhance the use of technology in medical education, a laptop program has been implemented, providing for standard equipment and configurations. Leasing of the equipment provides for regular updates and renewal in order to assist in ensuring that students and staff continue to use updated technology. Introducing technology tools in order to assist physicians in improving processes supporting patient care is an essential element of the curriculum. With the tools come the challenges of reasonable protocols that balance need and cost-effectiveness.

Facilities: On Time, On Budget

New medical school facilities were funded at each of the two campuses. The funds flowed to NOSM, and the buildings were owned by the two host universities.

With the assistance of planning consultants who engaged university academic leaders, physical plant leads, administrative leads, and the dean and associate deans of NOSM, functional plans were prepared for the new buildings at each site. These plans supported the curriculum delivery, which utilized small group learning through case-based problem solving. Smart classroom design facilitated topic-oriented sessions that, through the appropriate technology, were distributed across the sites. This technology also supported clinical skills labs utilizing electronic dummies. State of the art research laboratories were constructed and equipped with the generous support of a special grant from FedNor, a federal government agency with responsibility for economic and social development in Northern Ontario.

At the time of the capital construction, both Sudbury and Thunder Bay had major hospital construction projects that had attracted significant public attention due to large cost overruns. NOSM's Board of Directors, committed to ensuring that the capital projects of the medical school would be constructed within budget, approved the establishment of the Building and Acquisitions Committee. This committee was responsible for acting in the best interest of NOSM, and it played an active role in monitoring the progress of the construction (which was managed by the host universities) and ensured the accountability of all parties. The result was the completion of all facilities on time and under budget.

Change orders required the approval of NOSM management under the governance of the Building and Acquisitions Committee. Upon substantial completion of the construction contract, funding flowed from NOSM to the university. The requirement for lease and service agreements was reinforced in correspondence from the Ontario Ministry of Training, Colleges and Universities to ensure that NOSM had unfettered use of the requisite facilities. Service and lease agreements were negotiated with both universities. The universities were to provide facility services – including all utilities, heat, telephone, cleaning, maintenance, parking, snow removal, signage, and security – to NOSM for a reasonable cost. Since the completion of the buildings, the school has entered into additional agreements with the universities for the buildings occupied by NOMP and NOMEC, which are to be integrated with NOSM. Building support services provided by the universities allow NOSM staff to focus on the development and delivery of medical education.

Bursary Funds for NOSM Students

NOSM's tuition fees were to be comparable to tuition fees at other Ontario medical schools. However, financial assistance beyond the traditional Ontario Student Assistance Program was significantly lacking. Established medical schools were awarding, on average, at least 50 percent of tuition fees through bursaries and scholarships. How would NOSM attract the necessary endowment funds to yield the income to support its students? NOSM is a not-for-profit corporation without charitable status. How does it accept donations? Was this the time to become a registered charity? The logistics and governance required to attain charitable status, never mind its implementation, would divert scarce resources from what was most crucial – bursary funding for students.

NOSM's community of supporters – government, host universities, businesses, and the people of Northern Ontario, rose to the challenge. The Ministry of Training, Colleges and Universities recognized that NOSM's development would be spread over a number of years, and so the school was permitted to carry over the unspent development funds. The investment of these funds yielded income, which the board dedicated to the General Bursary Fund at the rate of approximately $467,000 per year.

The Board of Directors also approved a bursary fund campaign entitled "The Northern Solution," which yielded, with matching government funds, $13 million. The success of this endeavour is due to the fact that the two campaign co-chairs – one from the Northeast and one from the Northwest – were able to work together to engage communities, businesses, and people both inside and outside of Northern Ontario to invest in medical students who would ultimately improve the health outcomes of individuals in rural, remote, and northern communities. The support of the host universities, which worked with the NOSM development officer and communications unit, was critical. Their expertise in endowment contracts, in legacy giving, in donation tracking, and in the issuance of charitable receipts was invaluable. Although universities compete with each other in fundraising efforts, the development leads were able to find a mechanism to ensure that their own fundraising prospects were not compromised and that NOSM students would benefit.

The Northern Ontario Heritage Fund Corporation provided $5 million in matching funding. Hence, for every dollar given, two dollars were actually placed in the bursary fund. This incentive significantly increased the giving by many small and large community service groups and individual donors across Northern Ontario. Similarly, the Ministry of Training, Colleges and Universities allocated to the NOSM an annual amount under the Ontario Trust for Student Support (OTSS) funds available to match donations.

Negotiation to align investment rates on NOSM bursary funds deposited with the host universities, determination of the allocation of large corporate donations between the two host universities, and the challenges of encouraging donors to structure endowment contracts that were not university- or city-specific in order to provide opportunities to the maximum number of medical students were all hurdles that were successfully cleared. Service contracts were implemented in this area, and the benefits of the increased endowments within each of the host universities were wins for all parties.

Where Are We Today?

In January 2006, a relationship agreement was signed by NOSM and Laurentian and Lakehead, and it confirmed the benefits of the structure and set out guiding principles. NOSM has implemented many service agreements with both host universities. An ongoing challenge is the establishment and measurement of service standards that will meet the school's requirements. For the host universities, the role of service provider is new.

Board of Directors Support

Unlike other faculties of medicine, NOSM has the additional responsibility of meeting all of the corporate requirements set out in the bylaws and the Business Corporations Act of Ontario. These requirements include working closely with and supporting Board of Directors committees and providing regular reports and updates on corporate activities, including regulatory compliance. This is an additional responsibility for senior staff, and it requires dedicated support staff and senior administrative time to attend to the matters with due diligence.

Sustainability of the Structure

The existing structure provides the opportunity for leveraging resources, including people, systems, and best practices, in order to capitalize on other pan-northern initiatives to the benefit of all of Northern Ontario. Benchmarking against the founding principles while adapting to changes – political, environmental, and funding – will be critical in supporting sustainability. The structure has enhanced collaboration and planning on other potential pan-northern initiatives, from health information resources to research ethics to interprofessional health education. Opportunities are as great as are the collective creativity and energy and will of the future leadership of the two universities and NOSM to collaborate.

PART THREE
The Lessons

9

Socially Accountable Medical Education and the Making of the NOSM

GEOFFREY L. HUDSON AND DANIEL HUNT

I have the audacity to believe that peoples everywhere can have three meals
a day for their bodies, education and culture for their minds, and dignity,
equality and freedom for their spirits. I believe that what self-centred men
have torn down other centred men can build up.

Martin Luther King

INTRODUCTION

Social accountability in medicine is related to the growth of state involvement in the support of medicine in Europe and elsewhere since
the late nineteenth century. State intervention for the purpose of
fostering national health insurance schemes and socialized medicine
were part of a broad socio-political movement to make health care
available to all citizens based on need rather than on ability to pay.
For the state, this was, in part, a recognition that fit citizens were fit
workers (and, if necessary, fit soldiers). In many countries, social-
ism, or the desire to avoid it, was also a factor.

Over the course of the twentieth century the medical profession
in all developed countries except the United States came to support
health care systems administered by the state. Indeed, physicians,
many of whom were active in public and community health, have
been influential in these developments since the mid-nineteenth century. With the Second World War, and the terrible complicity of
physicians in medical abuses in Nazi Germany, the medical profession internationally embraced a renewed emphasis on ethics and

social responsibility, both for the profession and individual physicians, as exemplified by the 1948 Geneva Oath (World Medical Association 1948).

Concern about the poor and socially marginalized found international expression in the Alma-Ata Declaration of 1978, which affirmed that "health, which is a state of complete physical, mental and social wellbeing, and not merely the absence of disease or infirmity, is a fundamental human right and that the attainment of the highest possible level of health is a most important world-wide social goal whose realization requires the action of many other social and economic sectors in addition to the health sector" (Conference on Primary Health Care 1978). The sentiments behind this ringing challenge were echoed internationally. The World Health Organization (WHO) called on all medical schools around the world to be socially accountable in all of their activities: research, education, and health care. The 1995 WHO definition of social accountability has been widely accepted: "[Medical Schools have] the obligation to direct their education, research and service activities towards addressing the priority health concerns of the community, region, and/or nation they have a mandate to serve. The priority health concerns are to be identified jointly by governments, health care organizations, health professionals and the public." (World Health Organization 1996). The 2003 World Federation for Medical Education Conference attracted participants from eighty-eight countries and endorsed a series of accreditation and other standards, including socially accountable medical education (World Federation for Medical Education 2003).

Internationally based researchers, published by the WHO, have suggested criteria based on the study of best practice. Richards, Fulop, and Bannermann (1987), for example, suggest five criteria to determine the community orientation of a medical school: (1) the extent to which its guiding principles are community-oriented; (2) the emphasis the curriculum places on concepts and knowledge of what constitutes a community and a population, how to measure and cope with health needs, and how to take proper account of socio-cultural background; (3) the extent to which community-based learning forms part of the curriculum; (4) the degree of community involvement in the training program; and (5) the organizational linkages between the school and the health services systems. C. Boelen and Heck suggest that there are five players that must take part in social accountable medical education: the policy makers, the health professionals, the health administrators, the communities, and the academic institutions (Boelen and Heck 1995; see also Woollard 2006; Association of American Medical Colleges 2005; WHO 1995).

In Canada, the Association of Faculties of Medicine (AFMC) has been engaged in a national strategy to encourage social accountability (AFMC 2002–06; AFMC 2004; Parboosingh 2003). The Canadian government is responding locally and nationally, with the assistance of the Primary Health Care Transition Fund. This initiative is sponsored by Health Canada and is dedicated to supporting the renewal of health care delivery across Canada. Provinces are also involved. In 2001, Health Canada published *Social Accountability: A Vision for Canadian Medical Schools,* a report developed by a task force comprised of multiple stakeholders, including Canada's medical schools. The social accountability vision incorporated in that report sees an important leadership role for medical schools in key areas, including: the establishment and promotion of innovative practice patterns to better meet individual and community needs; the reinforcement of partnerships with other stakeholders, including academic health centres, governments, communities, and other relevant professional and lay organizations; and advocacy for the services and resources needed for optimal patient care (Health Canada 2001).

Medical schools have been engaged for some time in activities that would meet the definition of "social accountability," and, beginning in 2003, the AFMC developed a database of such activities in order to raise awareness of the role of medical schools in meeting the needs of the various publics and to stimulate and support collaborative activities across schools (AFMC 2006).

All of these ideas and activities had a role in the creation and early development of NOSM. Of course, the slippage between theory and practice can be marked. In this chapter, we examine what being socially accountable means in practice. What challenges did it entail? What is the nature of the conflicts that arose as a result of pursuing social accountability? How did NOSM address the conflicts and challenges that arose? What might other medical schools learn from NOSM's experience? We also look at how social accountability is reflected in NOSM's curriculum and its engagement with the rural North and with people with varying health needs related to cultural and linguistic heritages, faculty recruitment, research, and governance.

CURRICULUM MODEL AND SOCIAL
ACCOUNTABILITY:

In the database submitted on behalf of NOMS to the Liaison Committee on Medical Education (LCME) in November 2004, the school made explicit comments about social accountability:

Recently, Health Canada and the Canadian medical schools have considered principles of social accountability by which Canadian medical schools should function. The NOMS objectives include attention to those principles:

That through appropriate training and evaluation "Medical schools emphasize to their faculty and students the need to maintain their competence, the importance of the patient physician relationship, and an understanding of professionalism and its obligations."

(Covered in part by objectives related to Theme 2)

That "Medical schools respond to the changing needs of the community by developing formal mechanisms to maintain awareness of these needs and advocate for them to be met." (Covered in part by objectives related to Theme 1)

That "Medical schools conduct curiosity-driven research and provide evidence-based care, testing new models of practice that translate the results of research into practice."

(Covered in part by objectives related to Theme 3)

That "Medical schools work together and in partnership with their affiliated health care organizations, the community, other professional groups, policy makers and governments to develop a shared vision of an evolving and sustainable health care system for the future." (Covered in part by objectives related to Theme 3). (NOSM 2004c)

The NOSM draft database submission was reviewed by external senior medical educators, and one reviewer commented:

First of all, I am impressed with the breadth of objectives that have been selected to guide the program. I also support the inclusion of the emphasis on social accountability. Not only are these objectives all stated; the curriculum is consistent with them and they are included in a way that supports their value. The five themes seem appropriate and inclusive, and provide a workable framework for the design of an integrated curriculum as is planned. The five themes of Northern and Rural health; personal and professional aspects of Medical Practice; social and population health; foundations of medicine and clinical skills in health care appear to include those objectives that will prepare the graduate for the demands of medical practice in the north, and in rural and remote communities elsewhere. (NOSM 2004a)

In chapter 6, Joel Lanphear outlines the structure and processes of the curriculum. Perhaps the most important element with regard to the viability of the social accountability mandate was the prior successful experience of the Northwestern Ontario Medical Program (NOMP) and the Northeastern Ontario Medical Education Corporation (NOMEC). These had engaged northern physicians, health organizations, and communities and made possible the community-based model upon which NOSM was founded (McCready et al. 2004; Rourke 2002).

COMMUNITY AND STUDENT LEARNING

An important component of NOSM's curriculum as it relates to the social accountability mandate involves the community learning sessions (CLSs). Each week there is one three-hour session dedicated to providing students with a wide range of community-based clinical experiences: observing and interacting with patients under the guidance of a preceptor, students visit patients in their homes, in hospitals, in long-term care centres, in doctors' offices, in pharmacies, in rehab centres, and so on. These experiences involve the content of all five of the school's themes (see chapter 6) and provide a focus for interprofessional learning.

Community learning is divided into three streams: (1) physician offices, (2) interprofessional health care teams, and (3) community and social service settings. Over the course of each year, students complete at least one CLS in each of these three streams.

The physician stream allows the student to learn among family physicians and medical specialists in physicians' offices, during hospital rounds, and in specialty out-patient clinics. The interprofessional stream allows the students to explore the practices of health professionals who are providing care and services in the community. This includes access to learning opportunities in acute care and rehabilitation institutions, long-term care facilities, and private practice. The community and social services stream provides students with the opportunity to explore community resources and to deepen their understanding of the culture of each community setting. Learning settings include social service agencies, shelters, mental health agencies, health care support services, addictions services, and eating disorder clinics.

In spring 2006, Sue Berry, the director of undergraduate community learning at NOSM (and a previous long-term NOMP manager and staffer), was interviewed for the school's newsletter. She commented: "The CLS gives students a chance to observe and interact with health care providers, patients or community users of a service in different settings and in a wide variety of community conditions"(NOSM 2006e).

Specific examples of locations in which CLSs are available include Thunder Bay District Health, a community health resource made up of a multidisciplinary team of health professionals that promotes healthy lifestyles and injury and disease prevention. Another example is the NorWest Community Health Centre, which provides health care and health promotion to people who are at high risk or who have difficulty finding health care due to language/cultural barriers and/or poverty or isolation. Yet another example is the Concurrent Disorders Program at the St Joseph's Care Group (Lakehead Psychiatric Hospital), in which students explore the role of the health care provider through both the Outreach to Recovery Program and the Community Support Program. Clinical staff members in the Concurrent Disorders Program include people from psychiatry, family medicine, nursing, occupational therapy, therapeutic recreation, and vocational counselling. A final example of a CLS location is the Anishnawbe Mushkiki, which provides culturally sensitive primary health care for Aboriginal people, combining Western care with Aboriginal philosophies and practices (NOSM 2007a).

Interviewed by Geoffrey Hudson, Siobahn Farrell, the new manager of community-based learning for NOSM, commented that the CLSs are very much a part of the school's social accountability mandate and that part of that mandate includes an increased emphasis on familiarizing students with marginalized populations.

In NOSM's first year, a dozen students applied for and won summer research scholarships and a number of them worked on projects related to the school's social accountability mandate. One student reviewed the use of fibrinolytics and other cardiac medications in the treatment of acute myocardial infarctions in remote northern communities in comparison to their use in larger, more urban, Northern Ontario communities. This student looked at what tools/resources can be used in these remote communities to improve the care given in situations involving heart attacks. A second student focused on the relationship between primary health care providers and Aboriginal communities in Northern Ontario, employing epidemiological methods and specific determinants of health to study the complex societal factors involved in specific medical conditions within Aboriginal communities. A third student examined how interprofessional (e.g., physician and nursing) issues shape health care delivery in northern and remote communities, studying archival collections and reports of health care delivery in remote settings to evaluate the historic role of interprofessional contributions in care (NOSM 2005d).

SOCIAL ACCOUNTABILITY AND ABORIGINAL NORTHERN ONTARIO

As early as 2000, Lakehead University president Dr Fred Gilbert approached the Nishnawbe Aski Nation (NAN) and asked it to participate in the development of a proposal for a new school in the North. The negotiations were tough, and NAN passed a resolution setting out its principles with respect to such involvement on 20 July 2000 (NAN 2000). NAN's participation was subject to three conditions: (1) First Nations must be included in the governance structure; (2) First Nations must be involved in the development of the program curriculum; and (3) First Nations must be guaranteed an agreed number of seats in the program (Morris 2000).

In many respects these principles were respected. In June 2003, Aboriginal people were invited to attend a consultative workshop ("Follow Your Dreams") so that they could provide their views on the development of NOSM, and they attended a workshop in order to provide input into the development of the school. The planning committee for the workshop included representatives from the major Aboriginal peoples in Northern Ontario as well as NOSM. The delegates heard speeches and sat in circles to discuss their recommendations, which included:

- The need for a pathway that encourages and nurtures Aboriginal peoples into and through medical school.
- The need for NOMS (faculty, staff, programs, etc.) to acknowledge and respect Aboriginal history, traditions, and cultures. This included cultural competency and recognizing issues such as the effects of colonization and residential schools, consultation with elders, the role of spirituality in health, languages, cultural taboos, and cultural practices.
- The need to recognize expertise and resources in Aboriginal communities that could assist in the growth and development of NOMS. These include traditional healing, professional services, and the incorporation of culturally appropriate settings.
- The need to provide opportunities for collaboration and partnerships to the mutual benefit of Aboriginal communities and NOMS. This would involve research and development initiatives that would improve health, the active recruitment of Aboriginal students, and the inclusion of Aboriginal peoples on the board, on the faculty, and in administration.
- The need to recognize that it is not enough to have students read about Aboriginal people; rather, they needed to live with them. Thus, the curriculum should include, for all students, placements in Aboriginal communities.
- The need to recognize the nature and challenges posed by specific health priorities of the Aboriginal communities, including diabetes, mental health, suicide, grief, and other outcomes of colonialism.

Subsequently, NOSM (2003c) produced a report on the workshop and made it publicly available. In July 2003, the Accredited MD Program Group started the process of following up on the recommendations, and it decided on an Aboriginal placement for students in first year – a daunting but highly significant decision. It was also decided that an Aboriginal director would be appointed to NOSM and that an Aboriginal advisory group would follow up on the workshop's recommendations. In addition, it was decided to make it a priority to hire a vice-dean from Lakehead/Thunder Bay who had demonstrated a commitment to Aboriginal peoples, to include Aboriginal participation in module writing groups, to develop admissions and student affairs processes, and to recommend to the Interim Academic Council that it should have two designated Aboriginal representatives (NOSM 2004f). Almost all these objectives would be met within the year. An early indication of what this would mean in practice is illustrated in an exchange recorded in the faculty development workshop on student assessment in July 2003. The dean called for an assessment that would recognize the high degree of competition between medical students and that would enable NOSM to compare its students with those from other schools. An Aboriginal member of the group, Ms Darcia Borg, who would later be NOSM's student affairs officer at the Lakehead/Thunder Bay campus, immediately commented that "competitiveness is not in the Aboriginal culture" (NOSM 2004b). Social accountability had arrived.

Later, an Aboriginal reference group and an Aboriginal affairs unit were created to carry out the recommendations of the workshop and to work with Dr Dan Hunt, the vice-dean at Lakehead/Thunder Bay and second author of this chapter, to ensure meaningful collaboration with Aboriginal communities, to assist in the recruitment of Aboriginal students, and to recruit Aboriginal host communities for medical students. The Aboriginal Reference Group was formed following two three-day workshops in which the membership and terms of reference were developed. This group went on to meet three times a year, providing input and guidance to NOSM's leadership regarding the curriculum.

As has been mentioned, one of the most challenging curriculum-related recommendations that came out of the Follow Your Dreams Workshop was the creation of a required placement for first-year students in Aboriginal communities. In order to better understand the issues involved, a pilot placement project was designed for June 2005. The authors (the pilot module coordinators and vice-dean Hunt) took part in the preparation and delivery of the pilot, along with staff from the Aboriginal affairs, undergraduate medical education, and student affairs offices. Fifteen medical students and nursing students were selected from schools in southern Ontario and Manitoba and were assigned to seven Aboriginal communities across Northern Ontario (which were selected to represent the challenges of communities both with and without road access).

The four-week pilot provided a sharp lesson for NOSM. It was clear that the students expected that the experience would be more clinically based than community-based. Areas in which there was a lack of coordination and administrative support were identified, and it was recognized that the video-conferencing of the small group sessions was overly complex. What was also revealed was the need to involve a wider group of participants in each of the communities.

So lessons were learned, and the response was to engage with the communities earlier in the following year, to prepare the way in a more systematic fashion, to create a module working group that would begin months in advance, to hire Aboriginal regional community coordinators, and to train local community coordinators more thoroughly. Students were given more preparation, including discussions with Aboriginal peoples and researchers regarding Aboriginal health and healing, the history of relations between Aboriginal and non-Aboriginal peoples, and the impact of the residential school system as well as other colonialist practices. In addition, a self-study project was introduced in order to help students reflect upon their experiences and to determine what to do to best practise medicine in Aboriginal communities.

Because of the pilot experiences and the important improvements that it produced, the first-year class – all fifty-six members – were sent in pairs out to communities across Northern Ontario (including fly-in reserves) for a month. They found the learning experience both intense and meaningful as they mastered their curriculum and lived among Aboriginal people for the last month of their first year. This was a truly innovative example of socially accountable medical education (Hudson 2007).

NOSM was also involved at the national level in AFMC social accountability initiatives. Vice-dean Dan Hunt participated in the Aboriginal Health Task Group, which had its first meeting in early 2005 in Halifax. This meeting led to the creation of two national work groups on Aboriginal health topics, both of which had active leadership from NOSM. The Aboriginal admissions work group eventually published an Aboriginal admissions tool kit, which is now in use in many Canadian medical schools. The second work group, which focused on curriculum, subsequently published a consensus-derived set of learning objectives that has been recommended for incorporation into all Canadian medical schools (AFMC n.d.[a]).

INFORMATION TECHNOLOGY
AND SOCIAL ACCOUNTABILITY

As touched on above, the June 2005 Aboriginal placement pilot allowed NOSM to try out distributed educational methods, many of which were tied to new information technologies. The plan for the pilot consisted of the use of asynchronist web-based discussion boards for small group learning as well as the digital recording of lectures in advance of the two-week community placement (with the recordings being available via the internet). In addition, the internet was the vehicle for student access to the curriculum as well as to resources (such as scholarly articles and e-books). At the beginning of each week, all the students gathered with the pilot coordinator via video-conference (VC) across Northern Ontario to preview the curriculum for the week and to discuss student questions and concerns.

During the pilot, several difficulties with the technology emerged. There was little if any meaningful discussion via the web-based discussion boards as students and faculty found them difficult to navigate. Instead, students simply posted reports that were read and commented upon by the faculty, usually the next day. Students found the web-cast three-hour lectures to be incredibly boring, and the faculty were not adequately trained in dealing with follow-up questions. Broadband internet did not work in all communities all the time, and sometimes the mainframe computers were down at NOSM itself. These two problems combined to make it impossible for students to gain access to the curriculum and resources on a reliable basis. The use of VC for the start-of-week sessions with the pilot faculty coordinator proved to be problematic as the VC systems in the Aboriginal communities were often some distance away from student accomodation, necessitating, for a number of students, long journeys by car very early on Monday mornings. It was also difficult, and in some cases impossible, to book the VC as these services were at times over-subscribed.

As a result of the pilot experience a different model was developed for the charter class students of 2006. Instead of web-based discussion boards for small groups and the weekly meetings with the faculty coordinator, teleconferences were utilized and supplemented by web-based discussion boards. This permitted small classroom discussions and weekly coordination meetings on a reliable and effective basis. In addition, a distributed tutorial session (DTS) was developed by Dr Brian Ross, a medical scientist who had used this curriculum model when teaching in the University of the Highlands and Islands in Scotland. The DTS replaced the recorded "talking head" lectures with a much more interesting interactive model (PowerPoint with audio discussion, study questions, and resources for the students, along with a teleconference take-up). The curriculum was pre-packaged on the students' laptops, and resources were provided on paper and/or preloaded on a CD before their placement began. This ensured that all students had reliable access to the curriculum while staying in re-mote communities. Since 2005, Dr Geoffrey Hudson has been approached on a number of occasions by an Aboriginal organization that provides broadband access to remote communities and that has asked him to rely on the internet for the delivery of the curriculum. This has not been possible, however, as NOSM cannot allow students to have unreliable, inequitable access to the curriculum and resources while on placement. It is anticipated that, in time, information technology across the North will be reliable enough for the model developed after the 2005 pilot to be adjusted significantly. But for now, social accountability to northern communities cannot be allowed to trump students' educational needs.

SOCIAL ACCOUNTABILITY AND FRANCOPHONE NORTHERN ONTARIO

The WHO definition of social accountability states that concerns need to be "identified jointly by governments, health care organizations, health professionals and the public." In the case of francophone Northern Ontario, the concerns of the government and the community differ, and this resulted in challenges for NOSM.

In Canada, governments provide services in French in certain areas and institutions. In Ontario, the University of Ottawa is uniquely mandated to provide an MD program in both English and French; it is the only medical school in North America to do so. The school was given neither the mandate nor the resources to provide medical education in both languages. Given that there is a large francophone population in northeastern Ontario, this would become a political challenge for NOSM.

NOSM's mandate from the provincial government was to encourage applications from francophone students; to provide, where feasible, opportunities for small group learning experiences in a French environment; to explore French language learning tools; to collaborate with francophone medical schools; and to ensure that the board had francophone representation. NOSM created an advisory community group that included representatives from francophone groups across the North.

An initial meeting of francophone community representatives occurred on 27 June 2002, and the facilitator, Geoff Tesson, outlined the mandate that NOSM had received from the provincial government. Members immediately expressed the view that at least 30 percent to 40 percent of the Board of Directors should be francophone. Follow-up meetings were held, including one on 28 August 2003, at which representatives stressed the need to recruit francophone students and to facilitate teaching resources. In particular, a concern was raised about the need to "avoid assimilation" – a concern that reflects the widespread cultural desire of francophones to preserve their language and culture amidst a larger anglophone population. As part of the discussion concerning admissions, it was mentioned that the MCAT favoured anglophones and should therefore not be used (NOSM 2003b).

In 2003, NOSM expanded the francophone community group and established it as the Francophone Reference Group. Nicole Ranger, from le Collège Boréal in Sudbury, was selected as the group's president. In addition, NOSM created a francophone coordinator position in 2004. As part of its curriculum development work, the school committed to creating a first-year module centred on a francophone community. In March 2004, it signed a five-year agreement with the University of Ottawa, in which it was agreed that students who wished to study in French were to be encouraged to study at that university.

At a meeting of the reference group in May 2004, tensions erupted and a number of motions passed. On reporting on community comments, members said that NOSM had never had a champion for the francophone portfolio as it had for the Aboriginal portfolio and that "people in the community are insulted, and angry towards NOSM and its commitment to francophone services." The group asked for a meeting with the dean and clarification not only of the agreement with the University of Ottawa but also of NOSM's relationship with the community. It also passed a motion that read: "due to the blatant lack of respect towards the francophone culture from the directors of NOSM, the Francophone Reference Group recommends that the Campus Deans-East be francophone."

In addition, the reference group passed a motion recommending to the dean that, on the admissions committee, there should be at least two francophone representatives for every Aboriginal representative. This motion again revealed tensions between the two communities with respect to their role and influence within the school (NOSM 2006b). At a meeting of the Accredited MD Program Group in

August 2003, the minutes note that "the Aboriginal people see Francophones as a minority within the dominant culture in Canada and
consequently are concerned with any suggestion that the situation of
Francophones is similar to that of Aboriginal people in this country."
This observation occurred within the context of a discussion of the
advisability of teaching "medical Ojibwa" and other Aboriginal languages as well as medical French (NOSM 2004h).

Subsequently, the dean met with the Francophone Reference
Group, asking for patience and reiterating NOSM's commitment to
the needs of the francophone community. A statement was produced
from the school's senior management, outlining its commitment to be
accountable to francophone communities by encouraging students
and securing francophone placements, study groups, and mentors.

At the May and June meetings of the reference group, motions
were passed and concerns raised: all NOSM support services should
be available in French, all committees must have francophone representatives, and francophone students must be encouraged to come to
the Sudbury campus. At the June 2004 meeting of the group, objec-
tions were raised to encouraging Northern Ontario francophone students to apply to the University of Ottawa. At the September
meeting, the group objected to the hiring of a staff member responsible for the francophone community at the coordinator level, pointing
out that the "person responsible for the Aboriginal portfolio" had
been appointed at "the Director's level." At the October meeting, this
issue arose again, with the dean quoted as explaining that the position of director of Aboriginal affairs was necessary because of the academic dimensions of Aboriginal health and research. It was the
position of the Francophone Reference Group that the same dimensions existed for their community. However, the dean was quoted as
stating that, even if NOSM agreed, there was no core funding for a di-
rector-level post and that external funding would need to be found
(NOSM 2004i).

In May 2005, a symposium was held on the topic of francophones and NOSM. Speakers included faculty and students from
local high schools and universities as well as the dean of the University of Ottawa Medical School, and the francophone medical training coordinator and associate dean of the University of Shebrooke.
Seventeen recommendations were made. A key recommendation
was predictably challenging, given the provincial government's
mandate and funding: NOSM should offer an MD program in both

French and English. This was especially so now that most of the full-time faculty and administrative staff had been hired on the understanding that the school's language of instruction was English. The report published by the school had the apt title *A Community Vision* (NOSM 2005a).

Subsequently, however, the Francophone Reference Group would highlight other recommendations found in the report, focusing, in late 2005 and 2006, on securing more francophone members on the Board of Directors; securing a quota of twelve francophone students each year (out of fifty-six); grouping all francophone students in academic, clinical, and associative activities; and, most of all, ensuring that there were francophone placements in francophone communities. In addition, the reference group welcomed student members and was glad to hear from them, at its May 2006 meeting, that the francophone module, as well as other elements of the first-year curriculum, included a wide range of learning opportunities appropriate for future physicians of francophone Northern Ontario. Indeed, it was reported that some students were so motivated by these elements that they were considering a French-speaking community for their second-year placement (NOSM 2006b).

SOCIAL ACCOUNTABILITY AND THE RURAL, REMOTE NORTH

NOSM also sought to be responsive to rural and remote Northern Ontario (COFM, NORMS Liaison Council, Tesson, Rourke). This goal moved the school to involve community physicians and others in a variety of ways. The Board of Directors has from the beginning included physicians from rural and remote areas. The Academic Council also includes twelve elected clinical faculty members from across Northern Ntario, and rural and remote representatives were appointed to the admissions committee. The senior leadership engaged in a wide range of community visits across the North on an ongoing basis, in part to develop a network of distributed academic sites. The goal was that, in each location in which NOSM had significant education, research, and other academic activities, a local NOSM group would be formed to provide leadership for school activities and programs. Later members of the northern communities would be recruited to participate on an almost daily basis in the medical education program as standardized and volunteer patients.

With regard to curriculum development, as early as 2002 NOSM decided to involve a wide variety of northern participants in a workshop. An invitation to attend a three-day workshop was extended to health care providers and other interested citizens of Northern Ontario, including faculty members at Laurentian and Lakehead universities. The planned workshop was to be held in Sault Ste Marie from 16 to 18 January 2003. There was an overwhelming response, with over 500 persons indicating interest in attending.

The list of people who eventually did go to the workshop (only 300 of the 500, due to space limitations) included physicians from across the North, university faculty, researchers, Aboriginal community members, students and residents, local government members, political representatives, and NOMS staff. Information regarding the workshop, including a package of pre-readings, was sent to all participants. A questionnaire invited people to identify characteristics needed by physicians in Northern Ontario, and the information collected from it was used to shape the activities of the workshop.

The approach taken over the three days involved a variety of presentations by experts in the field of community-based medical education and five two-hour working group sessions, which followed the formal presentations. The five working group sessions focused on possible goals and related objectives of the undergraduate MD program, including: the learning needs of medical students studying in the Northern Ontario community context; the requisite supports that students, their teachers, and communities would need, given the circumstance of community-based medical education; and the curriculum choices that would need to be met, given the Northern Ontario setting (NOSM 2003a).

Initially, it was thought that NOSM would have four course themes: (1) personal and professional aspects of medicine, (2) social and population health, (3) basic science (a.k.a. foundations of medicine), and (4) clinical medicine. After the conference, it was decided to create a fifth course: northern and rural health. In July 2003, NOSM placed an advertisement looking for people to contribute to curriculum development in northern and rural health. A variety of individuals responded, starting their work as the northern and rural health curriculum writing team in early August 2003, the day southern (but not most of Northern) Ontario suffered a blackout. The group met on several occasions over the coming months. Kristen Jacklin, a member of the group who would later be appointed chair of the Course Committee, commented in an interview with Dr Geoffrey Hudson (21 September 2007) that a crucial factor was that they were in no way restricted to coming up with recommendations that would be compatible with the Medical Council of Canada's licensing exam; rather, their sole concern was to come up with recommendations that would turn medical students into good doctors for rural and Northern Ontario. According to Jacklin: "We thought the sky was the limit." And the group proceeded on that basis. Jacklin sought "to send them paddling," with the result that the group strongly recommended an Aboriginal community placement for all students.

Jacklin also commented that it was very helpful to have an experienced curriculum instructional designer, Holly Rupert, join the group. Rupert expertly converted goals into clear educational objectives. Everyone agreed on the importance of having Aboriginal-specific objectives, but there was significant debate regarding whether francophone-specific objectives should also be created, with some arguing that the francophone experience would best be placed within the wider context of all the major ethnic and linguistic groups that stemmed from European settler populations. In the end, the group decided, on the senior leadership advice of Dr Richard Denton, to proceed with francophone-specific objectives, partially because health records and services in some areas in Northern Ontario were in French, a unique and pedagogically significant circumstance.

The group also identified the need for NOSM to be attentive to international health as well as rural and northern health. In other words, it was to place the Northern Ontario situation within a wider context. However, NOSM rejected this recommendation.

In 2004, the formal Northern and Rural Health Course Committee was struck, picking up on the curriculum recommendations made by the 2003 development group. The committee's first meeting was in July 2004, with the founding members being Dr Richard Denton, Ms Joyce Atcheson, Ms Joyce Helmer, Dr Andre Hurtubise, Ms Bev Lafoley, Ms Holly Rupert, Mr Richard Witham, and Ms Orpah Mckenzie. The course committee soon got down to business, creating a course description and syllabus over the coming months. The course description included the following introductory remarks:

The course will help students to understand the rewards and challenges of medical practice in northern and rural communities ...

It is designed to introduce students to the social, cultural, economic and environmental realities of Northern Ontario. Students
will gain an appreciation for the ways in which these realities
shape the delivery of health care and the practice of medicine in
the northern and rural context ... Through case scenarios, standardized patients and clinical encounters, students will gain an
understanding of the social and cultural realities of Aboriginal,
Francophone and European people living in the north. This emphasis on cultural differences aims to build cultural competency
and foster deeper awareness of the various perspectives that
shape the individual's concept of wellness and experience of
illness. (NOSM 2005h)

In part to meet these course objectives, NOSM, in addition to the
Aboriginal placement, created two integrated community experiences for students in rural and remote communities in their second
year, each of four weeks duration and with a number being in francophone communities.

SOCIAL ACCOUNTABILITY
AND FACULTY RECRUITMENT

In 2003, the process of recruiting clinical as well as full-time medical
and human sciences faculty involved a great deal of discussion and
debate. It was concluded in favour of hiring a combination of both,
with the hope that a number of full timers would be from, or have
connections with, the North. In early February 2004, it was reported
that, for the initial nine full-time positions in the Medical and Human
Sciences, approximately 200 applications had been received from inside and outside the country. Several applicants had connections with
the North, and this may have helped in the hiring process.

Faculty positions in the Division of Clinical Sciences had been ad-
vertised as well, and many local clinicians in Northern Ontario had
shown interest. The goal was to appoint around fifty clinical faculty
in and around Thunder Bay and Sudbury as teachers of year 1 of
the MD program, with hundreds more following in the coming
months (NOSM 2004d). Although no full-time francophone non-
management faculty were hired in the first two years, by September
2005 there were more than twenty-five francophone faculty in the
clinical division.

It was agreed that, at the long/medium listing stage of the search process, Aboriginal background and/or experience of working with and/or research with Aboriginal people would be used as criteria for appointment. Two researchers of Aboriginal health were hired on a full-time basis in the Human Sciences Division in the next round of hiring, which was in 2005. Dr Geoffrey Hudson had the following question included in the standardized interview as part of the hiring process in the Human Sciences: "The Northern Ontario School of Medicine was created in part to address the needs and interests of all the people of Northern Ontario. How would you define socially accountable medical education and to what degree do you believe it is relevant to a career at the School?" (NOSM 2005c).

SOCIALLY ACCOUNTABLE RESEARCH

In July 2003, in preparing the section on research for the Accreditation Database, the NOSM accreditation team decided that, prior to the arrival of the associate dean of research, the database needed to demonstrate that "there should be ample evidence of 'curiosity driven research' and general scholarly activity" and that this "may include medical education research" (NOSM 2004e). With the arrival of an associate dean of research, Dr Greg Ross, would come the formulation of research priorities that would, in 2005, include "creating a research environment optimized for discovery and innovation to improve the health of Northern Ontario" as well as the facilitation of "partnerships to undertake cross-disciplinary health research across Northern Ontario." In addition the associate dean sought to "encourage innovation and technology transfer to develop effective biotechnology-based therapeutics, which will improve the quality of life and stimulate economic growth in Northern Ontario" (NOSM 2005g).

Later in 2005, NOSM published a report entitled *Creating a Sustainable Health Research Industry in Northern Ontario*. This report was written by a consulting firm that was hired by NOSM, and its goal was to provide an overview of the strategies and potential opportunities to enable Northern Ontario's health research industry to grow. It highlights the role that NOSM and private- and public-sector organizations could play in contributing to the outcome of these research strategies and in facilitating their implementation. The report made a number of recommendations, including creating a northern community-based health research network. In addition, it recommended a project related to bio-prospecting for pharmaceutical compounds in the North (this would subsequently cause some concern among Aboriginal groups) (NOSM 2005e).

NOSM has also developed a research relationship with the Centre for Rural and Northern Health Research (CRaNHR), which is an academic centre with sites at Laurentian (with Dr Raymond Pong as director) and at Lakehead (with Dr Bruce Minor as director). CRaNHR's mandate was of significant interest to NOSM, and it was "to conduct interdisciplinary research on rural health with a view to improving health services, access to health care, particularly in rural and northern communities, and enhancing our understanding of the health care system" (CRaNHR 2008). That mandate led to a number of NOSM faculty, including the founding dean, joining CRaNHR as well as to the development of joint initiatives. One example of this is a multi-year tracking study, which was initiated to follow the 2005 charter class over a number of years in order to study changes in academic interests, career aspirations, practice location decisions, and practice profile (CRaNHR n.d.).

In March 2006, NOSM's wet and dry research labs, funded by the federal government, were opened. According to Dr Greg Ross, "Research performed in these labs will focus on Northern health issues and will equip future physicians with the skills needed to deal with the unique health concerns facing Northerners" (NOSM 2006d).

The first annual Northern Health Research Conference was held in Sault Ste Marie from 2–3 June 2006. Presenters came from across Northern Ontario and included research scientists (e.g., from forestry and cancer centres), faculty from NOSM, faculty from the two host universities as well as other universities in the province; local physicians, nurses, and dieticians; telehealth coordinators; and district health unit members. Unfortunately, the first day of the two-day conference was held on NOSM's final day of term, which meant that many of the school's faculty and students could not attend.

In mid-2006, a report by a consultancy firm, paid by the federal government grant and the town of Sault Ste Marie, recommended the creation of a NOSM clinical research institute in that town. Some months later, NOSM would endorse the feasibility report. The mayor of Sault Ste Marie, whose predecessor had been quoted in the media in 2002 complaining that his town was being neglected in plans for the school, expressed his support for the further development of NOSM programs and services in Sault Ste Marie (NOSM n.d.[a]).

Socially accountable research and curiosity-driven research survived and thrived, with faculty being encouraged, but not forced, to
conduct research attuned to Northern Ontario. Indeed, the associate dean made it clear that any research that NOSM faculty conducted in Northern Ontario was, by definition, research by and for
Northern Ontario, no matter what was being researched (NOSM
2005f). This broad definition satisfied faculty (and NOSM's objective of being vigilant in defence of academic freedom).

A crucial part of any medical school is the library. At NOSM the
Health Information Resource Centre (HIRC) drew on the experience
of its predecessor and colleague library at NOMP, the Northern
Ontario Virtual Library. Both were developed to provide a range of
electronic resources as well as the necessary texts for student, resident, physician, and faculty research, teaching, and learning across
Northern Ontario. Resources have been ordered appropriate to rural and northern medical education and research, with Aboriginal
and French materials included (NOSM 2005b).

COMMUNITY INVESTMENT:
THE BURSARY CAMPAIGN

NOSM also connected with the communities across Northern Ontario
to raise money for a bursary fund, encouraging the community to be
socially accountable to its medical students. Separate community-
based committees were established in places such as North Bay, Parry
Sound, Sault Ste Marie, and Timmins. Such a community-based
fundraising initiative was necessary because of Ontario's decision,
made in the late 1990s, to let professional school tuition in the juris-
diction rise to historically very high rates: approximately $15,000 per
annum. Given that NOSM was attempting to encourage rural and
northern applicants, who had fewer resources than did southern applicants, a bursary fund was deemed essential. Indeed, when the new
full-time medical school faculty met for the first time in August 2004
on the west campus, the need for a bursary fund was the first subject
of conversation. NOSM's Board of Directors responded to this need
by establishing a fundraising committee, which worked in collaboration with the host universities. A wide range of individuals and
groups gave to the fund: municipalities; northern companies; trade
unions; Lions clubs; individuals, faculty, and staff at NOSM; university alumni associations, northern physicians (both as individuals and
in groups); and, of course, international pharmaceutical companies.

The provincial government matched these donations. By April 2006, the Bursary Fund Campaign was closed, with $13 million having been raised (probably short of what was needed to provide bursaries to all the medical students who would need them over the four years of the program). An interesting example of a community group is the Clubs Richelieu du Moyen-Nord, which established a medical school bursary for francophone students. Dr Allaire of Laurentian University explained: "Considering the high Francophone population in Northern Ontario, it makes sense to have more French-speaking doctors. This is why we have designated the Bourse Richelieu as a Francophone bursary" (NOSM n.d.[b]).

SOCIAL ACCOUNTABILITY AND GOVERNANCE

The final section of this chapter deals with social accountability and governance. As is discussed in chapter 8 of this volume, NOSM is unique in its governance structure as it serves as the faculty of medicine for two universities. In other ways it is traditional. It has a bicameral structure, with an academic council responsible for academic matters and a board of directors responsible for operations.

The Academic Council's constitution speaks to its "deliberations and decisions," being mindful that the "primary focus" is "responsive to the individual needs of students and to the healthcare needs of the people of northern Ontario" (NOSM 2007b). There are two spots on the council for Aboriginal academics, and at least four of the council's eighteen elected faculty must be francophone. Given that the full-time faculty in Medical and Human Sciences are anglophones, this means that four of the twelve elected clinical faculty must be francophone. In addition, there is a requirement that the Academic Council maintain geographic balance between northwestern and northeastern Ontario.

The Board of Directors is also socially accountable with regard to its membership, with members being appointed by municipalities, the provincial government, Aboriginal groups, and a francophone group. It also has representatives from various medical and health communities. Its goal of responding to the needs of the people of Northern Ontario is similar to that of the Academic Council.

NOSM is also socially accountable through the high standard of its commitment to academic freedom. Medical schools in Canada have experienced a number of internationally high-profile academic freedom cases concerning the undue influence of pharmaceutical companies and other interests inhibiting teachers and researchers from communicating findings to the academic community and general public. In a ground-breaking move, NOSM's Board of Directors agreed to incorporate into its constitution a schedule entitled "Academic Freedom and Integrity of Research," which clearly puts the interest of society (and patients) front and centre in several respects, including research funding, free expression, and the liberty to publish findings (NOSM 2006a). The school's Board of Directors and the newly certified Faculty Association subsequently used the board's schedule on academic freedom as the basis for an article on academic freedom that appeared in the first collective agreement, which was negotiated in 2006 (NOSM 2006f). The article would later be highlighted in a national bargaining advisory on the subject of academic freedom that was published by the Canadian Association of University Teachers and sent across Canada to all faculty associations (CAUT 2007). Acting to establish a high standard of academic freedom revealed NOSM's commitment to social accountability within the academic setting.

NOSM's management structure has gone through a number of changes. A September 2004 document cited three bodies: the Executive, the Senior Management Group, and the Senior Academic Leadership Group. The latter was to include all academic directors. In the autumn of 2004, the Executive merged the Senior Management Group and Senior Academic Leadership Group to create the Senior Leadership Group (SLG), which is a management-only group that excludes all faculty and librarians in senior academic leadership roles who are not also managers (including, for example, the director of assessment and evaluation). The SLG responded to a request from the Aboriginal Reference Group to include two Aboriginal elders, who met with it beginning in January 2006. NOSM issued a news release on 2 May 2006, stating that the elders were in attendance at the SLG "to provide guidance and an Aboriginal perspective on NOSM activities" (NOSM 2006c).

The Board of Directors and the Academic Council have promulgated numerous statements on guiding principles and strategic directions, several of which have social accountability objectives. The Vision and Mission statement for 2005–06 to 2008–09 states, for example, that NOSM will seek out "qualified students who have a passion for living in, working in and serving Northern and rural communities" and that it "will be vigilant in the protection of academic freedom." In addition, the school is committed to pursuing "a culture of inclusiveness and responsiveness within the medical communities, the northern communities, the rural communities, and the Aboriginal and Francophone communities."

NOSM's strategic plan for 2006 to 2009 has three strategic directions, the second of which is social accountability. The plan states that NOSM will "continue to develop relationships with all the communities (Aboriginal, francophone, rural), clinicians and other health care providers, hospitals and health centres, the two universities, government at all three levels, media and other medical schools." The other strategic directions also incorporate social accountability goals. For example, the first strategic direction – academic accountability – states that NOSM will be socially accountable and will rely on community-based faculty (which, so Dr Geoffrey Hudson was told in a division meeting in 2006, permanently excludes the full-time faculty hired and now living with their families in Thunder Bay and Sudbury).

The strategic plan also includes a number of initiatives, one of which is to "increase community engagement, including Francophone, Aboriginal, rural and remote communities," partially via an increase in the "number of visits to develop relations with community groups." Another initiative is to "increase Community (sic) engagement, including Francophone, Aboriginal, rural and remote communities, and establish a structure (network) that enhances local community involvement in the academic and administrative aspects of the school." An additional objective is the "establishment and development of a network of NOSM Local Groups" in each community. NOSM is also committed to the "successful development and implementation of high school level enrichment programs with particular emphasis on Aboriginal, Francophone, remote and rural communities high school students" (NOSM 2006h).

The Academic Council developed a set of academic principles in 2006, several of which deal with matters related to social accountability. One principle deals with community orientation, which is defined as "the conceptual and pragmatic understanding of the dynamics of communities in the North and the creation of meaningful, enduring partnerships between all Northern Communities and NOSM" (NOSM 2006g).

CONCLUSION

With regard to international and Canadian definitions of social accountability, as well as with regard to the literature and activities related to socially accountable medical education, where does NOSM fit? Sometimes, social accountability objectives can be defined without adequate consultation with the faculty who must execute them. For example, NOSM's strategic plan commits to developing "a plan for and funding of a research centre of excellence focused on Aboriginal Health." This objective came as a surprise to the two full-time tenure-track faculty who were conducting Aboriginal research in Northern Ontario when they heard about it at a division retreat in mid-2006. This indicates a disconnect between the full-time faculty and the Board of Directors (NOSM 2006h). There is no question that social accountability drives NOSM in that the school exists in order to satisfy the needs of Northern Ontario and has striven, with a significant amount of success, to consult and to incorporate that area's perceived needs and concerns in its governance, curriculum, and research activities. These needs and concerns are complex and, at times, contradictory. It is not possible to satisfy everyone, and, as the literature suggests, any organization involved in such activities needs to avoid a drift into isolation and mutual recrimination between the different sectors involved. An example: despite NOSM's being very clear to the francophone community as to what is possible with regard to the provision of an MD program in the French language, the lack of such provision continues to be a source of tension. This conflict is likely impossible to resolve, given the long history of concern over the delivery of services in both French and English in Ontario. What is evident is that NOSM has very clearly told the francophone community that it is not possible to meet its wishes, given the school's mandate from the government and the resources available. And, at the end of the day, social accountability must be subject to the needs of the people as expressed by its representatives in the Legislative Assembly. The government has the final say on public funding and the administration of medical education and health care services.

NOSM is exemplary in its dedication to academic freedom within the medical school context. However, for all its concern with rural and remote social accountability, NOSM needs to pay more attention to the social accountability concerns of Thunder Bay and Sudbury.

The community learning sessions are important in that they provide a way to encourage students to learn the fundamental values of healing and human concern in practice. The AFMC database reveals that many medical schools have fostered informal student-initiated activities in communities – activities that focus on greatly needed services (AFMC n.d.[b]). Social accountability is not just about the institution: it is also about the graduates, the future physicians. At this stage, NOSM has yet to see a great deal of student-initiated activity in this area, the focus having been on the top-down creation and management of the curriculum. One of many remaining challenges for NOSM is to enable its students and future alumni to influence the context, incentives, and culture of the societies within which they learn, practise, and conduct research.

10

Beyond NOSM: Lessons for Others

GEOFFREY TESSON AND ROGER STRASSER

INTRODUCTION

At the time of writing, it has been over seven years since the Ontario
government announced the creation of the Northern Ontario School
of Medicine in May 2001. Each stage in its development – from the
decision itself, to the hiring of the founding dean, the construction of
the buildings, the creation of the curriculum, the arrival on campus of
the first group of students, the successful accreditation visits, and the
first graduating class – has been an occasion for celebration and an
increasing sense that, in spite of widespread scepticism, this was indeed a valid approach to creating a medical school. But the passage
of time also gives some distance from these feelings of satisfaction
and provides an appropriate occasion for sober reflection and for
looking back to see what lessons might be learned from all of this. In
an important sense, NOSM represents an experiment in adapting
medical education to meet the needs of a culturally and economically
diverse population spread over a million square kilometres. It also offers lessons regarding how the skill sets of physicians and their relationships with other health professionals might be reconfigured to
advantage. It is an experiment that should be instructive for many
other regions that are contemplating new ways of ensuring that dispersed populations have the health care that they need.

THE UNIQUE CHARACTER OF MEDICAL SCHOOLS

Before proceeding with the analysis, it is perhaps worthwhile to
reflect on the special character of faculties of medicine. Medical

education programs, while grounded in universities, depend heavily for clinical learning on settings, such as hospitals, medical practices, and community clinics, that lie outside of the university. These resources are expensive and require, in almost all countries, heavy government subsidization. So a decision to create a medical school must involve a commitment on the part of the requisite government to fund the substantial clinical components of the program. No other aspect of university activity is so heavily dependent on direct government approval.

The practical implication of this significant government role is that an important part of the energy needed to start a new medical school has to be directed, for better or for worse, towards the political arena. One might wish that something as socially significant as the creation of a medical school would be inspired by a detailed vision of how the health needs of a large, underserved area could be met in new and creative ways. And, indeed, for many of the key actors, especially those within the medical community, this was in fact the case. But the dynamics of the political decision-making process itself do not always reflect such a vision, or they do so, at best, in a truncated manner. However, without politics, there would be no new school. Still, once the decision is taken, then the door is open to creativity and imagination. The evolution of NOSM's vision has been an iterative process as the founding dean and his academic leaders worked their way through the process by communicating with community groups, the developing clinical faculty, and, ultimately, the students. Our analysis, therefore, has two parts: (1) the decision to create the school and (2) the implementation of that decision.

THE DECISION TO CREATE A NEW SCHOOL

The development of NOSM occurred over time and in stages, each stage laying the ground for subsequent developments. The first stage involved the creation of northern clinical placements for both undergraduate and postgraduate students of established medical schools, along with the establishment of relatively independent agencies for the administration of these programs. Once they were built, these independent organizations became the basis for the development of other programs. The second stage started with the McKendry Report's recognition of serious physician shortages, especially in rural and northern regions of Ontario (McKendry 1999), and it culminated in the development of the proposal for a northern medical school (NORMS Liaison Council 2000). The third stage involved the resolution of the choice between having the northern program develop as a satellite of existing medical schools, as recommended by the government's Expert Panel (Ontario 2001), or starting from scratch with a whole new stand-alone school. The fourth stage, once the government had made its commitment to an entirely new school, involved the development of an implementation plan and the resolution of decisions regarding governance and where the school would be located. Finally, there was the building of the program itself, the hiring of faculty and administrative staff, the development of a curriculum, and the admission of the first class of students.

Policy analyses

What were the policy considerations that lay behind the decision to create a new school? First, there is the evidence regarding the linkage between physician supply and the number of funded places in the province's medical schools. Canada's current physician shortage is often blamed on a 1993 reduction in medical school enrolment based on the advice of a report by Barer and Stoddart (1991); although, as these same authors point out, there are many other factors, now widely acknowledged, that account for the shortfall (Stoddart and Barer 1999). Robert McKendry's (1999) report, which triggered the move to create the Northern Ontario school, also highlighted the complexity of the issue of physician supply, pointing up the need to take into account factors such as the kinds of services physicians provide, the number of hours a week they work, and the age structure of working physicians. He nevertheless concluded that Ontario suffers from a shortage of physicians and that this shortage is exacerbated in rural and northern areas due to the maldistribution of physicians (McKendry 1999). The government's Expert Panel, convened to review McKendry's report and other relevant data, largely concurred with his findings on two major issues of interest to the North: (1) that there was indeed an overall shortage of physicians in Ontario compounded by maldistribution, leaving rural and northern areas short of services, and (2) that the long-term answer to this issue lay in changing the way in which physicians were educated: "Experience in other jurisdictions indicates that rural physicians do not just happen, they have to be nurtured and developed. For example, physicians are more likely to choose to practice in rural, remote or underserviced areas when they come from rural areas, receive a significant portion of their training in rural or remote areas, and participate in a dedicated rural training scheme" (Ontario 2001, 6)

McKendry's report and that of the Expert Panel differed in one important respect, however. McKendry recommended the creation of a new medical school located in Northern Ontario, with a mandate to prepare its students for rural and northern practice. The Expert Panel took the more cautious approach of recommending a decentralization of components of Ontario's existing medical schools to create "clinical education campuses" in underserved areas, adding the lure of potential new medical schools in the distant future: "Once the capacity for rural medical education is developed, the system will have the potential to develop free-standing rural medical schools, if required" (Ontario 2001, 6). From a general policy perspective, this difference might appear as a nuance; for northerners who had come to expect their own school, it was a slap in the face. What seemingly convinced the government to take the bolder step was not more analysis but, rather, politics.

The political factor

A decision to create a new school of medicine is of sufficient fiscal importance that it cannot simply be made as the outcome of an administrative review process. It is necessarily a political decision and, as such, is affected by processes of political influence and persuasion. As noted in chapter 1, the lobbying for the new school was centred in the activity of the northern mayors. When the possibility of a new school in the North was raised by the McKendry Report, the mayors of the five major municipalities in the North spoke with a single voice in support of it. This may not seem like a big thing, but it needs to be viewed in the context of regional politics.

Northern Ontario is a huge hinterland, the size of France and Germany together. Most of the population and its associated infrastructure is concentrated in the south of the province, while the North's economy is largely resource-based (forestry and mining) and subject to the vagaries of global commodity markets. Northern communities seeking help to build much-needed infrastructure often find themselves as supplicants to a southern-based political machine, and, as such, they regard each other as rivals, not for want of a more generous view but, rather, because they are competitors for resources that are few and far between. So it was a matter of some moment when northern municipal leaders presented a common front to the government and gained a hearing.

The government was receptive to the case for a northern school for a number of reasons. The Mike Harris Conservative government had gained a reputation for toughness in the early years of its mandate, sharply reducing expenditures in the public sector, including for the universities. But it was nearing the end of its mandate, its fiscal situation was improving, and it was looking, as governments do in such circumstances, for projects that might have electoral appeal. In its relationship with the postsecondary sector, the government had taken the view that the province's universities were doing a poor job of meeting the province's human resource needs. The appeal of this new project was that it was targeted at meeting a very specific need that, it was widely conceded, the established universities had not done a good job of meeting. It should be added that the premier himself was from the North and might, as a consequence, be thought to be more attentive to northern needs. The other major political parties in Ontario, the Liberal Party and the New Democratic Party, also supported the creation of the new school. And, while their support was not a factor in convincing the government, it was an indication of the general popularity of this measure. It was particularly significant, given that the Liberal Party won power in the next election and subsequently followed through with longer-term funding for the school.

The role of the federal government

In Canada, health care and postsecondary education is a provincial responsibility, although both are partly financed through transfer payments from the federal government. For this reason, the majority of the lobbying activity was directed at the provincial government. Nevertheless, even though its role was constrained, the federal government was more than a simple bystander. The expansion of Canada's medical schools in the 1970s, which saw the establishment of new schools at McMaster University, the University of Calgary, Memorial University, and Université de Sherbrooke, received significant direct funding from the federal government under the rationale that it had an overall responsibility for health capacity in Canada. Since that time, the dynamic of federal-provincial relations has changed, and the provinces have generally preferred federal government help in the form of increased transfer payments rather than in the form of direct intervention.

Nevertheless, at the time of the proposed northern school, the federal ministry responsible for health (Health Canada), under the leadership of Minister Allan Rock, was taking an active interest in issues of rural health care. In 1998, it had established the Office for Rural Health, which was headed up by Dr John Wootton, a long-time advocate for rural physicians. Both Health Minister Rock and Dr Wootton visited Northern Ontario to offer their encouragement, although they were careful not to trespass in an area of provincial responsibility. Concrete help to aid in the development of the project came in the form of a grant from FedNor (an Industry Canada agency responsible for regional economic development).

Community input

Part of the source of the political momentum was the high level of interest and enthusiasm for this project in communities throughout the North. Communities that had long fought losing battles to attract and retain family doctors could easily identify with the goals of this project, which promised to offer a long-term solution to their problems. It is one of the benefits of a community-based model of distributed clinical education that many communities, which had previously felt estranged from the medical establishment, could realistically hope to have a medical school presence in their midst. And, as a consequence of this, they acquired a sense of pride and ownership in the project. In fact, this powerful identification of communities across the North with the goals of NOSM was an important element fuelling the politics that made the creation of the school possible in the first place. Different communities could overcome their traditional regional rivalries because they could see that the benefits of the school would not simply accrue to a single centre but, rather, would be spread around to each and every community. This is what held the mayors' coalition together, and it also explains why there was such an outcry when the government, in its initial announcement, named Sudbury as the main hub of the school.

Growing capacity

For some thirty years before the creation of NOSM, there had been, in Northern Ontario, a growing presence of clinical placements for students of established medical schools. In 1991, McMaster University in the Northwest and the University of Ottawa in the Northeast developed full two-year family medicine residency programs, in which residents spent the whole of their training in Northern Ontario clinical settings. The goal of these residency programs was to prepare graduates for practice in the North by maximizing their exposure to northern clinical settings during their clinical education. These programs proved highly successful. A study of practice locations of Ontario graduates who had participated in the northwestern program even for a period as short as one month showed that they were seven times more likely to practise in northwestern Ontario than were their peers who had not spent time in the North (McCready et al. 2004). Tracking of graduates of the subsequent full two-year family medicine program has shown an impressive rate of 67.5 percent who have opted for subsequent rural or northern practice (Heng et al. 2007).

These northern clinical programs paved the way for the development of NOSM in three important ways. First, they involved an increasing number of northern physicians in medical education through their role as preceptors (in chapter 4, John Mulloy captures some of the enthusiasm that those pioneers felt for their role as mentors); second, they necessitated the development of an administrative infrastructure in both Thunder Bay and Sudbury to manage the increasingly complex logistics; and, third, their success, not only in offering high-quality education but also in recruiting graduates to practise in the North, led to an undoubted sense of regional pride and was also an important factor in convincing the provincial government of the value of distributed medical education.

Economic impact

An important consideration in building a new medical school involves taking into account its economic impact. Prior to the development of NOSM, a study of the economic impact of key health-sector institutions in the Sudbury region showed that they were responsible for over 13,000 jobs and a net impact of nearly $500 million per year

(McKracken et al. 2001). No estimates were made for the impact of the proposed medical school, but there is little doubt that it would be considerable, particularly for the two host cities.

A recent study of the economic impact of the 125 accredited schools and their related teaching hospitals the in United States estimates that every dollar spent on a medical school or teaching hospital generates an additional $1.30 when it is re-spent on other businesses or individuals. The total impact of all schools in the Unites States is assessed at a massive $451.6 billion (AAMC 2007). Doubtless, some sense of the anticipated impact of a new medical school on the Northern Ontario economy was a significant factor in the popular enthusiasm for the project. And, almost certainly, it figured in the strong support of community and business leaders. Business leaders noted, for example, that the government's investment in a new medical school in the region was an expression of confidence in the area's future and that, further, the presence of the school would make it easier to attract highly qualified personnel to Northern Ontario.

LESSONS LEARNED

Multiple factors

With hindsight, it is difficult to identify any single factor that could be seen as determinant in the decision to create NOSM. The data on northern and rural physician shortages in the region, coupled with evidence from other successful experiments in rural medical education (such as the University of Washington's WWAMI program, James Cook University's new program, and Flinders University's Parallel Rural Community Curriculum) certainly point to the need (Tesson et al. 2006), but they did not in themselves dictate the solution. Politics was also important. Without the willingness of municipal politicians to take up the cause, and of the provincial government to respond, nothing could have happened. Clearly, too, the prior history of clinical placements in the North paved the way by creating a network of interested and enthusiastic physician teachers across the region, along with an administrative structure to support them. The presence of this network and the substantial success of its programs certainly lent an important element of credibility to the capacity of the region to undertake more ambitious projects. However, no single one of these factors was the deciding one.

Importance of collaboration

What did make the difference, however, was that the various agencies involved – the physician networks, the municipalities, the Aboriginal organizations, the universities, and the hospitals – were able to work together collaboratively to ensure that the opportunity presented by the demonstrated need and the government's attention was not lost. None of this was obvious at the outset. When the northern family medicine residency programs were established in the 1990s, the government funded the construction of health sciences buildings on the Lakehead and Laurentian campuses; however, the programs were managed relatively independently from the universities, both from the academic sponsors (the University of Ottawa and McMaster University) and from their physical hosts (Lakehead and Laurentian). Relationships between universities and their host municipalities often fall into, at best, an uneasy cohabitation between "town and gown," partly because of their quite different cultures of decision making. Making the case for the new schools of medicine required that these agencies work together seamlessly without any single one dominating the process. The vehicle for this collaboration was, in the initial phase, the Northern Rural Medical School Liaison Council, which included all the key academic and health-sector stakeholders and which produced the original NORMS proposal (NORMS Liaison Council 2000). Once the government announced the intention to create the school, the emphasis shifted to the political arena with the creation of the Implementation Management Committee. The ability of these groups to advance their case effectively depended on the willingness of the individuals involved to set aside their institutional proclivities and to work together for the common goal.

More challenging than institutional territoriality were the regional loyalties and, especially, the historical rivalry between Sudbury in the Northeast and Thunder Bay in the Northwest. These are the two largest cities in Northern Ontario, each has its own university, and each serves as the centre for health and social services in the area that surrounds them. In the eyes of southern Ontarians, and especially those in government, they are viewed as natural allies, as northern neighbours with a commonality of culture and of purpose. In reality, they are a thousand kilometres apart and have little in common except their geographic remove from the urban industrial south.

When McKendry first floated the idea of NOSM, it was as a pan-northern venture with campuses at both Thunder Bay and Sudbury. It was assumed that the case for a joint proposal would be so much stronger than would the case for a proposal from either region on its own. A liaison committee was struck with equal representation from the Northwest and the Northeast, and the proposal it submitted reflected the dual campus pan-northern model. When the government announced its intention to fund a main campus in Sudbury with only a satellite campus in Thunder Bay, this created a crisis for the Liaison Committee and reawakened old enmities. While a carefully crafted solution was eventually found, giving equal status to both communities, the memory of what the Northwest undoubtedly saw as a betrayal still smoulders just beneath the surface. In reality, a school of medicine that aims to distribute many of its functions across different centres throughout an area as large as Northern Ontario is bound to be constantly addressing issues as to whether one centre is being favoured over another. And that is not necessarily a bad thing. Indeed, a school of medicine that is designed to be responsive to communities can expect to experience tension as it is pulled in different directions by competing demands. The key is to work hard to ensure that the tension does not get out of hand and become dysfunctional for the school as a whole.

Stand-alone or satellite campuses: One model does not fit all

In a recent article reviewing the applicability of Australian models of rural medical education to the European context, Richard Hays (2007) observes that there are measures short of the establishment of stand-alone schools that may achieve many of the goals of reinvigorating rural practice. It was a matter of considerable importance to Northern Ontarians that, at the outset, they be granted their own school rather than an embryonic model that may or may not develop full stand-alone status at some unspecified time in the future. The pay-off has been the freedom to create a school that has been custom-designed for its regional mandate, and it is this that makes the school so unique. However, it does need to be acknowledged that excellent results have been achieved by satellite models in other areas (Tesson et al. 2005) and that not all underserved regions may need a stand-alone school. A determining factor will be the size and the dispersion of the population to be served and the availability of a critical mass of physicians to form the basis of a clinical faculty. Whatever the model, it is important to have sufficient control over the admissions process so as to enhance the recruitment of bright young people from the region to be served and to provide as much clinical experience in the area as the system will allow.

IMPLEMENTATION

There was great excitement in the North when the government made its announcement, which was then followed by the realization that a huge task lay ahead to create a high-quality program that had to achieve three key goals. First, it had to meet rigorous accreditation standards; second, it had to deliver more doctors for rural and northern regions; and third, and perhaps most important, it had to embody a new vision for health care that would represent a more effective use of resources in addressing the health issues of Northern Ontario and other similar regions. And all of this had to be accomplished within the very short time frame established by both political and public expectations. The first priority involved the search for a founding dean to lead the academic process and, thus, signal the transition from issues of politics and funding to those of curriculum and academic quality. But an equally important issue involved determining the governance structure for the new school.

Governance

The development of NOSM's governance structure posed some unique problems. Two important issues had to be resolved. First, there were two universities in the North, Laurentian in Sudbury and Lakehead in Thunder Bay, both of relatively equal stature and each with a range of programs that would make them viable candidates for housing a faculty of medicine. Second, how could the school's governance be organized to make it more responsive to the communities it was designed to serve?

NOSM's governing structure is discussed in detail in chapter 8. Here, suffice it to point out that not only does it address the problem of answering to two different universities but it also allows for more community input than is ordinarily the case. In attempting to satisfy a widely acknowledged need for greater social accountability in medical education (WHO 1995; Health Canada 2001), many medical schools have appointed advisory bodies to guide them, but rarely do these bodies have real power. The NOSM board has real authority over the management of the school's affairs, and this makes NOSM more responsive to the region it serves than is usually the case with medical schools.

Establishing a faculty

Designers of a new medical education program are faced with a chicken-and-egg problem. The first priority is to have a curriculum that will meet rigorous accreditation standards and the faculty to deliver it. However, in order to build a curriculum, there has to be a dean and a faculty team already in place to do the work. In addition, provisional accreditation has to be attained before students may be invited to apply for admission, which effectively means that this must occur at least a year ahead of the planned opening date. The provincial government and municipal leaders, keen to see their initiatives bear fruit, were pressing for an early start-up date. An international search for a dean was instigated in January 2002. Following the northern and rural mandate proposed in the NORMS model and subsequently endorsed in the business plan, what was wanted was an academic leader with a substantial profile in rural medical education. Dr Roger Strasser was appointed in April 2002. Using an audio-link from Australia, he participated in the finalization of the implementation plan during the summer and came on campus to take up his full duties in August 2002. To meet the government's announced start-up date of September 2004, Dr Strasser would have had to recruit his academic leadership team, write a new curriculum from scratch, and attain provisional accreditation all in less than a year – a next to impossible task. Seeing the immensity of the task, and reassured that the process was in good hands and well under way, everyone, including the provincial government, readily agreed to a delayed 2005 start-up date.

If enthusiastic early planning had underestimated the time that would elapse between the appointment of the founding dean and the admission of the first group of students, it had also not acknowledged how difficult it would be to build an appropriate academic leadership team (see chapter 8). In retrospect, the decisions taken during this time were critical in enabling NOSM to meet its goals, not only with regard to having to meet the tight accreditation deadlines but also with regard to establishing the innovative nature of the school. Certainly, the recruitment of Dr Strasser, who had

played a central role in establishing rural medical education programs in Australia, ensured that the vision of a distributed model
tailored to the needs of northern communities would remain the
school's dominant direction. Once appointed, the dean had to work
largely alone to build his team, using the transitional support of
Laurentian's Office of Health Initiatives and ad hoc search committees (staffed by those on the two campuses and within the physician
community who had the most expertise in medical education). It
was not an easy task, but, notwithstanding the difficulties with
some of the early appointments (see chapter 8), the school was able
to attract highly qualified staff and faculty whose commitment to
its vision and willingness to work under intense time pressures and
within an administrative structure that was in the process of being
developed was impressive. Full-time faculty members with special-
izations in education informatics, Aboriginal community health, the
history of medicine, and population health were hired to give substance to the commitment to reflect NOSM's special mandate. Administrative staff were recruited, some from the outside, some from
the existing medical education programs in the Northwest and
Northeast, but all showed a high level of dedication to the goals of
the school.

The admissions process

From the outset, NOSM decided to create an admissions process that
would reflect the social composition of Northern Ontario and, particularly, its Aboriginal and francophone populations:

> The mandate of the School's Admissions Committee is to reflect
> the demographics of Northern Ontario in the medical school
> class profile.... Applicants from within Northern Ontario, rural
> and remote areas in the rest of Canada, and Aboriginal and Fran-
> cophone applicants will have an advantage in the admissions pro-
> cess. (OMSAS 2007)

The admissions process is described in detail in chapter 5. The
most impressive feature of this process is the high rate of application, as discussed in chapter 7. As a consequence of this overall rate,
and especially the high proportion of students from northern and
rural backgrounds, NOSM has been able to meet its commitment to

reflect northern demographic profiles and, at the same time, maintain high standards of academic excellence, as reflected by a mean weighted grade point average (WGPA) of 3.69 on a four-point scale for the first intake.

In setting and maintaining these standards, NOSM has based its procedures on the available evidence from other schools as well as on significant input from the communities it serves. Because of the historically low rates of Aboriginal applications to Canadian medical schools, NOSM has introduced a series of initiatives directed at raising the profile of medical careers to school-age Aboriginal populations. In addition, the school has established an Aboriginal admissions subcommittee that makes recommendations for admissions to the Aboriginal stream. There is broad community representation on the admissions committee, including francophone and Aboriginal representatives, and community members are invited to participate in interview panels.

Developing a curriculum for northern, rural and remote communities

As we have already noted, one of the advantages of being a new stand-alone school is the freedom to innovate and to develop a curriculum suited to the setting and the mandate of the school. While the original push for a new school was based on the need for more doctors in the North, the building of a new curriculum opened the door to a transformation of thinking about health roles in a northern rural environment. The details of curriculum development are described in chapter 6; however, the following features are worthy of particular attention because they take the school much further along the road promised in the first proposal:

- True to NOSM's social accountability mandate, an important part of the curriculum development process involved consultation with communities across the North and, especially, with the Aboriginal and francophone communities. This level of community consultation was time-consuming and it was not always possible to accommodate the perceived needs of each community; however, it served to remind the designers of a principle fundamental to the conception of NOSM and established the legitimacy of the program in the eyes of those whom it was designed to serve.

- The school's northern mandate is also reflected in the curriculum content, which is centred on the five themes that organize the students' learning in each year of the program: (1) northern and rural health, (2) personal and professional aspects of medical practice, (3) social and population health, (4) foundations of medicine, and (5) clinical skills in health care. Thus the students are constantly exposed to issues relating to northern and rural health delivery as well as to the social and population health characteristics of northern communities.

- Students learn primarily in small groups, with the emphasis on self-directed learning and a faculty tutor acting as a facilitator. The curricular attention to northern and rural issues is complemented by a thorough immersion of students in a wide range of community clinical experiences, where they observe and interact with patients under the guidance of a clinician teacher. Their learning is distributed across the North during integrated community experiences in the first and second years. The third year comprehensive community clerkship sees students assigned to primary care practice settings in small- to medium-sized communities throughout Northern Ontario for the full academic year. This part of the program is modelled on the PRCC at Flinders University in South Australia, and, while it is as yet untested in Canada, the success of the Flinders program (Worley et al. 2004) provides grounds for expecting that it will be equally successful here.

- This pattern of distributed learning is supported by a sophisticated communication technology system. There is an extensive network of video-conferencing sites that have been developed by Contact North (a provincial agency that manages a wide-ranging northern educational network) and North Network (one of Canada's foremost telehealth networks). The whole network is serviced through ORION, Ontario's ultra high-speed research and education network. Thus, students from different sites across the region are regularly linked for interactive group sessions. The network also supports extensive electronic library holdings that are available to students, faculty, and health professionals through the Northern Ontario Health Information Network.

- Recognizing the growing importance of interprofessional collaboration in health care, NOSM's Curriculum Workshop identified "being a team player" as a key characteristic of northern physicians. Subsequently, the NOSM Academic Council included "interprofessional" as one of the six key Academic principles, and interprofessional education is a significant component of the undergraduate curriculum. This follows a long-established desire to see the school as a first step in a broad range of health sciences programs being offered in Northern Ontario. In fact, NOSM has already established the Northern Ontario Dietetic Internship Program and is working with McMaster University to expand the northern studies stream in physiotherapy and occupational therapy so that it may become pan-northern with a francophone component.

LESSONS LEARNED FROM IMPLEMENTATION

The general picture

It needs to be said that, in spite of the challenges that had to be overcome in establishing NOSM, the start-up years show every sign of success. While NOSM has yet to prove itself in the long term, and that proof will come when we see well-qualified and clinically skilled doctors establishing practices across the North, it has already overcome some substantial hurdles. Sceptics worried that the school might have been created as a political whim and that it would have difficulty attaining sustainable government funding. There was a concern about the new school's ability to attract high-calibre faculty at a time when the established schools were experiencing difficulties doing so. Finally, in the very prestige-conscious world of medical education, there was a risk that the school might not attract a sufficient number of high-ability students to maintain its academic credibility. As NOSM is approaching its fourth year of operation, it is now possible to say that these early fears have largely been allayed. Although an election led to a change of party in government, the flow of funding has been maintained and appears to be both adequate and stable. Northern Ontario physicians have embraced their new clinical teaching responsibilities with sufficient enthusiasm to ensure a vigorous start to the school, and the rate of students applying for places in NOSM has enabled it not only to recruit top students but also to meet its targets for students from northern and rural backgrounds.

Perhaps most important of all, however, the fundamental principles that animated the development of NOSM have received a further boost. Both the research literature and the concrete experience of the northern physicians in the early residency programs have proven to be solid building blocks upon which to establish the school. The evidence so far is not definitive, but it is very promising. It is particularly encouraging to see how the students have bought into the model, share its assumptions, and show evident satisfaction in their rural clinical experience.

The time factor

A number of chapters in this volume indicate that time pressure was an issue. The high level of political investment in the NOSM project, both at the municipal and the provincial levels, raised expectations that, once the go-ahead had been given, quick progress would be made in achieving tangible results. In retrospect, some of the time expectations were shown to be unrealistic, particularly bearing in mind that, in a program of this kind, issues of academic quality are paramount. Inability to satisfy accreditation criteria both for the program and for the ability of the faculty to deliver it would have seriously undermined the credibility of the project. There were some signs of impatience on the part of the political participants in the process when dealing with how academic institutions make decisions, both with regard to appointments and with regard to approving structures and programs. However, in the end, all involved recognized the need to delay the opening date from 2004 to 2005 in order to accommodate the complex steps that had to be taken in order to ensure provisional accreditation of the program. This was particularly important given the commitment to have community input into curriculum development and the admissions procedure. In fact, the pressure of looming deadlines can be an energizing factor, encouraging people to leave aside disputes over small issues in the interest of focusing on the bigger picture.

The not-for-profit corporation as a vehicle for innovation

The Northwestern Ontario Medical Program (NOMP) and the Northeastern Ontario Medical Education Corporation (NOMEC), the highly successful building blocks of medical education in the North, were not part of any traditional academic structure. Academically, the programs offered by NOMP and NOMEC were still answerable to their parent universities, McMaster and the University of

Ottawa, respectively; however, they were physically located on the northern university campuses of Lakehead (NOMP) and Laurentian (NOMEC), and they developed governance structures that reflected partnerships between the parent universities, local physicians, and new northern campus partners.[1] These hybrid organizations had a fair degree of autonomy with regard to the management of their funds, and they fostered a real sense of ownership among the participants in the programs that they managed. They were hybrid in the sense that they were not solely the instruments of the parent universities (the academic sponsors), or of the Ministry of Health (which funded most of their operations), or of the northern universities (on whose campuses they were located). These organizations developed identities of their own and bred among their participants a real sense that they could get things done in the North in a way that larger institutions could not. They certainly produced results. In fact, one might say, ironically, that they were so successful that they made themselves redundant as the full-fledged medical school that they spawned took over their functions. It is reasonable to ask whether this could have happened if these early medical education programs had been solely under the control of either their northern hosts or their traditional medical school sponsors.

Similarly, it may be argued that the unique governance structure of NOMS ensures that its commitment to the health needs of the communities of the North, its fundamental mandate, will not at some point in the future be rendered subordinate to the institutional ambitions of its academic sponsors. It is probably the case that the universities involved sometimes find themselves ill at ease with the relative autonomy of NOSM as the school has its own source of funds and its own decision-making processes. There are probably days when each might wish that it had its own school of medicine uncomplicated by the presence of the other. But it is doubtful that this is a realistic expectation, which is why they joined together in the first place. More important, however, NOSM's status as an independent entity answerable to its own board makes it much more responsive to community needs than would be the case if it were part of a traditional academic structure. NOSM has a unique ability to

---

1 While NOMEC was, in fact, established as an independent not-for-profit corporation, NOMP was simply established through an agreement between the main stakeholders. But, in effect, both organizations were relatively autonomous.

focus on its mandate, which, after all, is its raison d'être. Lakehead and Laurentian, for their part, might take some comfort in the fact that they are insulated from fiscal responsibility for NOSM, which, if times were to get hard, could be a huge responsibility for relatively small universities.

References

CHAPTER ONE

Government of Ontario, Ministry of Health and Long-term Care. 2001a. *Shaping Ontario's Physician Workforce: Building Ontario's Capacity to Plan, Educate, Recruit and Retain Physicians to Meet Health Needs.* Toronto. Available at http://www.health.gov.on.ca/english/public/pub/ministry_reports/workforce/workforce.html (viewed 6 March 2008)

– 2001b. *Harris Government's 21–Step Action Plan.* Toronto: Press Office, April 24.

– 2001c. *Harris Government Announces New Northern Medical School and Increased Medical School Enrolment.* Toronto: Press Office, May 17.

Heng, D., R.W. Pong, B.T.B. Chan, N. Degani, T. Crichton, J. Goertzen, W. McCready, and J. Rourke. 2007. "Graduates of Northern Ontario Family Medicine Residency Programs Practise Where They Train." *Canadian Journal of Rural Medicine* 12 (3): 146–52.

Kaufman, A. 1990. "Rurally Based Education: Confronting Social Forces Underlying Ill Health. *Academic Medicine 65*: S18–S21.

McKendry, R. 1999. *Physicians for Ontario: Too many? Too few? For 2000 and Beyond.* Toronto: Government of Ontario, Ministry of Health and Long-term Care. Available at http://www.health.gov.on.ca/english/public/pub/ministry_reports/mckendry/mckendry.html. (viewed 6 March 2008)

NORMS Liaison Council. 2000. "A Northern Rural Medical School: Increasing Rural Medical Graduates in Ontario – A Preliminary Proposal. Submitted by Laurentian and Lakehead universities to the Expert Panel on Health Professional Resources.

NOSM. 2005. *Inaugural: Breaking New Ground for Northern Ontario.* NOSM Communications.

Rosenblatt, R.A., M.E. Whitcomb, T.J. Cullen, D.M. Lishner and L.G. Hart. 1992. "Which Medical Schools Produce Rural Physicians?" *Journal of the American Medical Association* 268 (12): 1559–65.

Rourke, J. 1996. *Education for Rural Medical Practice: Goals and Opportunities – An Annotated Bibliography*. Moe, Australia: Monash University.

Sullivan, P., and M. O'Reilly. 2002. "Canada's First Rural Medical School: Is It Needed? Will It Open? *Canadian Medical Association Journal* 166 (4): 488.

Walker D. 2001. "Docs Don't Always Practice Where They Studied Med." Letters to the Editor, *Medical Post* 37: 15.

CHAPTER TWO

Allaire, G., and L. Picard. 2005. *Deuxiéme rapport sur la santè des francophones de l'Ontario*. Sudbury: Institute franco-Ontarien et Programme de recherche, d'éducation et de développement en santé publique.

Anderson, M., and M.W. Rosenberg. 1990. "Ontario's Underserviced Area Program Revisited: An Indirect Analysis. *Social Science and Medicine* 30: 35–44.

Badgley, R.F. 1991. "Social and Economic Disparities under Canadian Health Care." *International Journal of Health Services* 21: 659–71.

Barer, M.L., and G.L. Stoddart. 1991. *Toward Integrated Medical Resource Policies in Canada*. Winnipeg: Manitoba Health.

Brooks, R.G., M. Walsh, R.E. Mardon, M. Lewis and A. Clawson. 2002. "The Roles of Nature and Nurture in the Recruitment and Retention of Primary Care Physicians in Rural Areas: A Review of the Literature. *Academic Medicine* 77 (8): 790–8.

Chan, B.T.B. 2002. *From Perceived Surplus to Perceived Shortage: What Happened to Canada's Physician Workforce in the 1990s?* Ottawa: Canadian Institute for Health Information.

Coates, K., and W. Morrison. 1992. *The Forgotten North: A History of Canada's Provincial Norths*. Toronto: James Lorimer.

Dauphinee, W.D. 1996. "Medical Workforce Policy Making in Canada: Are We Creating More Problems for the Future? *Clinical and Investigative Medicine* 19 (4): 286–91.

Dauphinee, W.D., and L. Buske. 2006. "Medical Workforce Policy-making in Canada, 1993–2003: Reconnecting the Disconnected." *Academic Medicine* 81 (9): 830–6.

Denz-Penhey, H., S. Shannon, J.C. Murdoch, and J.W. Newbury. 2005. "Do Benefits Accrue from Longer Rotations for Students in Rural Clinical Schools? *Rural and Remote Health* 5: 414.

DesMeules, M., R.W. Pong, C. Lagacé, D. Heng, D. Manuel, R. Pitblado, R. Bollman, J. Guernsey, A. Kazanjian and I. Koren. 2006. *How Healthy Are Rural Canadians? An Assessment of Their Health Status and Health Determinants.* Ottawa: Canadian Institute for Health Information. Available at: http://secure.cihi.ca/cihiweb/dispPage.jsp?cw_page=cphi_e#pubs (viewed 11 March 2009).

Di Matteo, L., J.C.H. Emery, and R. English. 2006. "Is It Better to Live in a Basement, an Attic or to Get Your Own Place? Analyzing the Costs and Benefits of Institutional Change for Northwestern Ontario." *Canadian Public Policy* 32 (2): 173–95.

Diverty, B., and C. Pérez. 1998. "The Health of Northern Residents. *Health Report* 9 (4): 49–55.

Dunk, T.W. 1991. *It's A Working Man's Town: Male Working-class Culture.* Montreal and Kingston: McGill-Queen's University Press.

Expert Panel on Health Professional Human Resources. 2001. *Shaping Ontario's Physician Workforce: Building Ontario's Capacity to Plan, Educate, Recruit and Retain Physicians to Meet Health Needs.* Toronto: Ontario Ministry of Health and Long-Term Care.

Fair, M. 1992. "Health of the Rural Population: Occupational Mortality Patterns. In *Rural and Small Town Canada*, ed. R. Mendelson and R.D. Bollman, 293–8. Toronto: Thompson Educational Publishing.

Heard, S. 1999. "The City of Elliot Lake to 1991: Before the Roof Fell In." In *Boom Town Blues: Elliot Lake – Collapse and Revival in a Single-industry Community*, ed. A.M. Mawhiney and J. Pitblado, 21–35. Toronto: Dundurn Press.

Health Canada. 2003. *A Statistical Profile on the Health of First Nations in Canada.* Ottawa: Health Canada.

Heng, D., R.W. Pong, B.T.B. Chan, N. Degani, T. Crichton, J. Goertzen, W. McCready, and J. Rourke. 2007. "Graduates of Northern Ontario Family Medicine Residency Programs Practise Where They Train. *Canadian Journal of Rural Medicine* 12 (3): 146–52.

Hensel, J.M., M. Shandling, and D.A. Redelmeier. 2007. "Rural Medical Students at Urban Medical Schools: Too Few and Far Between? *Open Medicine* 1 (1): 19–23.

Hutten-Czapski, P., J.R. Pitblado and S. Slade. 2004. "Scope of Family Practice in Rural and Urban Settings." *Canadian Family Physician* 50: 1548–50.

Lalonde, M. 1974. *A New Perspective on the Health of Canadians.* Ottawa: Department of Health and Welfare.

Lucas, R.A. 1971. *Minetown, Milltown, Railtown: Life in Canadian Communities of Single Industry.* Toronto: University of Toronto Press.

McKendry, R.J. 1999. *Physicians for Ontario: Too Many? Too Few? For 2000 and Beyond.* Toronto: Ministry of Health and Long-term Care.

Mitura, V., and R.D. Bollman. 2003. "The Health of Rural Canadians: A Rural-urban Comparison of Health Indicators." *Rural and Small Town Canada Analysis Bulletin* 4 (6): 1–21. Available at: http://www.statcan.gc.ca/pub/21–006–x/21–006–x2002006–eng.pdf (viewed 11 March 2009).

Olatunde, S., E.R. Leduc, and J. Berkowitz. 2007. "Different Practice Patterns of Rural and Urban General Practitioners Are Predicted by the General Practice Rurality Index. *Canadian Journal of Rural Medicine* 12 (2): 73–80.

Pampalon, R. 1991. "Health Discrepancies in Rural Areas in Quebec." *Social Science and Medicine* 33 (4): 355–360.

Pathman, D.E., B.D. Steiner, B.D. Jones and T.R. Konrad. 1999. "Preparing and Retaining Rural Physicians through Medical Education." *Academic Medicine* 74: 810–20.

Pong, R.W. 2008. "Strategies to Overcome Physician Shortages in Northern Ontario: A Study of Policy Implementation over 35 Years. *Human Resources for Health* 6 (24). Available online at www.human-resources-health.com/content/6/1/24.

Pong, R.W., and J.R. Pitblado. 2005. *Geographic Distribution of Physicians: Beyond How Many and Where.* Ottawa: Canadian Institute for Health Information.

Pong, R.W., B.T.B. Chan, T. Crichton, J. Goertzen, W. McCready and J. Rourke. 2007. "Big Cities and Bright Lights: Rural- and Northern-trained Physicians in Urban Practice. *Canadian Journal of Rural Medicine* 12 (3): 153–60.

Probert, A., and R. Poirier. 2003. "The Health Status of First Nations People." *Health Policy Research Bulletin* 5: 6–10.

Raphael, D. ed. 2004. *Social Determinants of Health: Canadian Perspectives.* Toronto: Canadian Scholars' Press.

Romanow, R.J. 2002. *Building on Values: The Future of Health Care in Canada.* Saskatoon: Commission on the Future of Health Care in Canada.

Rourke, J.T.B., and R. Strasser. 1996. "Education for Rural Practice in Canada and Australia. *Academic Medicine* 71 (5): 464–9.

Rourke, J.T.B., F. Incitti, L.L. Rourke, and M. Kennard. 2005. "Relationship between Practice Location of Ontario Family Physicians and Their Rural Background or Amount of Rural Medical Education Experience." *Canadian Journal of Rural Medicine* 10 (4): 231–9.

Rosenblatt, R.A., M.E. Whitcomb, T.J. Cullen, D.M. Lishner and L.G. Hart. 1992. "Which Medical Schools Produce Rural Physicians?" *Journal of the American Medical Association* 268 (12): 1559–65.

Stymeist, D.H. 1975. *Ethnics and Indians: Social Relations in a North-western Ontario Town*. Toronto: Peter Martin Associates Limited.

Tepper, J. 2004. *The Evolving Role of Canada's Family Physicians, 1992–2001*. Ottawa: Canadian Institute for Health Information.

Tesson, G., V. Curran, R. Strasser, and R. Pong. 2006. "Adapting Medical Education to Meet the Physician Recruitment Needs of Rural and Remote Regions in Canada, the US and Australia. In *National Health Workforce Assessment of the Past and Agenda for the Future*, ed. A. Rotem, G. Perfilieva, M.R. Dal Poz, and B.D.H. Doan, 327–46. Paris, France: Centre de Sociologie et de Démographie Médicales.

Weller, G.R. 1985. "Political Disaffection in the Canadian Provincial North." *Bulletin of Canadian Studies* 9 (1): 58–86.

– 1990. "Politics and Policy in the North." In *The Government and Politics of Ontario*, ed. G. White, 275–92. Toronto: Nelson.

Weller, G.R., and P. Manga. 1988. "The Feasibility of Developing an Integrated Health Care Delivery System in the North: The Case of Northwestern Ontario. In *Health Care Issues in the Canadian North*, ed. David E. Young, 140–50. Edmonton: Boreal Institute for Northern Studies, University of Alberta.

Wilkin, R. 1992. "Health of the Rural Population: Selected Indicators. In *Rural and Small Town Canada*, ed. R. Mendelson and R.D. Bollman, pp. 285–91. Toronto: Thompson Educational Publishing.

Wilkinson, R., and M. Marmot, eds. 2003. *Social Determinants of Health: The Solid Facts*. Copenhagen: World Health Organization.

Worley, P., C.A. Silagy, D.J. Prideaux, D. Newble and A. Jones. 2000. "The Parallel Rural Community Curriculum: An Integrated Clinical Curriculum Based in Rural General Practice. *Medical Education* 34: 558–65.

Young, T.K. 1988. *Health Care and Cultural Change: The Indian Experience in the Central Subarctic*. Toronto: University of Toronto Press.

CHAPTER THREE

Boelen, C. 1995. "Prospects for Change in Medical Education in the Twenty-first Century." *Academic Medicine* 70 (7): S21–S28

Brazeau, N.K., M.J. Potts, and J.M. Hickner. 1990. "The Upper Peninsula Program: A Successful Model for Increasing Primary Care Physicians in Rural Areas." *Family Medicine* 22 (5):350–5.

Flexner, A. 1910. Medical Education in the United States and Canada: A Report to the Carnegie Foundation for the Advancement of Teaching. The Carnegie Foundation, bulletin no. 4.

Gibbs, T. 2004. "Community-based or Tertiary-based Medical Education: So What Is the Question?" *Medical Teacher* 26 (7): 589–90.

Green, Larry A., George E. Fryer Jr, Barbara P. Yawn,David Lanier, Susan M Dovey. 2001. "The Ecology of Medical Care Revisited." *New England Journal of Medicine* 344 (26): 2021–5.

Habbick, B.F., and S.R. Leeder. 1996. "Orienting Medical Education to Community Need: A Review." *Medical Education* 30: 163–71.

Hays, R., and T.S. Gupta. 2003. "Ruralising Medical Curricula: The Importance of Context in Problem Design." *Australian Journal of Rural Health* 11: 15–17.

Hays, R., J. Stokes, and C. Veitch. 2003. "A New Socially Responsible Medical School for Regional Australia." *Education for Health* 16 (1): 14–21.

Health Canada. 2001. *Social Accountability: A Vision for Canadian Medical Schools.* Ottawa: Health Canada.

Hogenbirk, J.C., F. Wang, R.W. Pong, G. Tesson, and R.P. Strasser. 2004. *Nature of Rural Medical Practice in Canada: An Analysis of the 2001 National Family Physician Survey.* Sudbury: Centre for Rural and Northern Health Research, Laurentian University.

Howe, A., and G. Ives. 2001. "Does Community-based Experience Alter Career Preference? New Evidence from a Prospective Longitudinal Cohort Study of undergraduate Medical Students." *Medical Education* 35: 391–7.

Inoue, K., Y. Hirayama, and M. Igarashi. 1997. "A Medical School for Rural Areas." *Medical Education* 31: 430–4.

Jeffries, M. N.d. "The History of Distance Education." Available at http://www.digitalschool.net/edu/DL_history_mJeffries.html (Viewed 11 March 2009).

Kenny, N.P., and B.L. Beagan. 2004. "The Patient as Text: A Challenge for Problem Based Learning." *Medical Education* 38: 1071–9.

Magnus, J.H., and A. Tollan. 1993. "Rural Doctor Recruitment: Does Medical Education in Rural Districts Recruit Doctors to Rural Areas?" *Medical Education* 27: 250–3.

Neufeld, V.R., R.F. Mandsley, R.J. Pickering, J.M. Turner, W.W. Weston, M.G. Brown, and J.C. Simpson. 1998. "Educating Future Physicians for Ontario." *Academic Medicine* 73: 1133 – 48

Oswald, N., and Anderson, S. Jones. 2001. "Evaluating Primary Care as a Base for Medical Education: The Report of the Cambridge Community-based Clinical Course." *Medical Education* 35: 782–8.

Papa, F.J., and P.H. Harasym. 1999. "Medical Curriculum Reform in North America, 1765 to the Present: A Cognitive Science Perspective." *Academic Medicine* 74: 154–64.

Rabinowitz, H.K., J.J. Diamond, F.W. Markham, and N.P. Paynter. 2001. "Critical Factors for Designing Programs to Increase the Supply and Retention of Rural Primary Care Physicians." *Journal of the American Medical Association* 286 (9): 1041–8.

Ramsey, P.G., J.B. Coombs, D.D. Hunt, S.G. Marshall, and M.D. Wenrich. 2001. "From Concept to Culture: The WWAMI Program at the University of Washington School of Medicine." *Academic Medicine* 76 (8): 765–75.

Rourke, J.T.B. 2001. "Rural Practice in Canada." In *Textbook of Rural Medicine*, ed., J.P. Geyman, T.E. Norris, and L.G. Hart, 395–409. New York: McGraw-Hill.

Ruiz, J.G., M.J. Mintzer, and R.M. Leipzig. 2006. "The Impact of E-Learning in Medical Education." *Academic Medicine* 81 (3): 207–12

Schmidt, H.G. 1983. "Problem Based Learning: Rationale and Description." *Medical Education* 17: 11–16.

Stewart, Moira, J.B. Brouwn, W.W. Weston, I.R. McWhinney, C.L. McWilliam, and T.R. Freeman. 2003. *Patient Centered Medicine: Transforming the Clinical Method*. Abingdon: Radcliffe Medical Press Ltd.

Strasser R. 1992. "The Attitudes of Victorian Rural General Practitioners to Country Practice and Training." *Australian Family Physician* 21 (7): 808–12

Strasser, R.P., R.B. Hays, M. Kamien, and D. Carson. 2000. "Is Australian Rural Practice Changing? Findings from the National Rural General Practice Study." *Australian Journal of Rural Health* 8: 222–226

Strasser, S., and R. Strasser. 2007. "The Northern Ontario School of Medicine: A Long-term Strategy to Enhance the Rural Medical Workforce." *Cahiers de Sociologie et de Démographie Médicales* 47 (4): 469–90.

Strasser, R.P. 2001. "Training for Rural Practice – Lessons from Australia." The Carl Moore Lecture. Hamilton: McMaster University.

Verby, J.E. 1988. "The Minnesota Rural Physician Associate Program for Medical Students." *Journal of Medical Education* 63: 427–37.

Working Group on Postgraduate Education for Rural Family Practice. 1999. *Postgraduate Education for Rural Family Practice: Vision and Recommendations for the New Millennium*. Mississauga, ON: College of Family Physicians of Canada.

Worley, P., C. Silagy, D. Prideaux, D. Newble, and A. Jones. 2000. "The Parallel Rural Community Curriculum: An Integrated Clinical Curriculum Based in Rural General Practice." *Medical Education* 34: 558–65

Worley, P.S., O.J. Prideaux, R.P. Strasser, C.A. Silagy, and J.A. Magarey. 2000. "Why We Should Teach Undergraduate Medical Students in Rural Communities." *Medical Journal of Australia* 172: 615–17.

Worley, P., A. Esterman, and D. Prideaux. 2004. "Cohort Study of Examination Performance of Undergraduate Medical Students Learning in Community Settings." *British Medical Journal* 328: 207–10.

Worley, P., D. Prideaux, R. Strasser, R. March, and E. Worley. 2004. "What Do Medical Students Actually Do on Clinical Rotations?" *Medical Teacher* 26 (7) :594–98

Worley, P., R. Strasser, and D. Prideaux. 2004. "Can Medical Students Learn Specialist Disciplines Based in Rural Practice? Lessons from Students' Self Reported Experience and Competence." *Rural and Remote Health* 4 (online):338. Available at http://www.rrh.org.au/articles/subviewnew.asp?ArticleID=338 (viewed 11 March 2009).

Worley, P., D. Prideaux, R. Strasser, A. Magavey, and R. March. 2006. "Empirical Evidence for Symbiotic Medical Education: A Cooperative Analysis of Community and Tertiary Based Programmes." *Medical.Education* 40: 109–16

CHAPTER FIVE

Albanese, M.A., P. Farrell, and S.L. Dottl. 2005. "A Comparison of Statistical Criteria for Setting Optimally Discriminating MCAT and GPA Thresholds in Medical School Admissions." *Teaching and Learning in Medicine* 17 (2): 149–58.

Bates, J., V. Frinton, and D. Voaklander. 2005. "A New Evaluation Tool for Admissions." *Medical Education* 39 (11): 1146.

Brieger, G.H. 1999. "The Plight of Premedical Education: Myths and Misperceptions – Part 2: Science 'versus' the Liberal Arts." *Academic Medicine* 74 (11): 1217–21.

Caplan, R.M., C. Kreiter, and M. Albanese. 1996. "Preclinical Science Course 'preludes' Taken by premedical Students: Do They Provide a Competitive Advantage?" *Academic Medicine* 71 (8): 920–2.

Eva, K.W., J. Rosenfeld, H.I. Reiter, and G.R. Norman. 2004. "An Admissions OSCE: The Multiple Mini-Interview." *Medical Education* 38 (3): 314–26.

Julian, E.R. 2005. "Validity of the Medical College Admission Test for Predicting Medical School Performance." *Academic Medicine* 80 (10): 910–7.

Kreiter, C.D., P. Yin, C. Solow, and R.L. Brennan. 2004. "Investigating the Reliability of the Medical School Admissions Interview." *Advances in Health Sciences Education: Theory and Practice* 9 (2): 147–59.

Lumsden M.A, M. Bore, K. Millar, R. Jack, and D. Powis. 2005. "Assessment of Personal Qualities in Relation to Admission to Medical School." *Medical Education* 39 (3): 258–65

Mitchell, K., R. Hayne, and, J. Koenig. 1994. "Assessing the Validity of the Updated Medical College Admission Test." *Academic Medicine* 69 (5): 394–401.

Neufeld, V.R., R.F. Maudsley, R.J. Pickering, J.M. Turnbull, W.W. Weston, M.G. Brown, and J.C. Simpson. 1998. "Educating Future Physicians for Ontario." *Academic Medicine* 73 (11): 1133–48

Owen, J.A., G.F. Hayden, and A.F. Connors Jr. 2002. "Can Medical School Admission Committee Members Predict Which Applicants Will Choose Primary Care Careers?" *Academic Medicine* 77 (4): 344–9.

Rabinowitz, H.K. 1988. "Evaluation of a Selective Medical School Admissions Policy to Increase the Number of Family Physicians in Rural and Underserved Areas." *New England Journal of Medicine* 319 (8): 480–6.

Rabinowitz, H.K., J.J. Diamond, F.W. Markham, and N.P. Paynter. 2001. "Critical Factors for Designing Programs to Increase the Supply and Retention of Rural Primary Care Physicians." *Journal of the American Medical Association* 286 (9): 1041–8.

Rourke, J., D. Dewar, R. Harris, P. Hutten-Czapski, M. Johnston, D. Klassen, J. Konkin, C. Morwood, R. Rowntree, K. Stobbe, and T. Young. 2005. "Strategies to Increase the Enrollment of Students of Rural Origin in Medical School: Recommendations from the Society of Rural Physicians of Canada." *Canadian Medical Association Journal* 172 (1): 62–5.

Tilleczek, K., R. Pong, J. Konkin, and D. Cudney. 2006. "An Examination of the Northern Ontario School of Medicine Student Selection Process." Unpublished report.

Woloschuk, W., and M. Tarrant. 2004. "Do Students from Rural Backgrounds Engage in Rural Family Practice More Than Their Urban-raised Peers?" *Medical Education* 38 (3): 259–61.

CHAPTER SIX

*All internal NOSM documents cited in this chapter have been donated to the NOSM Archives in Thunder Bay, Ontario.

Barrows, H., and R. Tamblyn. 1980. *Problem Based Learning: An Approach to Medical Education.* New York: Springer Publishing Co.

Elstein, A., L. Schulman, and S. Sprafka. 1978. *Medical Problem Solving: An Analysis of Clinical Reasoning.* Cambridge: Harvard University Press.

Fisher, L.A., and C. Levine. 1996. *Planning a Professional Curriculum.* Calgary: University of Calgary Press.

Harden, R. 1989. A presentation to the Faculty Council of the United Arab Emirates (author's recollection).

Mandin, H., P.H. Harasym, C. Eagle, and M. Watanabe. 1995. "Developing a Clinical Presentation Curriculum at the University of Calgary." *Academic Medicine*, 70:186–93.

Northern Ontario School of Medicine (NOSM). 2000. "A Northern Rural Medical School: Increasing Rural Medical Graduates in Ontario – A Preliminary Proposal." The NORMS Liaison Council of Laurentian University and Lakehead University. Presented to the Expert Panel on Health Professions Resources, June.

– 2002a. NOMS Business Plan, August. Northern Ontario Medical School Implementation Management Committee, Price Waterhouse Consulting Publisher, Sudbury, Ontario.

– 2002b. The Social Accountability Mandate. The Social Accountability Mandate. Principles and Framework for Working Arrangements Involving Lakehead University, Laurentian University, and the Northern Ontario School of Medicine.

– 2003a. "Proposal for the Curriculum of the Northern Ontario Medical School, Ontario Institute for Studies in Education (Course TPS 1813), 2003, Western Ontario." Ed. Janet Wilson and Doug Ross. 32 pp., University of Western Ontario.

– 2003b. "A Flying Start: Report of the NOMS Curriculum Workshop 'Getting Started in the North,' January 16–18, 2003." Sault Ste. Marie. 11 pp. NOSM Archives.

– 2003c. LCME Accreditation Data Base (2003–2004), Binder #2. NOSM Archives.

– 2004. Report on the Aboriginal Pilot Project, February. NOSM Archives.

– 2005a. Appendix: Part 2 (Specific Issues) LCME/CaCMA Limited Accreditation Site Visit, 13–17 March, 78–9. NOSM Archives.

– 2005b. Aboriginal Pilot Placement Report. NOSM Archives

Papa, F.J., and P.H. Harasym. 1999. "Medical Curriculum Reform in North America, 1765 to the Present: A Cognitive Science Perspective." *Academic Medicine* 74 (2), 154–164.

Parboosingh, J. 2003. "The Association of Canadian Medical Colleges' Working Group on Social Accountability: Medical Schools' Social Contract: More Than Just Education and Research." *Canadian Medical Association Journal* 168 (7): 852–3.

Southern Illinois University. 1976. *Curricular Objectives*. Fort Worth: Evans College Publication Service.

Toohey, S. 2002. *Designing Courses for Higher Education*. Philadelphia: Open University Press.

Worley, P., C. Silagy, D. Prideaux, D. Newble, and A. Jones. 2000. "The Parallel Rural Community Curriculum: An Integrated Clinical Curriculum Based in Rural General Practice." *Medical Education* 34: 558–65.

CHAPTER SEVEN

Association of American Medical Colleges. 2005. *Minority Students in Medical Education: Facts and Figures XIII.* Available at https://services.aamc.org/publications (viewed 11 March 2009).

Association of Faculties of Medicine of Canada. 2007. *Canadian Medical Education Statistics.* Vol. 29. Ottawa: AFMC

Bowman, R.C. 2007. "New Models or Remodeling Students or Both?" *Rural and Remote Health* 7: 722. Available at http://www.rrh.org.au (viewed 11 March 2009).

Deacon, T. 1997. *The Symbolic Species: The Co-evolution of Language and the Brain.* New York: W.W.Norton & Co.

Dhalla, I.A., J.C. Kwong, D.I. Streiner, R.E. Badour, A.E. Waddell, and I.L. Johnson. 2002. "Characteristics of First Year Students in Canadian Medical Schools." *Canadian Medical Association Journal* 166 (8): 1029–35.

Gold, J. 2002. *The Story Species: Our Life-Literature Connection.* Markham: Fitzhenry and Whiteside.

Northern Ontario School of Medicine (NOSM). 2005. *Inaugural: Breaking New Ground for Northern Ontario.* NOSM Archives, Thunder Bay, Ontario.

Talley, R.C. 1990. "Graduate Medical Education and Rural Health Care." *Academic Medicine* 65: S22–S25.

Wright, B., I. Scott, W. Woloschuk, F. Brenneis. 2004. "Career Choice of New Medical Students at Three Canadian Universities: Family Medicine versus Specialty Medicine." *Canadian Medical Association Journal* 170 (13): 1920–24.

Yates, M., and J. Youniss, eds. 1999. *The Roots of Civic Identity: International Perspectives on Community Service and Activism in Youth.* Cambridge: University of Cambridge Press

CHAPTER EIGHT

Kastor, J.A. 2001. *Mergers of Teaching Hospitals in Boston, New York, and Northern California.* Michigan: University of Michigan Press.

McKendry, R. 1999. *Physicians for Ontario: Too many? Too few? For 2000 and beyond.* Toronto: Government of Ontario, Ministry of Health and Long-term Care.

NORMS Liaison Council. 2000. *A Northern Rural Medical School; Increasing Rural Medical Graduates in Ontario: A Preliminary Proposal.* Submitted by Laurentian and Lakehead universities to the Expert Panel on Health Professional Resources. NOSM Archives, Thunder Bay, Ontario.

Northern Ontario School of Medicine (NOSM). 2002. *Principles and Framework for Working Arrangements Involving Lakehead University, Laurentian University, and the Northern Ontario Medical School.* NOSM Archives, Thunder Bay, Ontario.

– 2003. *Alternative Strategies for the Cooperation of Laurentian and Lakehead Universities with the Northern Medical School (NOMS) in Matters Relating to Human Resources.* NOSM Archives, Thunder Bay, Ontario.

Ontario, Ministry of Health and Long-term Care. 2001. *Shaping Ontario's Physician Workforce: Building Ontario's Capacity to Plan, Educate, Recruit and Retain Physicians to Meet Health Needs.* Toronto: Ministry of Health and Long-term Care.

CHAPTER NINE

*All internal NOSM documents cited in this chapter have been donated to the NOSM Archives, Thunder Bay, Ontario.

Association of American Medical Colleges. 2005. *Achieving Accountability: A Proactive Process for Academic Medical Centers.* Washington, DC.

Association of Faculties of Medicine of Canada (AFMC). N.d.(a). *Social Accountability: Aboriginal Health Needs.* Available at: http://www.afmc.ca/social-aboriginal-health-e.php (viewed 1 July 2008).

– N.d.(b). Social Accountability Initiatives Database. Available at: http://www.afmc.ca/search_tool/step1–e.php (viewed 1 July 2008).

– 2002–06. AFMC Forum.

– 2004. Proceedings of the Inaugural Meeting of Partners' Forum on Social Accountability of Canadian Medical Schools, Halifax, Nova Scotia.

– 2006. "Enhancing the Health of the Population: The Role of Canadian Faculties of Medicine." Paper presented to the Council of Deans of Faculties of Medicine from the AFMC Public Health Task Group, January.

Boelen C., and Heck J.E. 1995. *Defining and Measuring the Social Accountability of Medical Schools.* Geneva: Division of Development of Human Resources for Health, World Health Organization.

Centre for Rural and Northern Health Research (CRaNHR). N.d. http://www.cranhr.ca/ (viewed 1 July 2008).

Canadian Association of University Teachers (CAUT). 2007. The Freedom to Publish/The Freedom to Disclose Risks. *CAUT Bargaining Advisory*, no. 18, April.

Conference on Primary Health Care. 1978. Declaration of Alma-Ata, USSR. Available at: http://www.who.int/hpr/NPH/docs/declaration_almaata.pdf. (viewed 21 June 2008).

Council of Ontario Faculties of Medicine (COFM). 1999. *Educating Physicians for Rural and Northern Communities: A Provincial Plan for the New Millennium*. Report prepared by COFM Task Force on Education of Physicians for Rural and Northern Communities.

Health Canada. 2001. *Social Accountability: A Vision for Canadian Medical Schools*. Ottawa: Health Canada.

Hudson, G. 2007. "Medical Education, Technology and a Northern Aboriginal Community Experience." Paper delivered at annual meeting of the Canadian Society of Telehealth, St John's, Newfoundland and Labrador.

McCready, W., J. Jamieson, M. Tran, and S. Berry. 2004. "The First 25 Years of the Northwestern Ontario Medical Programme." *Canadian Journal of Rural Medicine* 9 (2): 92–100.

Morris, J. 2000. Letter to F. Gilbert, President, Lakehead University, 20 July. Northern and Rural Medical School First Nations Governance Working Group Background Book. NOSM Archives, Thunder Bay, Ontario.

Nishnawbe Aski Nation (NAN). 2000. Resolution 00/16, Nishnawbe Aski Nation, re. Proposed Northern Medical School, 20 July. Northern and Rural Medical School First Nations Governance Working Group Background Book. NOSM Archives, Thunder Bay, Ontario.

NORMS Liaison Council, Laurentian University and Lakehead University. 2000. "A Northern Rural Medical School; Increasing Rural Medical Graduates in Ontario: A Preliminary Proposal." Presented to the Expert Panel on Health Professions Resources.

Northern Ontario School of Medicine (NOSM). 2003a. *A Flying Start: Report of the NOMS Curriculum Workshop "Getting Started in the North."* Sault Ste Marie, Ontario. NOSM Archives.

– 2003b. Minutes, Francophone Community Representatives Meetings, 2002–03. NOSM Archives.

– 2003c. *Report of the NOMS Aboriginal Workshop "Follow Your Dreams."* Wauzhushk Onigum First Nation, Ontario, 10–12 June. NOSM Archives.

– 2004a. *Accreditation Documents, Commentary and Critique, External Review.* NOSM Archives.

– 2004b. Medical Education Database 2003–04, Section 2, Appendix ED26, 114. LCME, NOSM.

– 2004c. Medical Education Database 2003–2004, Section 4, Appendix ED1, 3. LCME, NOSM.

– 2004d. Medical Education Database, 2003–04, Section 4, Appendix FA14, 1–5. LCME, NOSM.

– 2004e. Medical Education Database, 2003–04, Section 4, Appendix FA14, 56. LCME, NOSM.

– 2004f. Medical Education Database 2003–04, Section 4, Appendix FA14, 59. LCME, NOSM.

– 2004h. Medical Education Database 2003–04, section 4, Appendix FA14, 75. LCME, NOSM.

– 2004i. Minutes, Francophone Reference Group. NOSM Archives.

– 2005a. *A Community Vision: Report of the Symposium "Francophones and the Northern Ontario School of Medicine.* NOSM Archives.

– 2005b. Health Information Research Centre, Library Strategic Plan, 15 May. NOSM Faculty Handbook. Available at: http://www.normed.ca/uploadedFiles/About_Us/Organization/NOSM_Faculty/FacultyHandbook.pdf (viewed 15 February 2009).

– 2005c. Human Sciences Division Interview Questions, Spring. NOSM Archives.

– 2005d. *Northern Passages*, NOSM newsletter, Spring.

– 2005e. *Creating a Sustainable Health Research Industry in Northern Ontario.* Available at: http://www.normed.ca/research/general.aspx?id=5980 (viewed 15 February 2009).

– 2005f. NOSM Academic Council Research Committee Minutes, Spring. NOSM Archives.

– 2005g. Strategic Research Plan, 17 May 2005. NOSM Faculty Handbook.

– 2005h. Theme 1 Course Committee Minutes and Correspondence, 2004–05. NOSM Archives.

– 2006a. Consolidated NOSM by-laws as passed 27 September. NOSM Archives.

– 2006b. Minutes, Francophone Reference Group, 2004–06. NOSM Archives.

– 2006c. News Release, 2 May. NOSM Archives.

– 2006d. *Northern Passages.* NOSM Newsletter.

– 2006e. Interview with Sue Berry, *Northern Passages* (NOSM Newsletter), Spring, p. 4.

– 2006f. NOSMFA, Collective Agreement, 2006–08, Article 1.3. Available at: http://www.nosmfa.ca (viewed 21 July 2008).

- 2006g. *Report of Academic Principles, Academic Council*, 18 May. Available at: http://www.normed.ca/uploadedFiles/About_Us/Governance/Academic_Council/Documents_and_Information/06_05_18_Academic Principlesapproved.pdf (viewed 21 July 2008).
- 2006h. Strategic Plan, 2006–09. Available at: http://www.normed.ca/about_us/general.aspx?id=298&terms=vision+and+mission (viewed 21 July 2008).
- 2007a. CLS Database, 2006–07. NOSM Archives.
- 2007b. Constitution of Academic Council, revised April and May. Available at http://www.normed.ca/uploadedFiles/About_Us/Governance/Academic_Council/Documents_and_Information/NOSM_Academic_CouncilConstitution _2007.pdf (viewed 15 February 2009).
- N.d.(a). Evolution of NOSM Research. Available at: http://www.nosm.ca/research/general.aspx?id=3840 (viewed 1 July 2008)
- N.d.(b). *Ways to Give*. Available at: http://www.normed.ca/about_us/giving/general.aspx?id=730 (viewed 1 July 2008).
- Parboosingh, Jean, et. al., 2003. "The Association of Canadian Medical Colleges' Working Group on Social Accountability, Medical Schools' Social Contract: More Than Just Education and Research." *CMAJ* 168 (7): 852–3.
- Richards R, T. Fulop, and J. Bannerman. 1987. *Innovative Schools for Health Personnel: Report on Ten Schools Belonging to the Network of Community Oriented Educational Institutions for Health Sciences.* Switzerland: World Health Organization.
- Rourke J.T. 2002. "Building the New Northern Ontario Rural Medical School." *Australian Journal of Rural Health* 10: 112–16.
- Tesson G., V. Curran, R. Pong, and R. Strasser. 2005. "Advances in Rural Medical Education in Three Countries: Canada, the United States and Australia. *Education for Health* 18: 405–15.
- Woollard, Robert F. 2006. "Caring for a Common Future: Medical Schools' Social Accountability. *Medical Education* 40 (4): 301–13.
- World Federation for Medical Education. 2003. *WFME Global Standards for Quality Improvement.* Available at: http://www.wfme.org/ (viewed 21 June 2008).
- World Health Organization. 1995. *Defining and Measuring the Social Accountability of Medical Schools.* Geneva: World Health Organization.
- 1996. *Doctors for Health: A WHO Global Strategy for Changing Medical Education and Medical Practice for Health for All.* Geneva: World Health Organization.
- World Medical Association. 1948. *Declaration of Geneva adopted by the 2nd General Assembly.* Geneva: World Medical Association. Available at: http://www.wma.net/e/policy/c8.htm (viewed 21 June 2008).

CHAPTER TEN

Association of American Medical Colleges (AAMC). 2007. *The Economic Impact of AAMC Member Medical Schools and Teaching Hospitals.* Washington, DC: AAMC.

Barer, M., and G. Stoddart. 1991. *Toward Integrating Medical Resource Policies for Canada.* Winnipeg: Manitoba Health.

Hays, R. 2007 "Rural Medical Education in Europe: The Relevance of the Australian Experience." *Rural and Remote Health* 7 (683). Available at: http://rrh.deakin.edu.au (viewed 15 August 2008).

Health Canada 2001. *Social Accountability: A Vision for Canadian Medical Schools.* Ottawa: Health Canada Publications.

Heng, D., R.W. Pong, B.T.B. Chan, N. Degani, T. Crichton, J. Goertzen, W. McCready, and J. Rourke. 2007. "Graduates of Northern Ontario Family Medicine Residency Programs Practise Where They Train." *Canadian Journal of Rural Medicine* 12 (3): 146–52.

McCready, W., J. Jamieson, M. Tran, and S. Berry. 2004. "The First 25 Years of the Northwestern Ontario Medical Programme." *Canadian Journal of Rural Medicine* 9 (2): 92–100.

McKendry, R. 1999. *Physicians for Ontario: Too many? Too few? For 2000 and beyond.* Toronto: Government of Ontario, Ministry of Health and Long-term Care.

NORMS Liaison Council. 2000. *A Northern Rural Medical School; Increasing Rural Medical Graduates in Ontario: A Preliminary Proposal.* Submitted by Laurentian and Lakehead universities to the Expert Panel on Health Professional Resources. Sudbury: Centre for Research in Northern and Rural Health.

Ontario Medical School Application Service (OMSAS). 2007. Medical School Information. Available at: http://www.ouac.on.ca/omsas/pdf/b_omsas_e.pdf (viewed 30 August 2007).

Ontario, Ministry of Health and Long-term Care. 2001. *Shaping Ontario's Physician Workforce: Building Ontario's Capacity to Plan, Educate, Recruit and Retain Physicians to Meet Health Needs.* Toronto: MHLTC.

Stoddart, G., and M. Barer. 1999. "Will Increasing Medical School Enrolment Solve Canada's Physician Supply Problems?" *Canadian Medical Association Journal* 161 (8): 983–84.

Tesson, G., V. Curran, R.W. Pong and R. Strasser. 2005. "Advances in Rural Medical Education in Three Countries: Canada, the United States and Australia." *Rural and Remote Health* 5: 397. Available at: http://rrh.deakin.edu.au (viewed 20 August 2008). Also appears in *Education for Health* 18 (3): 405–15.

Tesson, G., V. Curran, R. Strasser, and R. Pong. 2006 "Adapting Medical Education to Meet the Physician Recruitment Needs of Rural and Remote Regions in Canada, the US and Australia." In *Proceedings of the International Symposium on the National Health Workforce: Assessment of the Past and Agenda for the Future*, 327–46. Paris: Centre de Sociologie et de Demographie Medicales.

World Health Organization. 1995. *Defining and Measuring the Social Accountability of Medical Schools*. Geneva: Division of Development of Human Resources for Health, World Health Organization.

Worley, P., A. Esterman, and D. Prideaux. 2004. "Cohort Study of Examination Performance of Undergraduate Medical Students Learning in Community Settings." *British Medical Journal* 328: 207–09.

Index

Aberman, A., xi, 16, 18, 134, 135, 141

Aboriginal communities, 9, 14, 21, 24, 45, 60, 69, 72, 76, 93, 121, 129, 163–6, 196

Aboriginal Curriculum Workshop, 69, 88, 163–5

Aboriginal history, 164

Aboriginal Reference Group, 45, 165

Aboriginal traditional healing, 162, 166, 175

academic freedom and research, 179

accreditation, vii, 16, 89, 94, 132, 135

admissions process, 43, 65–82; Aboriginal admissions stream, 70, 75–7, 79; Admissions Committee, 66, 71–2; affect on career choice, 65, 117, 126; applicant background, 68, 116, 120–4; interviews, 69, 78–9; policies, 73–5; Rural and Remote Suitability Score, 78

Albanese, M., 68, 210

Algoma College, 137n

Allaire, G., 24, 204

Alma-Ata Declaration of 1978, 158

Almond, R., 7, 9

Anawati, A., 119, 122

Anawati, J., 59

Anderson, M., 27, 204

Anishnawbe Mushkiki, 162

Association of American Medical Colleges (AAMC), 120, 132, 159, 190, 213, 214, 218

Association of Faculties of Medicine of Canada (AFMC), 121, 124, 159, 166, 213, 214

Atcheson, J., 173

Augustine, J., xv, 5, 7, 51–2

Aveni, O., 122

Badgley, R., 24, 204

Bannermann, J., 158, 217

Barer, M., 30, 185, 204

Barrows, H., 84, 211

Bates, J., 78, 210

Beagan, B., 34, 208

Berardi, P., 119

Berkowitz, J., 29, 206

Berry, S., 54, 162